Lightfoot to thi Via Frani Edition 6

Besançon
to
Vercelli
435 kilometres

Copyright 2014 Pilgrimage Publications All rights reserved.
ISBN : 978-2-917183-26-7

The Lightfoot Guide to the Via Francigena, written by Paul Chinn and Babette Gallard presents, in great detail, the official routes for cyclists, walkers and horse riders.

The European Association of Via Francigena (EAVF), founded in 2001, is the custodian of the Cultural Route Via Francigena. In 2006 it became the official body recognised by the Council of Europe for supporting, promoting and developing the route.

In France, the Association Via Francigena France (associated to the EAVF) manages the co-ordination of regional walking groups and liaison with other national organisations.

For more information and for downloading the Italian route see : www.viefrancigene.org"

Massimo Tedeschi
President
European Association of Francigena Ways

About the Authors
We are two very ordinary people who quit the world of business and stumbled on the St James Way during our search for a more viable, rewarding alternative to our previous lifestyle. Since then we have completed four pilgrimages, one of which was particularly tough and finally prompted us to create Pilgrimage Publications and the LightFoot guide series. We have no religious beliefs, but share a 'wanderlust' and need to know about and contribute to the world we occupy.

Pilgrimage Publications is a not-for-profit organisation dedicated to the identification and mapping of pilgrim routes all over the world, regardless of religion or belief. Any revenue derived from the sale of guides or related activities is used to further enhance the service and support provided to pilgrims.

The ethos of Pilgrimage Publications has 4 very basic aims:
To enable walkers, cyclists and riders to follow pilgrim routes all over the world.
To ensure LightFoot guides are as current and accurate as possible, using pilgrim feedback as a major source of information.
To use eco-friendly materials and methods for the publication of LightFoot guides and Travel Books.
To promote eco-friendly travel.

Also by LightFoot Guides
Riding the Milky Way
Riding the Roman Way
LightFoot Guide to the via Francigena - Besançon to Vercelli
LightFoot Guide to the via Francigena - Vercelli to Rome
LightFoot Companion to the via Francigena
LightFoot Guide to the Three Saints Way - Winchester to Mont St Michel
LightFoot Guide to the Three Saints Way - Mont St Michel to St Jean d'Angely
LightFoot Guide to Foraging - a guide to over 130 of the most common edible and medicinal plants in Western Europe
LightFoot Companion to the via Domitia- Arles to Rome
Your Camino - information, maps for Camino routes in France and Spain
Camino Lingo - 'cheats' guide to speaking Spanish on the Camino
Slackpacking the Camino Frances - provides all the information and advice you'll need to plan your perfect Camino.

LightFoot Guides are designed to enable everyone to meet their personal goals and enjoy the best, whilst avoiding the worst, of following ancient pilgrimage routes. Written for Walkers, Cyclists (mountain bikes) and Horse Riders, every section of this LightFoot guide provides specific information for each group.

The authors would like to emphasise that they have made great efforts to use only public footpaths and to respect private property. Historically, pilgrims may not have been so severely restricted by ownership rights and the pressures of expanding populations, but unfortunately this is no longer the case. Today, even the most free- spirited traveller must adhere to commonly accepted routes. Failure to do so will only antagonise local residents, encourage the closure of routes and inhibit pilgrims following on behind.

Please let us know about any changes to the route or inaccuracies within this guide book. mail@pilgrimagepublications.com

Our special thanks go to:
We would like to thank François Louviot and all the members of the Association Via Francigena France for their commitment to sign posting.
Adelaide Trezzini for her contribution to the development and mapping of the via Francigena route. http://www.francigena-international.org/

Openstreetmap: The maps in this book are derived from data (c) Openstreetmap (http://www.openstreetmap.org) and its contributors and are made available under the Creative Commons agreement http://creativecommons.org/licenses/by-sa/2.0/

Maperitive for the creation of an indispensable tool used in the drawing of our maps. http://igorbrejc.net/about

Contents

Your LightFoot Guide to the via Francigena

This book traces the Via Francigena from Canterbury to Besançon. You will find an introductory section followed by ?? chapters, each of which covers a segment of the route.

Each chapter contains:
- A Route Summary
- Detailed instructions
- Map
- Altitude profile
- Addresses and contact information for accommodation and other facilities

Layout

The entire distance has been divided into manageable sections of approximately 22 kilometres, but accommodation (where it exists) is listed for the entire length of the section so that is up to you and your body where you decide to stop.

Instructions

The entire route has been GPS traced and logged using way point co-ordinates. On this basis, it should be possible to navigate the route using only the written instructions, though a map is provided for additional support and general orientation. Use of a compass is recommended.

Each instruction sheet provides

- Detailed directions corresponding to GPS way point numbers on the map - GPS waypoint data can be downloaded from www.pilgrimagepublications.com
- Verification Point - additional verification of current position
- Distance (in metres) between each way point
- Cross Reference to GPS and Compass direction to next waypoint

Each map provides:

- A north/south visual representation of the route with way point numbers
- Altitude Profile for the section
- Icons indicating facilities en route (see Map symbols)
- A map scale bar. The scale differs from map to map.

Accommodation Listings:

The price banding is based on the least expensive option for two people in each establishment - accurate at the time of entry, but subject to change. For simplicity, the listing is divided into 3 price bands:

A = (€/£) 70+ **B** = (€/£) 35 - 70 **C** = (€/£) 0 - 35 **D** = Donation

1

There are no listings above 80£/€ per night, unless nothing else is available in the area. Accommodation is listed in ascending order (i.e. cheapest first). Prices may or may notinclude breakfast and some establishments charge a tariff for dogs. In general, dogs are not welcome in Youth or Religious Hostels. Similarly, the general rule for accommodation in Religious Houses is that reservations must be made 24 hours ahead of arrival. Note: **Donation** means just that, you are expected to give what you can and think the accommodations warrants.

Accommodation is classified as follows:

Pilgrim Hostel
Hostel that specifically offers accommodation to via Francigena pilgrims. Usually with dormitory accommodation, kitchen facilities and shared bathrooms. The hostels may be run by commercial, municipal or religious authorities.

Religious Hostel
A facility with accommodation managed by a religious group which may have space for via Francigena pilgrims. Usually with dormitory accommodation, kitchen facilities or the possibility of prepared meals and shared bathrooms.

Church or Religious Organisation
Places where limited, basic accommodation or assistance may be offered.

Commercial Hostel
Commercial or municipal hostel including gîte d'etape in France. Usually with dormitory accommodation, kitchen facilities and shared bathrooms.

Hotel and Bed and Breakfast
More expensive commercial accommodation including chambres d'hôtes in France and Agriturismos in Italy. Usually double or family sized rooms with the possibility of a private bathroom. Hotels normally are priced by room while bed and breakfast and chambres d'hôtes may charge by room or by person. Bed and Breakfasts and Agriturismos may be isolated from shops and restaurants. Often dinner can be provided if requested in advance. Kitchen access may be possible. Where there is a choice of room types the price band is given for the room type with the lowest price. In some situations there may be seasonal premiums.

Following the route :

France is administered on a hierarchical basis of nation, region, department and commune. Work is in hand to have the via Francigena adopted as a national facility in the form of a route Grand Randonée – the GR145. The process requires a negotiation between all levels of the hierarchy and with implementation e.g. signposting taking place at a regional level.

In France the route passes through 4 regions Nord-Pas-de-Calais, Picardie, Champagne-Ardenne and Franche-Comté. The implementation of the GR145 and its signposting have been completed in some areas, though not all. The GR signposting comprises red and white painted or adhesive signs sometimes also showing the number of the GR. Beware of confusion where 2 GR routes intersect it is often unclear to which route the signs refer. On the GR145 the red and white signs have been supplemented with bi-directional via Francigena signs on metal poles. These are normally located at main intersections where access is possible for the installation crews and are typically between 1 and 3 kilometres apart.

In populated areas both types of sign are subject to vandalism. In agricultural areas free standing signs have been damaged by farm machinery. Unfortunately it is not possible to rely on every junction being signposted.

In Picardie signs only exist where a local group have adopted the route or where the route happens to overlap with existing local or national routes.

In Franche-Comté the stencilled yellow and white pilgrim is extensively used. While there is also some GR signs where the route overlaps with the existing GR595 and GR5.

The books primarily follow the GR145 where it exists. This we call the « Official Route » but we also propose a large number of Alternative Routes that either reduce distance or have greater historic relevance.

In Switzerland a regional walking route has been established as Swissmobility Route N° 70. There are good clear signposts at most intersections showing this name and often with time or distance measurements to the next commune. Between these signs yellow diamonds indicate that you are on the route.

Unfortunately Route N° 70 follows an earlier interpretation of the historic pilgrim route and has not yet been updated and so we will only follow it in part.

In Italy signposting has been undertaken at a national, regional and community level as well as by many volunteer groups. As a result you will find many types of signpost with some pointing in conflicting directions. In the Aosta valley the signposting is of good quality with a similar style to the Swiss signs i.e. yellow signs with time and distance measurements, but with the addition of a pilgrim emblem.

From Ivrea you will encounter the large brown via Francigena road signs with with 2 hikers indicating a walking route, but also bike and car symbols for other groups. This is supplemented by smaller pilgrim signs on a yellow and brown background. In areas the signs have become the target of vandalism and trophy hunting.

A volunteer group have supplemented the official signs with painted signs showing red and white stripes with a small black pilgrim. These have often proved more durable.

Each year route numerous small modifications are proposed in Italy to improve safety or increase amenity of the route. We endeavour to keep up to date with these changes in each edition of the books, but there can be a lag in the authorities adapting the signposts to the changes.

From Ivrea you will encounter the large brown via Francigena road signs with with 2 hikers indicating a walking route, but also bike and car symbols for other groups. This is supplemented by smaller pilgrim signs on a yellow and brown background. In areas the signs have become the target of vandalism and trophy hunting.

A volunteer group have supplemented the official signs with painted signs showing red and white stripes with a small black pilgrim. These have often proved more durable. Each year route numerous small modifications are proposed in Italy to improve safety or increase amenity of the route. We endeavour to keep up to date with these changes in each edition of the books, but there can be a lag in the authorities adapting the signposts to the changes.

Where we describe the « Official Route » then this is the route agreed by the national managing authority and where signposting should be most complete.

The Basics in France

Currency:
Euro. Standard banking Hours: Monday-Friday 09.30-12.00 and 14.00-16.00. Closed on Sundays and usually Monday, with half day opening on Saturday morning Post Offices (La Poste): Standard opening hours Mon - Fri - 09.30-12.00 and 14.00-17.00. Half day opening on Saturday morning.

Emergencies
112 will give you access to the following services: Fire, Police, Ambulance, Coastguard, Mountain Rescue or Cave Rescue. This is free and can be dialled from any telephone (including mobile phones).

Basic Business Hours
08.00-12.00 and 14.00-18.00. Almost everything in France - shops, museums, tourist ffices etc. - closes for two hours at midday. Food shops often don't reopen until half way through the afternoon, but close at 19.30 or 20.00. The standard closing days are Sunday and Monday in small towns, but you will find that many large supermarkets are now staying open throughout the day.

Post Offices (La Poste):
Standard opening hours Mon - Fri - 09.30-12.00 and 14.00-17.00. Half day opening on Saturday morning. You can make domestic and international phone calls from any public telephone box and can receive calls where there is a new logo of a ringing bell. Poste Restante. You can receive mail at the central post offices of most towns. It should be addressed (preferably with the surname first and in capitals) "Poste Restante, Poste office address, followed by the name of the town and its postal code. To collect your mail you will need a passport or other convincing ID, and there may be a charge of around a euro or less. You should ask for all your names to be checked, as filing systems are not brilliant. Uncollected mail is returned to sender after 15 days.

Health Care
All EU citizens are eligible for free health care if they have the correct documentation.

Food

In France, the best way of eating breakfast is in a bar or café, at a fraction of the cost charged by most hotels. Expect a croissant or some bread with coffee or hot chocolate. At lunchtime and sometimes in the evenings you'll find most cafés and restaurants offering a plat du jour, which is by far the cheapest alternative if you don't fancy cooking yourself.

Accommodation

In country areas, in addition to standard hotels, you will come across chambre d'hôtes and ferme auberge, bed and breakfast accommodation in someone's house or farm. These are rarely an especially cheap option, usually costing the equivalent of a two star hotel. Youth hostels (auberges de jeunesse) are great for travellers on a budget. They are often beautifully sited and they allow you to cut costs by preparing your own food in their kitchens or eating in cheap canteens. The majority will require that you are a member of the International Youth Hostel Federation.

Gites d'étape are basic but do not require membership and provide bunk beds with primitive kitchen and washing facilities at a reasonable price.

Campsites in France are nearly always clean and have plenty of hot water. On the coast there are superior categories of campsite where you will pay prices similar to those of a hotel for the facilities -bars, restaurants and usually elaborate swimming pools too. For horses, it is useful to know that campsite owners often allow horses to be tethered at the edge of the site.

The Basics in Switzerland

Currency:

Swiss Franc CHF. Standard banking Hours: 08:30–16:30 (Mon–Fri). Closed on Sundays
Swiss Post Standard Opening Hours: 07.30-1200 and 13.45-18.30 Monday to Friday.
Mon - Fri - 09.30-12.00 and 14.00-17.00. Half day opening on Saturday morning.

Post Offices

All post offices are open from Monday to Saturday from 8.15 to 13.30. Some are open all day from 8.15 to 18.00. Stamps can be bought in Post Offices and tobacconists' shops. Poste restante is available at any post office: all you need to know is that town's four figure postal code. We've given these in the guide chapters covering major cities and resorts, and they're displayed outside each post office, but Swiss phonebooks and www.post. ch list the lot. The correct format is, for example: Your Name, Poste Restante, CH-3920 Zermatt ("CH" is the standard postal designation for Switzerland). Liechtenstein shares the Swiss postal system, but uses its own prefix: Your Name, Poste Restante, FL-9490 Vaduz. To minimize confusion at pickup, you should ask anyone writing to you to print your surname in underlined capitals, and include only one initial. If you want to receive mail at a smaller countryside office in the German-speaking part of the country (where the term "Poste Restante" may be less understood), you should get your correspondents to add the German equivalent – Postlagernde Briefe – to the address. You need your passport to pick up your mail, and the service is always free. Uncollected mail is returned to sender after 30 days.

Emergencies

If you don't know where to call, dial the police on 117 who will tell you where to call or directly connect you. If you need an ambulance, dial 144.

Basic Business Hours
Monday, Tuesday, Wednesday, Friday 9 a.m. - 6:30 p.m. Shops in smaller towns and villages may close on Monday (either morning or all day). Thursday 9 a.m. - 8 or 9 p.m. (mainly in larger cities and towns). Saturday 9 a.m. - 4 p.m. Sunday and holidays closed (except for bakeries, which may be open in the morning).

Health Care
Switzerland has agreements with the EU states as well as the EFTA states Iceland and Norway, which provide for a so-called mutual benefits assistance. Citizens living outside these countries must arrange personal health insurance.

Food
Swiss cuisine draws heavily on its influences from its French, Italian and German neighbours. In the German-speaking region, the food takes its influence from the climatic and geographic conditions of the area and features soup and heavier kinds of food. There are also some good wines worth investigating, but watch out - nothing in Switzerland is cheap.

Accommodation
Swiss hotels are very similiar to the French,in terms of the types available. In addition to standard hotels, you will also find chambre d'hotes, ferme auberge and bed and breakfast accommodation in someone's house or farm. Youth hostels are a good, cheap option, but unfortunately there are not many on the Via Francigena route.
As you would probably expect, Swiss campsites are well equipped and provide just about everything the average camper will need. Price and location are the only possible drawbacks.

Currency:
Euro. Standard banking Hours: 08.30–13.30 and 14.30-16.00, Monday to Friday. Closed on Sundays.

The Basics in Italy

Currency:
Euro. Standard banking Hours: 08.30–13.30 and 14.30-16.00, Monday to Friday. Closed on Sundays.

Post Offices
 Standard Opening Hours: 08.30-19.30 and 13.45-18.30, Monday to Friday. Branches in smaller towns and villages close for an hour, 13.00-14.00.
Phone booths that still accept coins are hard find. If you're planning to use a public phone purchase of a telephone card is recommended.
Numbers beginning with 800 are free.
170 - English-speaking operator.
176 - International Directory Enquires.
 12 - Telephone Directory Assistance Number
112 - Carabinieri (national-level police who also perform military police duties)
113 - Emergency Police Help Number (also ambulance and fire)
115 - Fire Department
116 - A.C.I. (Italian Automobile Club) road assistance.
118 - Medical Emergencies

Note: Italian telephone numbers can include 4, 5, 6, 7, or even 8 digits, so don't automatically assume you have the wrong number if it looks strange. Since December 1998, calls to land lines in most cities, but not all, and all other points in Italy must include a leading '0' regardless of whether the call originates within or outside of Italy. However, the leading '0' is not required with mobile phones.

Letters can be sent **poste restante** to any Italian post office by addressing them "Fermo Posta" followed by the name of the town; your surname should be double-underlined for easier identification, when picking items up take your passport, and – in case of difficulty – make sure they also check under your middle names and initials.

Basic Business Hours
08.00-13.00 and 16.00-19.00, Monday to Friday. Shops in smaller towns may close on Saturday afternoons and Monday mornings.

Visiting churches and religious sites.
Most churches are open in the early morning for Mass and close around noon, opening up again at 16.00 and closing at 19.00 or 20.00. In some remote places, churches only open for early morning and evening services. Opening hours for museums are generally Tuesday to Saturday, 09.00 to 19.00 with a midday break.

Health Care
All EU citizens are eligible for free health care in Italy, if they have the correct documentation. Non EU Citizens must arrange personal health insurance.

Food
Pizza is now a worldwide phenomenon, but Italy remains the best place to eat it. Italian ice cream (gelato) is justifiably famous and available in every conceivable flavour. Traditionally Italian food consists of lunch (pranzo) and dinner (cena) starting with antipasto (literally before the meal), a course consisting of cold meats, seafood and vegetables. The next course, primo, involves soup, risotto or pasta, followed by secondo - the meat or fish course, usually served alone. Vegetables - contorni - are ordered and served separately.

Public Holidays
August, particularly during the weeks either side of Ferragosto (August 15) is a difficult time for travellers, because many towns are deserted, with shops, bars, hotels and restaurants shut.

Accommodation
Italian **hotels** fall into a number of categories, though the difference between each is gradually decreasing. Virtually all hostels (excepting Religious Hostels) are members of the International Youth Hostel Association and you'll need to be a member.

Agritourismo - basically an upmarket B&B in a rural area and usually a working farm (see Travel tips for more information)

Camping in Italy is popular and the sites are generally well equipped.

Useful Links

www.Pilgrimstales.com
PILGRIM TALES publishing is passionate about inspiring others with the possibility of discovery, understanding and peace through travel.

www.pilgrimstorome.org.uk
Practical information for the pilgrimage to Rome.

www.theexpeditioner.com
THE EXPEDITIONER popular travel-themed webzine featuring articles about travel, music and film.

www.eurovia.tv/
EUROVIA serves as a platform made by pilgrims, for pilgrims. Everybody is welcome to share their experiences withothers, and to contribute their views and opinions. Other pilgrims are always grateful to receive useful tips.

www.camminideuropageie.com
An Italian, Spanish, French collaboration.

www.groups.yahoo.com/group/viafrancigena/
VIA FRANCIGENA YAHOO DISCUSSION GROUP A lively discussion group with a large amount of useful information.

www.csj.org.uk
CONFRATERNITY OF ST JAMES providing a wealth of information about the many pilgrim routes to Santiago de Compostela in Spain as well as general guidance and advice to pilgrims. It is well worth visiting if this is your first pilgrimage.

www.francigena-international.org
INTERNATIONAL ASSOCIATION OF VIA FRANCIGENA publishes maps of the route in walking stages as well as route instructions and accommodation lists.

http://www.viefrancigene.org/
multilingual site containing: maps, GPS traces and accommodation information for the route in Italy sponsored by the European Association of the Via Francigena

http://www.francigena-international.org/
Multilingual site providing credentials, news and maps for the route in witzerland and Italy

http://www.viefrancigene.it/
Italian language site with integrated Google translation providing news, credentials, maps, GPS data and accommodation throughout the route.

http://www.movimentolento.it/
Italian language site providing information on pilgrim routes throughout Italy

http://www.regione.toscana.it/via-francigena

Italian language site with extensive information on the route in Tuscany

http://www.francigenalazio.it/ -
Multilingual site with extensive information on the route in Tuscany

http://www.wanderland.ch/en/routes/route-070.html
Multilingual site with interactive maps and travel information for route 70 in Switzerland

http://www.wanderland.ch/en/routes/route-070.html
Multilingual site with interactive maps and travel information for route 70 in Switzerland

http://pilgrim.peterrobins.co.uk/ – English language site with information on pilgrim routes throughout Europe

http://www.urcamino.com/ – English language site with accommodation information

Facebook groups:
Via Francigena – multilingual group for all with a valid interest in the route
Via Francigena España – Spanish language group

Recommended Reading

The Art of Pilgrimage	Phil Cousineau
Have Saddle Will Travel	Don West
The Essential Walker's Journal	Leslie Sansone
The Pilgrim's France - A Travel Guide to the Saints	Jonathan Sumption
Along the Templar Trail	Brandon Wilson
Rome: a pilgrim's companion	David Baldwin
The Age of Pilgrimage: The Medieval Journey to God	Jonathan Sumption
In Search of a Way: two journeys of spiritual discovery	Gerard Hughes
The Via Francigena Canterbury to Rome	Alison Raju
Traveling Souls: Contemporary Pilgrimage Stories	Brian Bouldrey (Editor)

Symbol	Description	Symbol	Description
	Pilgrim Hostel		Sigeric Route
	Religious Hostel		
	Church or Religious Organisation		Submansion
	Pilgrim Hosts		Main Route
	Commercial Hostel		Alternate Route
	B&B, Hotel, Gîte d'Etape		Motorway
	Camp Site		Main Road
	Equestrian Centre		Minor Road
	Town Hall or Tourist Information		Track
	Bank or ATM		Railway Track
	Public Transport Location		Restaurant
	Hospital		Supermarket
	Doctor		Public House
	Veterinary		Café
	Hiking Equipment Store		Site of Historic Interest
	Bicycle Store		
	Farrier		Church
	Railway Station		View-point

Pilgrim Hostel

Religious Hostel

Church or Religious Organisation

Pilgrim Hosts

Commercial Hostel

B&B, Hotel, Gîte d'Etape

Camp Site

Equestrian Centre

Town Hall or Tourist Information

Bank or ATM

Public Transport Location

Hospital

Doctor

Veterinary

Hiking Equipment Store

Bicycle Store

Farrier

Railway Station

Sigeric Route

LXI Sefui Submansion

Main Route

Alternate Route

Motorway

Main Road

Minor Road

Track

Railway Track

Restaurant

Supermarket

Public House

Café

Site of Historic Interest

Church

View-point

Besançon to Vercelli
435 kilometres

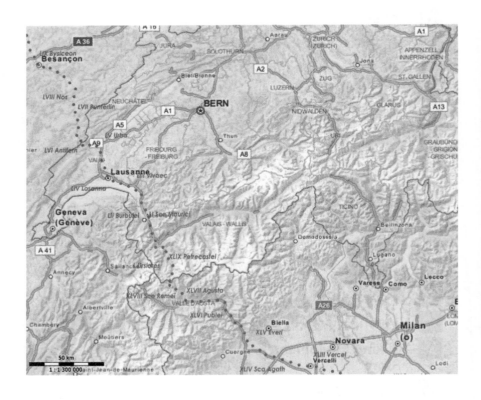

The World is a book, and those who do not travel read only a page.

Saint Augustin

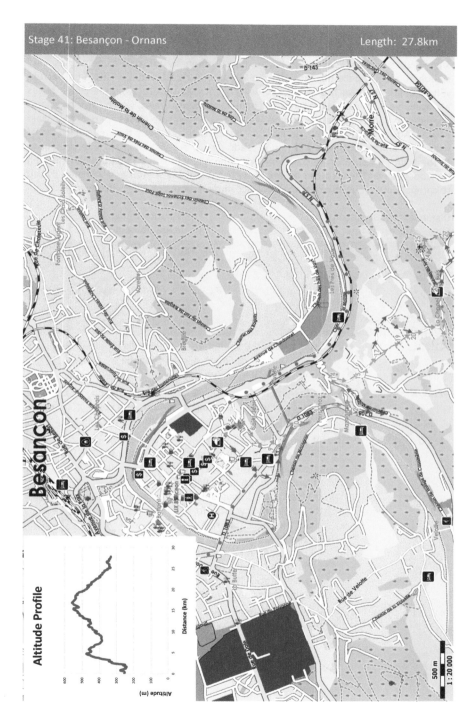

Stage Summary: on leaving Besançon the substantially off-road route climbs very steeply to the Chapelle des Buis and the Monument de Libération. This initial section will be challenging for heavily packed walkers and cyclists. To avoid the climb, buses are available from place St Jacques to Chapelle des Buis. Trains, which carry bikes, run regularly to Saône where the station is just 2.5km from the closest part of the Main Route. After the Monument de Libération the route proceeds through a mixture of woodland and farm tracks and minor roads. There are a number of interpretations of the "Official Route" in this area we will generally follow the most popular through the Loue valley. The area can be very busy in the holiday season and you are advised to carefully plan your itinerary and book accommodation 1 or 2 days in advance.

Distance from Besançon: 0km

Distance to Vercelli: 435km

Stage Ascent: 714m

Stage Descent: 635m

Waypoint	Distance between waypoints	Total km	Directions	Verification Point	Compass	Altitude m
41.001	0	0.0	From place du 8 Septembre, beside the Tourist Office, continue on Grande Rue	Towards La Citadelle	SE	253
41.002	250	0.3	At the junction with rue de la Préfecture, continue straight ahead	Pass Musée du Temps on your right	SE	251
41.003	190	0.4	At the junction with rue Ronchaux, continue straight ahead. Note:- the route ahead includes a steep flight of steps and is impassable for horses and cyclists. To avoid the steps, turn right on rue Ronchaux and at the T-junction, bear right over the pedestrian crossing to join the riverside track. Then turn left keeping the river on your right	Towards the small square and then uphill towards the archway	SE	252
41.004	140	0.6	Pass through the archway, la Porte Noire, and bear left	Keep the clock tower and cathédrale St Jean on your right	SE	261

Waypoint	Distance between waypoints	Total km	Directions	Verification Point	Compass	Altitude m
41.005	80	0.7	Continue to skirt the cathedral	Cathedral on your right and the citadel on your left	SW	268
41.006	140	0.8	At the junction with rue du Palais, continue straight ahead	On rue du Chapitre	SW	277
41.007	200	1.0	At the next junction bear left	Between high stone walls	S	261
41.008	80	1.1	Take the right fork downhill	Magnificent view of la Citadelle on your left	SW	258
41.009	120	1.2	At the foot of the steps turn sharp left towards the roundabout, cross the road using the pedestrian crossing, turn left and bear right towards the riverside	River on your right, pass tunnel entrance on your left	SE	245
41.010	270	1.5	Beside the flood tunnel in the rock face to your left, bear right down the ramp and turn left onto the bridge	Pass lock on your right	SE	249
41.011	400	1.8	At next bridge, continue beside river	Metal railings beside the ramp	S	247
41.012	250	2.1	Take the pedestrian crossing, turn right and then sharp left: Note:- the "Official Route" will climb a number of steep and long flights of steps. Horse-riders, cyclists and those wishing a slightly less steep climb should take the less sharp turning to the left, chemin de Malpas, and follow the signs to Chapelle des Buis	No Through Road, chemin de la Petite Creuse	E	249

Waypoint	Distance between waypoints	Total km	Directions	Verification Point	Compass	Altitude m
41.013	300	2.4	At the T-junction with the road at the top of the steps, turn left on the road. Note:- cyclists etc. join from the right	Wooden crash barrier on the right at the junction	NE	313
41.014	160	2.6	At the crossroads, turn sharp right	Direction Chapelle des Buis	S	328
41.015	400	2.9	Remain on the road and bear left joining chemin de la Chapelle des Buis	GR sign	SE	343
41.016	180	3.1	Take the right fork on the tarmac track. Note:- there are more steps ahead, to avoid these remain on the road and continue to follow the road signs for Chapelle des Buis	GR sign	SE	339
41.017	100	3.2	At the T-junction with a small road, cross over and climb the grassy track ahead	VF sign	SE	337
41.018	170	3.4	At the crossroads with a broad gravel track, continue straight ahead up the hill	GR sign	SE	365
41.019	60	3.4	At the crossroads with a tarmac road, continue straight ahead		SE	376
41.020	40	3.5	At the crossroads with the partially gravelled track, continue straight ahead		SE	382
41.021	40	3.5	At the crossroads with a tarmac road, continue straight ahead across the grass and bear right on the more major road. Note:- those taking the road route rejoin from the left	Pass house n° 44 on your right	S	386

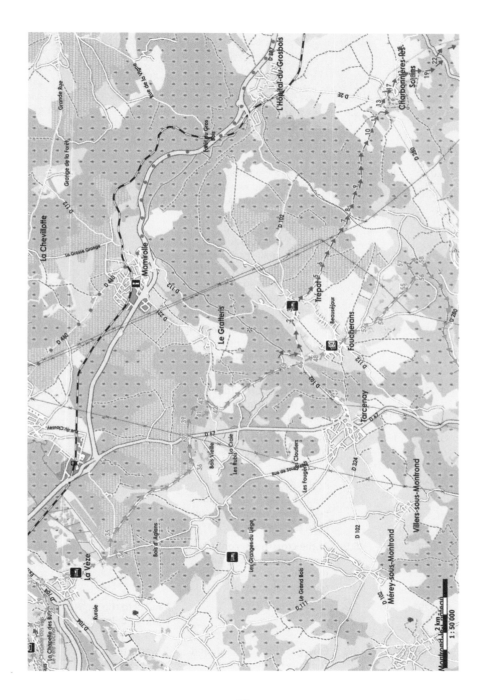

16

Waypoint	Distance between waypoints	Total km	Directions	Verification Point	Compass	Altitude m
41.022	300	3.8	Turn sharp left remaining on the road. Ignore the path to the right	Wooden crucifix in the trees on your right	E	420
41.023	400	4.2	Pass the Chapelle des Buis on your left and wonderful views over Besançon and la Citadelle and then immediately turn left. Note:- the track ahead includes a steep downhill section that could be difficult for cyclists in the wet. To avoid this remain on the D144 until the track emerges from the left	Direction Monument de la Libération	NE	450
41.024	300	4.6	With the metal bridge leading to the Monument de la Libération ahead, turn right on the stony track	VF sign	E	470
41.025	240	4.8	At the T-junction with the broad track, turn right downhill	VF sign	S	465
41.026	150	5.0	At the junction in the tracks, continue straight ahead	Avoid the turning to the right	S	454
41.027	100	5.1	At the T-junction with the road, turn left. Note:- those taking the road option rejoin from the right	VF sign	SE	451
41.028	400	5.5	At the crossroads, continue straight ahead briefly and then bear right on the stony track into the woods	Pass beside the gate of house n° 1	E	450
41.029	240	5.7	Take the right fork	Parallel to the highway below	NE	459
41.030	500	6.2	Emerge from the woods and continue on the tarmac	Towards the road below	E	446

Waypoint	Distance between waypoints	Total km	Directions	Verification Point	Compass	Altitude m
41.031	70	6.3	At the T-junction, turn right and with care take the 3rd exit from the roundabout	Direction la Vèze	S	436
41.032	240	6.5	Take the left fork	Direction la Vèze	S	427
41.033	700	7.2	Continue straight ahead on Grande Rue	Pass the restaurant le Vèzois	SE	395
41.034	1100	8.2	Turn left on the road. Note:- the signed route continues straight ahead, we prefer a more direct route	Airport runway on your left	E	386
41.035	600	8.8	Take the right fork onto the small tarmac road, towards the woods	Chemin de Bief d'Aglans	SE	385
41.036	2400	11.2	At the T-junction at the top of the hill, turn left on the road	Farmhouse on your left	E	459
41.037	700	11.9	At the T-junction with the busy D67, cross the road with care and bear left on the track then bear right after 50m keeping the hedge on your left	Restaurant to the right on the main road at the junction	E	445
41.038	400	12.2	Continue straight ahead with the woods on your immediate right	Field on your left	E	453
41.039	70	12.3	Continue straight ahead on the path	Into the corner of the woods	E	456
41.040	240	12.6	Take the first path to the right beside the tree with '19' painted in white. At the next junction keep straight ahead up the slope	Join the track at the top of the slope	S	463
41.041	280	12.8	At the junction in the tracks, turn left	Towards the road	SE	462
41.042	170	13.0	At the T-junction with the road, turn left	Trees on the left and right	E	482

Waypoint	Distance between waypoints	Total km	Directions	Verification Point	Compass	Altitude m
41.043	210	13.2	Turn sharp right up the hill leaving the principal road	"3 tonne Sauf Véhicule Agricole et Forestièr"	SE	490
41.044	2000	15.2	Take the right fork on the GR595. Note:- there is a stile in the route ahead which is not passable by horses. Riders should take the left fork and rejoin the Main Route on the D102 beside the lavoir	Denser woods on your right and a line of trees on your left	S	549
41.045	220	15.4	Beside the Chapelle St Maximin continue straight ahead down the grassy slope	GR and VF signs	S	548
41.046	130	15.6	At the bottom of the path cross the stile and continue across the field	Towards the road and the lavoir	SE	528
41.047	230	15.8	At the road junction, continue straight ahead on the D112e towards Foucherans. Note:- the "Official Route" follows the scenic vallée de la Loue. The route provides more options for eating and accommodation. However, while initially easy going for all groups, the route concludes with a very stiff climb through the Gorges de Nouailles to the Source de la Loue which is impassable for horse-riders and cyclists. Cyclists are advised to turn left and take the Alternate Route, although options are available to bypass the main obstacles these involve considerable additional distance. In the high season the valley is a very popular tourist attraction with increasing traffic levels and demand for accommodation	Yellow arrow	SE	521

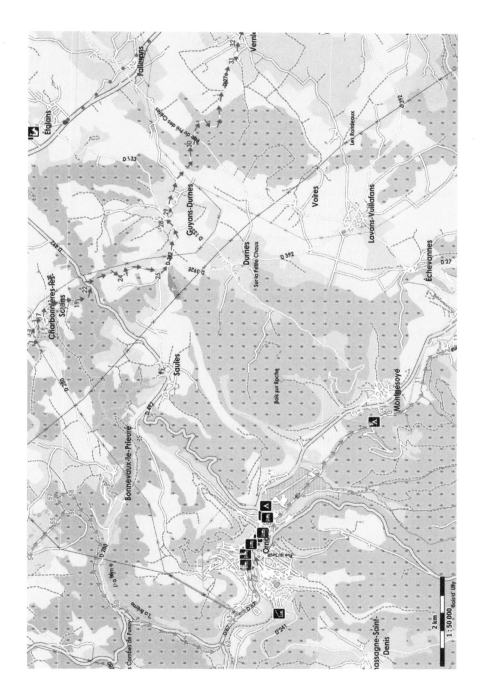

Waypoint	Distance between waypoints	Total km	Directions	Verification Point	Compass	Altitude m
41.048	130	15.9	Fork right onto the stony track up the hill	VF sign	S	524
41.049	280	16.2	Rejoin the road and continue uphill and enter the village of Foucherans	GR sign	SE	543
41.050	150	16.3	At the junction, continue straight ahead on rue de l'Eglise	Towards the church	SE	547
41.051	300	16.6	As the road forks with a stone crucifix in the centre, bear right and then turn left on rue de Bonnevaux	Pass clock tower on your right	SE	556
41.052	600	17.2	Fork right towards the old barn	VF and GR signs	SE	545
41.053	400	17.6	Take the right fork	Pass the farm, Luserole, on your left	SE	539
41.054	60	17.7	Take the left fork downhill	Yellow cross on the right fork	SE	539
41.055	1100	18.8	Continue straight ahead into the woods	Metal barrier	SE	528
41.056	270	19.0	At the crossroads, just before the main track bears right, turn left on the gravel track	VF sign, pass sign board and picnic table on your right	NE	523
41.057	400	19.4	At the T-junction at the foot of a steep descent, turn right	Pass cattle fencing on your left, VF sign	S	501
41.058	210	19.6	Take the left fork beside the cattle fencing	GR and VF signs	SE	489
41.059	60	19.7	At the crossroads in the track with a concreted area ahead, turn right on the disused railway	Ornans - 7.5km	W	486

Waypoint	Distance between waypoints	Total km	Directions	Verification Point	Compass	Altitude m
41.060	2900	22.5	At the crossroads with a tarmac road, continue straight ahead on the old railway	VF sign, pass wooden barriers	SW	413
41.061	900	23.4	At the crossroads with a tarmac road, continue straight ahead remaining on the old railway	Pass railway building n° 6 on your right	S	386
41.062	2000	25.4	At the crossroads with a tarmac road, continue straight ahead remaining on the old railway	Pass the road sign for Ornans on your left	SE	338
41.063	700	26.0	Beside the roundabout, with a large trout in the centre, continue straight ahead on the footpath on the left side of the road	Direction Ornans Centre, supermarket on the left	E	343
41.064	1200	27.2	At the roundabout with the steel turbine sculpture, bear right	Direction Centre Ville	E	337
41.065	260	27.5	At the crossroads with the D241, continue straight ahead. Note:- to avoid the steps leading to the footbridge in the centre of the town, horse and bike riders should turn right and cross the river, then turn left and continue to keep left until reaching the footbridge	Direction Pontarlier	E	336
41.066	300	27.8	Arrive at Ornans centre	Beside the statue of the boy with the harpoon		332

Stage Summary: Alternate Route via Nods (LVIII) following minor roads and farm and woodland tracks. The route is closer to the historic path, but unfortunately has fewer possibilities for accommodation

Stage Ascent: 928m   Stage Descent: 618m

Waypoint	Distance between waypoints	Total km	Directions	Verification Point	Compass	Altitude m
41A1.001	0	0.0	At the junction with the road turn left	Direction Trépot	E	523
41A1.002	1100	1.1	In the centre of Trépot take the right fork	Pass the church on your left	E	536
41A1.003	260	1.4	At the T-junction, turn right	Pass the Depot des Pompes on your left	SE	551
41A1.004	140	1.5	After passing the bar, take the left fork	White fencing on your right	SE	548
41A1.005	900	2.3	Continue straight ahead on the tarmac road and avoid the gravel track to your right	Pass wooden crucifix on your left	E	535
41A1.006	300	2.7	Again continue straight ahead and avoid the gravel track on the right		SE	533
41A1.007	1100	3.8	At the crossroads with the disused railway line continue straight ahead	Sign on your left "Doubs Chemin"	E	517
41A1.008	270	4.0	Take the left fork	Blue and yellow sign	E	527
41A1.009	600	4.6	Bear slightly right on the track across the field and pass through the gap between the trees	Blue and yellow sign	E	544
41A1.010	1300	5.9	Continue straight ahead	Mont Pelé normally visible directly ahead	SE	556

Waypoint	Distance between waypoints	Total km	Directions	Verification Point	Compass	Altitude m
41A1.011	300	6.3	Bear right downhill on the tarmac	Blue and yellow sign on your left	S	551
41A1.012	180	6.5	At the T-junction with the more major road, turn left	Towards the "Dino Zoo"	E	543
41A1.013	400	6.8	Turn right and then left into the parking area for "Dino Zoo"	Blue and Yellow sign	SE	532
41A1.014	210	7.0	Bear left up the hill	No Entry sign, parking on your right	S	532
41A1.015	50	7.1	Take the left fork, uphill	Pass stone well on your right	SE	534
41A1.016	80	7.2	Beside the bus shelter on rue du Château in Charbonnières-les-Sapins, bear left to the T-junction and then turn right	Towards village centre	SE	537
41A1.017	180	7.3	Take the right fork	Rue de la Chauderotte	SE	542
41A1.018	600	8.0	As the road bends to the right, take the 2nd left fork on the gravel track into the woods	Direction Pont de Fagot	S	558
41A1.019	300	8.3	At the crossroads in the track, continue straight ahead on the small track	Blue and yellow sign	SE	571
41A1.020	280	8.6	At the T-junction, turn left on the more defined track	Steeply downhill	E	541
41A1.021	170	8.7	At the T-junction with the road, turn right	Cross the bridge	SE	536
41A1.022	40	8.8	Turn left into the parking space and follow the broad track, uphill	Rock outcrop on your right	NE	535

Waypoint	Distance between waypoints	Total km	Directions	Verification Point	Compass	Altitude m
41A1.023	60	8.8	Take the right fork	Woods on your right, cattle fencing on your left	S	529
41A1.024	900	9.7	Bear left keeping the farm buildings close on your right and follow the tarmac road away from the farm	Le Gros Champagnole	S	559
41A1.025	900	10.6	At the junction, bear left		SE	601
41A1.026	140	10.8	Take the left fork on the road	Direction Guyans-Durnes	E	604
41A1.027	900	11.7	At the junction beside the church in Guyans-Durnes, continue straight ahead	D133, towards Vernierfontaine	NE	600
41A1.028	270	12.0	Turn right on rue de la Fruitiére	D27e, direction Vernierfontaine	E	599
41A1.029	300	12.3	Take the left fork	Pass stone crucifix on your right	E	597
41A1.030	1700	14.0	At the crossroads in the woods, continue straight ahead	Direction Vernierfontaine - 3 km	SE	
41A1.031	2500	16.6	With a tree in the centre of the road junction, bear left	Pass house n° 34 on your left	E	
41A1.032	400	17.0	Turn right and then left following the signs for Nods	Pass the Fromargerie de Vernierefontaine on your left	E	
41A1.033	400	17.4	Fork right towards the Auberge and Nods	Metal crucifix on your left	E	
41A1.034	1700	19.1	Continue straight ahead on the road	Avoid the turning on your right	SE	
41A1.035	400	19.5	At the T-junction, bear right		SE	725

Waypoint	Distance between waypoints	Total km	Directions	Verification Point	Compass	Altitude m
41A1.036	900	20.4	At the T-junction, in the centre of Nods, keep left on the D32	Towards the church, Toutes Directions	SE	715
41A1.037	220	20.7	At the crossroads, continue straight ahead	Pass the pharmacy on your left and the Mairie on your right	SE	707
41A1.038	700	21.4	Bear right and ignore the No Entry sign	VF sign	SE	715
41A1.039	110	21.5	Fork right on chemin de la Grosse Aige	VF Historic sign	S	714
41A1.040	110	21.6	Take the left fork between the trees	Forêt Communale de Nods	S	718
41A1.041	230	21.8	Bear right on the road	VF sign "Sigeric"	W	725
41A1.042	1000	22.8	Remain on the road	VF sign	SW	747
41A1.043	800	23.5	At the road junction, bear left on the tarmac	VF sign, direction Les Fermes d'Athose	SW	768
41A1.044	700	24.2	At the T-junction, turn left	Direction Les Fermes d'Athose	SE	784
41A1.045	600	24.8	At the crossroads, turn right towards the farm - Champey	VF sign	SW	817
41A1.046	800	25.6	With farm buildings on your left and the barn on your right , bear left downhill on the gravel track	Semont - pass through metal gate	SE	847
41A1.047	400	25.9	At the T-junction with the road, turn right	VF sign	SW	850
41A1.048	1000	26.9	After reaching a conifer plantation on your right, fork left on the gently rising track	VF sign beside the track	S	855
41A1.049	160	27.1	Keep to the right hand side of the clearing and take the track on the far side	Track will bear left	SE	866

Waypoint	Distance between waypoints	Total km	Directions	Verification Point	Compass	Altitude m
41A1.050	80	27.2	Take the right fork on the better defined track and then at the crossroads, continue straight ahead	VF sign	SE	874
41A1.051	100	27.3	Bear left	VF sign	E	872
41A1.052	180	27.5	Emerge from the woods into a grassed area. Cross the grass and bear right with the woods close on your left	VF sign	S	860
41A1.053	260	27.7	Join a gravel track and bear right down the hill		S	845
41A1.054	260	28.0	Turn left, downhill towards the woods	VF sign on the tree	SE	819
41A1.055	500	28.5	Continue on the road as it bends to the right	Avoid the track on the left	SE	796
41A1.056	500	29.0	Take the right fork downhill towards Aubonne	VF sign	S	757
41A1.057	1200	30.1	In the village, bear left and then take a rapid sharp left and right turn onto rue de l'Eglise		S	673
41A1.058	170	30.3	Continue straight ahead on the road	Pass the church on your left	SW	664
41A1.059	130	30.4	At the junction bear left onto the D269		S	659
41A1.060	2000	32.4	In Saint-Gorgon-Main, bear left, right and then left again following the main road	Direction la Main, D269	S	691

Waypoint	Distance between waypoints	Total km	Directions	Verification Point	Compass	Altitude m
41A1.061	600	32.9	At the crossroads turn left and then take the first right parallel to the busy Route Nationale	Pass VF sign on rubbish bin shelter	S	688
41A1.062	1600	34.5	At the tarmac crossroads continue straight ahead closeto the Route Nationale	Ignore the VF sign to the right	S	772
41A1.063	260	34.8	Enter the parking area and continue parallel to the main road		SE	775
41A1.064	400	35.1	At the end of the parking area continue along the gravel track	Parallel to the Route Nationale	SW	790
41A1.065	2000	37.1	At the crossroads in the tracks, continue straight ahead. Note:- the "Official Route" joins from the right	Grassed area to your left		833

Accommodation & Facilities .... Besançon - Ornans

Monastère Charité,131 Grande rue,25000 Besançon,Doubs,France; Tel:+33(0)3 81 82 00 89; Email:secretariatconseil.besancon@wanadoo.fr ; Web-site:www.suoredellacarita.org; Price:D; Note:Women only,

Franciscains de Besançon,Chemin de la Chapelle des Buis,25000 Besançon,Doubs,France; Tel:+33(0)3 81 81 33 25; Email:franciscains. besancon@wanadoo.fr ; Web-site:www.chapelledesbuis.org; Price:D

Association Diocésaine Sacré Cœur,14 avenue Carnot,25000 Besançon,Doubs,France; Tel:+33(0)3 81 80 90 55

Francis Geere,11 rue du Chateau,25330 Nans-Sous-Sainte-Anne,Doubs,France; Tel:+33(0)3 81 86 55 41; +33(0)6 68 47 25 81; Email:geerebox2001@yahoo.co.uk; Price:C; Note:Will collect and deposit pilgrims anywhere between Besançon and Jougne. 20€ per night per person including breakfast and collection and delivery, ; PR

Fmjt les Oiseaux,48 rue des Cras,25000 Besançon,Doubs,France; Tel:+33(0)3 81 40 32 00; Email:accueil@fjtlesoiseaux.fr; Web-site:www.fjtlesoiseaux.fr/auberge-de-jeunesse; Price:B

Gîte d'Etape de Musée,16 rue de l'Église,25620 Foucherans,Doubs,France; Tel:+33(0)3 81 86 73 20; Email:gite.foucherans25@gmail.com; Web-site:www.foucherans25.fr; Price:C

Gîte d'Etape - Domaine le Chanet,9 Chemin du Chanet,25290 Ornans,Doubs,France; Tel:+33(0)3 81 62 23 44; Email:contact@lechanet.com; Web-site:www.lechanet.com; Price:C

Hôtel Logis Florel,6 rue Viotte,25000 Besançon,Doubs,France; Tel:+33(0)3 81 80 41 08; Email:contact@hotel-florel.fr; Web-site:www.hotel-florel.fr; Price:A

Hotel Mercure Besancon Parc Micaud,3 avenue Edouard Droz,25000 Besancon,Doubs,France; Tel:+33(0)3 81 40 34 34; Web-site:www.accorhotels.com; Price:A

Hotel Ibis Besançon Centre Ville,21 rue Gambetta,25000 Besancon,Doubs,France; Tel:+33(0)3 81 81 02 02; Web-site:www.accorhotels.com; Price:A

Chambres d'Hôtes - Vue des Alpes,(Mme Sylvie Pasteur),14 rue de la Vue des Alpes,25660 Montfaucon,Doubs,France; Tel:+33(0)3 81 81 25 31; Email:vuedesalpes@orange.fr; Price:B

Hôtel du Nord,8 rue Moncey,25000 Besançon,Doubs,France; Tel:+33(0)3 81 81 34 56; Email:contact@hotel-du-nord-besancon.com; Web-site:www.hotel-du-nord-besancon.com; Price:B

Chambre d'Hôtes - le Magasin de Sel,9 rue Chifflet,25000 Besançon,Doubs,France; +33(0)6 51 75 46 92; Email:magasindesel@gmail.com; Web-site:www.lemagasindesel.fr; Price:B; Note:Open April to November,

Hôtel Granvelle,13 rue Gén Lecourbe,25000 Besançon,Doubs,France; Tel:+33(0)3 81 81 33 92; Email:info@hotel-granvelle.fr; Web-site:www.hotel-granvelle.fr; Price:B

Hôtel Auberge de la Malate,10 Chemin Malâte,25000 Besançon,Doubs,France; Tel:+33(0)3 81 82 15 16; Web-site:www.lamalate.fr; Price:A

Hotel les Marais,4 Grande rue,25660 Saône,Doubs,France; Tel:+33(0)3 81 55 70 64; Web-site:www.hotel-les-marais.com; Price:B

Chambre d'Hôtes - le Coin des Colverts,46 Chemin de Mazagran,25000 Besançon,Doubs,France; Tel:+33(0)3 81 52 34 78; +33(0)6 07 72 94 18; Email:lecoinddescolverts@orange.fr; Web-site:lecoindescolverts.free.fr; Price:B

Chambre d'Hôtes - le Jardin de Velotte,31 Chemin des Journaux,25000 Besançon,Doubs,France; Tel:+33(0)3 81 50 93 55; +33(0)6 87 14 20 75; Email:lejardindevelotte@orange.fr; Web-site:lejardindevelotte.free.fr; Price:B; Note:Reductions possible,

Chambre d'Hôtes,(Philippe Bercot),3 Grande rue,25660 La-Vèze,Doubs,France; Tel:+33(0)9 61 53 84 52

Auberge des Granges du Liège,(Isabelle & Guy Laut),Les Granges du Liège,25660 Mérey-Sous-Montrond,Doubs,France; Tel:+33(0)3 81 81 88 22; Email:contact@lesgrangesduliege.fr; Web-site:www.lesgrangesduliege.fr; Price:B

La Ferme 1839,18 rue du Château,25620 Trépot,Doubs,France; Tel:+33(0)3 81 39 03 14; +33(0)6 81 27 24 53; Email:info@laferme1839.com; Web-site:www.laferme1839.com; Price:B

L'Atelier du Peintre,37 place Gustave Courbet,25290 Ornans,Doubs,France; Tel:+33(0)9 80 44 94 86; +33(0)6 33 69 64 99; Email:latelierdupeintrornans@gmail.com; Web-site:www.latelierdupeintre-ornans.com; Price:A

Hotel de la Vallée,39 avenue du Président Wilson,25290 Ornans,Doubs,France; Tel:+33(0)3 81 62 40 43; Email:contact@ hoteldelavallee-ornans.com; Web-site:www.hoteldelavallee-ornans.com; Price:B

Hôtel de France,51 rue Pierre Vernier,25290 Ornans,Doubs,France; Tel:+33(0)3 81 62 24 44; Email:contact@hoteldefrance-ornans.com; Web-site:www.hoteldefrance-ornans.com; Price:A

Hôtel - la Table de Gustave,11 rue Jacques Gervais,25290 Ornans,Doubs,France; Tel:+33(0)3 81 62 16 79; Email:latabledegustave@orange.fr; Web-site:latabledegustave.fr; Price:A

Chambres d'Hôtes - le Jardin de Gustave,(Marylène Rigoulot),28 rue Edouard Bastide,25290 Ornans,Doubs,France; Tel:+33(0)3 81 62 21 47; Email:info@ lejardindegustave.fr; Web-site:www.lejardindegustave.fr; Price:A

Camping la Roche d'Ully,Allée Tour de Peilz,25290 Ornans,Doubs,France; Tel:+33(0)3 81 57 17 79; Web-site:www.camping-ornans.com; Price:C; Note:Tipis and bungalows also available for rent,

Domaine le Chanet,9 Chemin du Chanet,25290 Ornans,Doubs,France; Tel:+33(0)3 81 62 23 44; Web-site:www.camping-ornans.com; Price:C

Ferme Equestre,Chemin des Bas de Chailluz,25000 Besançon,Doubs,France; Tel:+33(0)6 70 31 30 43

Ecuries de Saint-Paul les,48 Chemin Fort Benoit,25000 Besançon,Doubs,France; Tel:+33(0)3 81 88 32 41

Desbiez-Piat Michèle,44 rue Édouard Bastide,25290 Ornans,Doubs,France; Tel:+33(0)3 81 62 03 73

Office du Tourisme,2 place de la 1Ère Armée Française,25000 Besançon,Doubs,France; Tel:+33(0)3 81 80 92 55

i Mairie,21 rue Six Septembre,25620 Mamirolle,Doubs,France; Tel:+33(0)3 81 55 71 50

i Office du Tourisme,7 rue Pierre Vernier,25290 Ornans,Doubs,France; Tel:+33(0)3 81 62 21 50

$ Banque Populaire,1 place 1Ère Armée Française,25000 Besançon,Doubs,France; Tel:+33(0)8 20 33 75 00; Web-site:www.bpbfc.banquepopulaire.fr

$ Credit Agricole,11 avenue Elisée Cusenier,25000 Besançon,Doubs,France; Tel:+33(0)3 81 82 29 38

$ Credit Agricole,11 avenue Elisée Cusenier,25000 Besançon,Doubs,France; Tel:+33(0)3 81 82 29 38

$ CIC,54 Grande rue,25000 Besançon,Doubs,France; Tel:+33(0)8 20 36 04 31

$ Société Générale,68 Grande rue,25000 Besançon,Doubs,France; Tel:+33(0)3 81 83 50 78

$ LCL,86 Grande rue,25000 Besançon,Doubs,France; Tel:+33(0)8 20 82 47 50

$ BNP Paribas,1 rue de la Préfecture,25000 Besançon,Doubs,France; Tel:+33(0)8 20 82 00 01

$ Crédit Agricole Franche-Comté,1 rue Croix de Mission,25660 Saône,Doubs,France; Tel:+33(0)3 81 55 71 25

$ Crédit Mutuel,2 Grande rue,25660 Saône,Doubs,France; Tel:+33(0)8 20 03 44 28; Web-site:www.creditmutuel.fr

$ Crédit Agricole,6 place Gustave Courbet,25290 Ornans,Doubs,France; Tel:+33(0)3 81 62 14 52

$ Crédit Mutuel,Place Jura,25290 Ornans,Doubs,France; Tel:+33(0)8 20 22 39 89

$ Banque Populaire,20 rue Jacques Gervais,25290 Ornans,Doubs,France; Tel:+33(0)3 81 57 35 30

🛤 Gare SNCF,1-7 avenue du Maréchal Foch,25000 Besançon,Doubs,France; Tel:+33(0)8 92 33 53 35; Web-site:www.sncf.fr

H Centre Hospitalier Universitaire de Besançon,2 place Saint-Jacques,25030 Besançon,Doubs,France; Tel:+33(0)3 81 66 81 66

H Hôpital Local Saint-Louis,2 rue Vergers,25290 Ornans,Doubs,France; Tel:+33(0)8 20 20 45 22

+ Médecins du Monde,7 rue Languedoc,25000 Besançon,Doubs,France; Tel:+33(0)3 81 51 26 47

+ Rijavec Boja,35 place Gustave Courbet,25290 Ornans,Doubs,France; Tel:+33(0)9 66 03 12 89

🐾 Clinique Vétérinaire du Docteur Loulier,24 avenue Montjoux,25000 Besançon,Doubs,France; Tel:+33(0)3 81 50 46 97

Megasport,18 rue Pasteur,25000 Besançon,Doubs,France;
Tel:+33(0)3 81 83 57 42

Cycles Pardon,14 rue Dole,25000 Besançon,Doubs,France;
Tel:+33(0)3 81 81 08 79

Lerelaisvelo,36 rue 7Eme Armée Américaine,25000 Besançon,Doubs,France;
Tel:+33(0)6 31 37 58 42

Sport Xtrême Loue,6 rue Pierre Vernier,25290 Ornans,Doubs,France;
Tel:+33(0)3 81 57 18 08

Sté Nle Taxis de la Licorne,40 rue Eugène Cusenier,25290
Ornans,Doubs,France; Tel:+33(0)3 81 57 14 14

Bougnon Vitte Corinne,24 Chemin des Justices,25000
Besançon,Doubs,France; Tel:+33(0)3 81 58 88 79

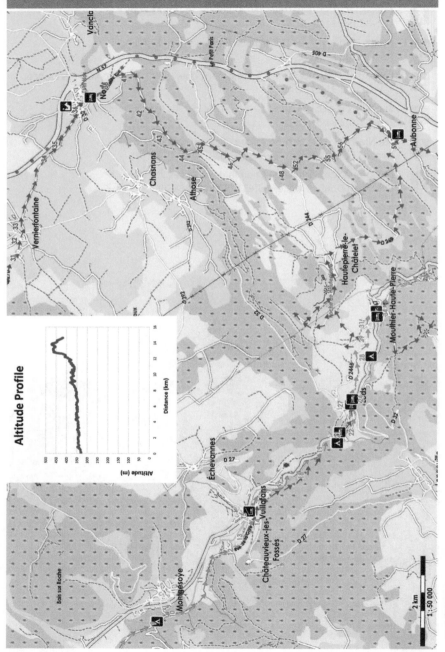

Altitude Profile

Stage Summary: this short section of the "Official Route" continues to follow tracks and small roads on both sides of the Loue river valley, passing through a number of villages offering tourist facilities.

Distance from Besançon: 28km   Distance to Vercelli: 407km
Stage Ascent: 407m   Stage Descent: 321m

Waypoint	Distance between waypoints	Total km	Directions	Verification Point	Compass	Altitude m
42.001	0	0.0	Beside the statue of the boy with the harpoon, bear right into the square, cross to the opposite corner and take the footbridge over the river		SE	331
42.002	180	0.2	After crossing the bridge, turn left on the road	Direction Musée Courbet	SE	330
42.003	130	0.3	At the junction beside the bridge, continue straight ahead across the square and into the narrow street	Pass Maison de Courbet on your left	SE	331
42.004	600	0.9	At the T-junction with the road, turn left on the road	Keep the river close on your left	E	342
42.005	50	1.0	At the fork in the road, bear left towards the bridge and then bear right on the road leading away from the river	Pass the fontaine on your right	SE	339
42.006	800	1.8	Take the left fork	GR595, Montgesoye - 3.5km	SE	343
42.007	600	2.4	At the junction, continue straight ahead	GR sign	SE	338
42.008	1600	4.0	Continue straight ahead under the bridge	VF sign	SE	342
42.009	230	4.2	At the T-junction with the road, turn left	VF sign	SE	354

Waypoint	Distance between waypoints	Total km	Directions	Verification Point	Compass	Altitude m
42.010	270	4.5	At the road junction beside the river bridge, continue straight ahead with the river on your left and then bear right remaining on the road	Direction Vuillafans	SE	345
42.011	1400	5.9	At the fork, keep right	Pass large stones at the entrance to the left fork	SE	346
42.012	800	6.7	Cross the bridge over the stream and continue straight ahead on the tarmac into Vuillafans	Modern houses on your left and right	SE	346
42.013	600	7.3	At the road junction, continue straight ahead	Rue de la Gare	E	351
42.014	400	7.6	At the crossroads bear left on rue Saint Claude. Note:- there are a number of obstacles ahead, that are not possible for horse or bike riders. To avoid the obstacles, turn right on the road. On the crown of the first hairpin to the right, turn left on the broad gravel track and follow the track to rejoin this route shortly before the river-side camp-site	No Entry sign	E	353
42.015	150	7.8	After crossing the place du Champ de Mars, turn right	Rue Gérard	SE	350
42.016	180	7.9	At the T-junction, turn left and continue to follow the route of the disused railway	Pass football pitch on your left	SE	355
42.017	1100	9.0	The tunnel ahead is blocked, walkers should follow the well-beaten path to the left		SE	382
42.018	400	9.3	Continue straight ahead on the disused railway		SE	373

Waypoint	Distance between waypoints	Total km	Directions	Verification Point	Compass	Altitude m
42.019	900	10.3	At the crossroads, bear left towards the river on the broad track. Note:- riders join from the right	Second tunnel entrance ahead	SE	379
42.020	300	10.6	Continue straight ahead	Pass the camp site on your right	SE	373
42.021	300	10.9	With the bridge on your left, bear right and climb the metal stairs to rejoin the disused railway. Note:- to avoid the stairs, bike and horse riders should cross the bridge and turn right on the main road to the bridge above the weirs in Lods		SE	362
42.022	80	10.9	At the top of the metal steps turn left on the old railway track		E	365
42.023	800	11.8	At the crossroads, turn left into the village of Lods	Cross the river bridge	NE	382
42.024	50	11.8	At the end of the bridge turn right and immediately left on the very narrow road. Note:- to avoid the steps ahead, riders should continue on the road and then turn left towards Athoze	Pass stone building on your left	E	377
42.025	50	11.9	At the top of the steps, turn left on the road		NW	382
42.026	260	12.1	Beside the Point de Accueil, turn right, uphill	Rue de l'Eglise	NE	394
42.027	70	12.2	At the junction, turn right	Rue du Château	E	406
42.028	1100	13.3	At the T-junction with the tarmac road, turn right downhill	Blue and yellow sign	SE	462

Waypoint	Distance between waypoints	Total km	Directions	Verification Point	Compass	Altitude m
42.029	600	13.9	At the junction, continue straight ahead on the road. Note:- to avoid the Gorges de Nouailles, cyclists should turn left to Hautepierre le Châtelet and follow the D269 to regain the Main Route at Aubonne. Horse riders can follow this route or a later cross country route involving a fairly steep climb	Direction Mouthier Haute Pierre	E	470
42.030	280	14.1	At the junction, continue straight ahead into Mouthier-Haute-Pierre	No Entry sign	E	444
42.031	50	14.2	At the junction, bear right	Rue Robert Dame	SE	446
42.032	210	14.4	At the crossroads, continue straight ahead	Grande Rue	S	434
42.033	100	14.5	Take the left fork	Remain on Grande Rue	SE	426
42.034	130	14.6	Arrive at Mouthier-Haute-Pierre at the junction with the main road	D67		416

Accommodation & Facilities .... Ornans - Mouthier-Haute-Pierre

Gîte d'Etape du Pré Bailly,Le Pré Bailly,25840 Vuillafans,Doubs,France; Tel:+33(0)3 81 60 91 52; Email:Mairie.vuillafans@wanadoo.fr; Web-site:www.vuillafans.fr; Price:C

Hôtel du Champ de Foire,30 rue Elisée Cusenier,25580 Étalans,Doubs,France; Tel:+33(0)3 81 59 21 01; Price:B

Chambre d'Hôtes,(Josette Mercier),1 le Coin du Bois,25580 Nods,Doubs,France; Tel:+33(0)3 81 60 03 79; +33(0)6 81 35 09 09; Price:B

Hotel la Truite d'Or,40 route de Besançon,25930 Lods,Doubs,France; Tel:+33(0)3 81 60 95 48; Email:la-truite-dor@wanadoo.fr; Web-site:www.truite-dor.fr; Price:A

Chambres d'Hôtes - au Fil de l'Eau,(Annick and Christophe Moreau),4 Chemin des Forges,25930 Lods,Doubs,France; Tel:+33(0)3 81 60 97 51; +33(0)6 45 98 94 33; Email:ch.moreau25@wanadoo.fr; Price:A

Hôtel de France,1 place Pézard,25930 Lods,Doubs,France; Tel:+33(0)3 81 60 95 29; Web-site:www.hoteldefrancelods.com; Price:B

Gîtes des Gorges,(Gérard Daumerie),14 route des Gorges de Nouailles,25920 Mouthier-Haute-Pierre,Doubs,France; Tel:+33(0)3 81 60 98 53; Email:gerard.daumerie@orange.fr; Web-site:www.gite-des-gorges.com; Price:B

Hôtel de la Cascade,4 route Gorges de Nouailles,25920 Mouthier-Haute-Pierre,Doubs,France; Tel:+33(0)3 81 60 95 30; Web-site:www.hotel-lacascade.fr; Price:B

Camping Aire Naturelle Municipale,Rue d'Achay,25111 Montgesoye,Doubs,France; Tel:+33(0)3 81 62 23 14; Email:montgesoyeanimationtourisme@yahoo.fr; Price:C

Camping le Champaloux,Ancienne Gare,25930 Lods,Doubs,France; Tel:+33(0)3 81 60 90 11; Email:mairie.lods@wanadoo.fr; Price:C

Camping - Essi,Les Oyes,25920 Mouthier-Haute-Pierre,Doubs,France; Tel:+33(0)3 81 60 91 39; Price:C

Boiston Christian,40 Grande rue,25580 Étalans,Doubs,France; Tel:+33(0)3 81 59 37 49

Gérard Hervé,Rue Pelerot,25580 Nods,Doubs,France; Tel:+33(0)3 81 81 26 95

Centre Equestre les Fauvettes,31 Bis rue Besançon,25270 Levier,Doubs,France; Tel:+33(0)3 81 49 52 55

Mairie,1 rue Granges,25580 Étalans,Doubs,France; Tel:+33(0)3 81 59 21 17

Bouveresse Jean-François,19 rue Champs de Foire,25580 Étalans,Doubs,France; Tel:+33(0)3 81 59 27 57

Maréchal Ferrant Méot e,21 rue Clos Dessus,25380 Belleherbe,Doubs,France; Tel:+33(0)3 81 44 31 20

Gauthe Eddy Paul Francois,24 rue Clair Logis,39600 Arbois,Jura,France; Tel:+33(0)6 30 87 55 62

Ambulance Vsl Taxi Philippe Vivot,26 Bis rue de l'Hôtel de Ville,25800 Valdahon,Doubs,France; Tel:+33(0)3 81 56 29 19

Altitude Profile

Stage Summary: the section starts with the beautiful, but very strenuous climb through the Gorges de Nouailles to the Source de la Loue. Unfortunately this is impassable for horse-riders and cyclists. From the head of the valley the route continues on a mixture of farm and woodland tracks to the outskirts of Pontarlier. The town of Pontarlier offers a full range of facilities.

Distance from Besançon: 42km   Distance to Vercelli: 392km
Stage Ascent: 958m   Stage Descent: 544m

Waypoint	Distance between waypoints	Total km	Directions	Verification Point	Compass	Altitude m
43.001	0	0.0	From the junction with the D67, cross over and bear right downhill on the small road towards the river	Rue de Charrière	W	415
43.002	160	0.2	At the junction, take the second turning to the left	Towards the river bridge	SE	400
43.003	230	0.4	At the junction, continue straight ahead with the river on your right. Note:- to avoid the climb through the gorges, cross the bridge to the right, then bear right uphill on the concrete road. Take the left turn at the top of the climb (GR590) and at the T-junction beside the restaurant Grange Carrée turn left and follow the road through Renédale to Ouhans to rejoin this route at the car park above the Source of the Loue	Beside the river bridge	SE	385
43.004	800	1.1	At the end of the road continue on the track		S	397
43.005	700	1.8	At the crossroads at the top of the hill, turn right on the road downhill	VF signs	S	453
43.006	400	2.2	Bear left through the barrier and join the forest pathway	Hydro-electric station to your right and straight ahead	S	411

Waypoint	Distance between waypoints	Total km	Directions	Verification Point	Compass	Altitude m
43.007	190	2.4	At the junction in the tracks, bear right and cross the wooden bridge and continue uphill	Metal bridge to your left, Source de la Loue 1hour 20min	SE	414
43.008	3500	5.9	Bear right and continue uphill	Source de la Loue to the left	S	563
43.009	600	6.5	In the parking area turn sharp left on the forest track	Café and restaurant "Chalet de la Loue"	NE	599
43.010	190	6.7	Take the right fork on the small pathway, steeply uphill	Chapelle Notre Dame - 15mins	NE	631
43.011	70	6.7	At the T-junction at the top of the steps, turn right on the narrow track	GR sign	SW	648
43.012	600	7.3	Pass through the gap between the fence posts and emerge from the woods. Continue straight ahead	Skirt the hill on your left surmounted by the chapel, VF sign	S	637
43.013	600	7.9	At the T-junction, with the tarmac road, turn right and continue downhill	Pass modern wooden house on your right	S	622
43.014	240	8.1	At the crossroads continue straight ahead slightly uphill, towards the forest	VF sign	SE	608
43.015	130	8.2	Continue straight ahead uphill towards the woods, avoiding the fork to the left	Pass yellow cross	SE	611
43.016	500	8.7	Take left fork into the woods	13% incline	E	664
43.017	400	9.1	Bear right and then left and remain on the tarmac	Avoid gravel track to the left	SE	727
43.018	300	9.4	Bear left to continue on the tarmac	Emerge from the woods into the pastures	E	761

Waypoint	Distance between waypoints	Total km	Directions	Verification Point	Compass	Altitude m
43.019	300	9.8	Beside the wooden cross, take the right fork and then bear left	Woods on your left, open field on your right	SE	787
43.020	500	10.2	Bear right on the well worn tarmac road	Keep the woods to your left	E	812
43.021	200	10.4	At the crossroads at the top of the rise, turn right on the stony track	Between fir trees	S	830
43.022	260	10.7	Continue straight ahead	Cross two grassy areas	S	844
43.023	800	11.5	At the crossroads with a broad gravel track, turn right. Note:- the Alternate Route via Nods joins from the left	Towards open fields	SW	833
43.024	700	12.2	Continue straight ahead	Cattle fencing on your left, small clearing and woods on your right	S	858
43.025	500	12.7	At the T-junction with the road, turn right	VF sign	W	862
43.026	250	12.9	At the double road junction on your left, take the first turning to the left	Pass sign "Forêt communale de Goux-Les-Usiers" on your right	SE	874
43.027	800	13.7	Take the left fork and then shortly afterwards take the right fork		SE	855
43.028	1400	15.1	At the crossroads, continue straight ahead. Note;- the signed VF route makes a loop through the woods to the right before returning to the road, we prefer to remain on the normally quiet road	VF sign	S	847

43

Waypoint	Distance between waypoints	Total km	Directions	Verification Point	Compass	Altitude m
43.029	1200	16.3	At the junction, continue straight ahead on the road. Note:- the loop through the woods joins from the right		S	879
43.030	1900	18.1	At the crossroads in Vuillecin, turn left	Pass the Mairie on your right	SE	811
43.031	500	18.6	At the T-junction, turn right	Exit the village	SE	805
43.032	1500	20.1	Just before reaching the roundabout, turn left on the tarmac track	Parallel to the highway on your right	NE	809
43.033	60	20.1	Bear right on the gravel track	Take the tunnel under the highway	SE	809
43.034	260	20.4	After emerging from the tunnel, turn left beside the roundabout and then turn right to cross the road. Turn right again and follow the cycle track	Pedestrian crossing	S	810
43.035	280	20.7	At the next roundabout, turn left remaining on the cycle track. Note:- 400m can be saved by continuing straight ahead with the Hypermarket on your left and rejoining at waypoint n° 39	Pass hypermarket on your right	NE	812
43.036	150	20.8	Just before the next roundabout, turn right to cross the road and proceed straight ahead in the hypermarket car park	Wooden tower in the centre of the roundabout	SE	809
43.037	230	21.1	At the mini-roundabout, bear right towards the large roundabout and turn right, direction Pontarlier	Follow the foot-way that passes between the large roundabout and the petrol station	S	813

Waypoint	Distance between waypoints	Total km	Directions	Verification Point	Compass	Altitude m
43.038	500	21.5	Shortly before the road divides, cross the road by the pedestrian crossing and continue on the left side	Beside the trees	S	817
43.039	210	21.7	As the road merges, recross the road and continue straight ahead on rue de Besançon	Again beside the trees	S	817
43.040	700	22.4	At the next roundabout continue straight ahead on rue de Besançon	Toutes Directions	S	821
43.041	600	23.0	Continue straight ahead	Church on your left	SE	828
43.042	300	23.3	Arrive at Pontarlier	Porte St Pierre		829

Accommodation & Facilities .... Mouthier-Haute-Pierre - Pontarlier

Sainte Bénigne,6 rue Tissot,25300 Pontarlier,Doubs,France; Tel:+33(0)3 81 39 00 37; Price:D

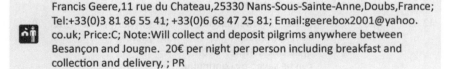

Francis Geere,11 rue du Chateau,25330 Nans-Sous-Sainte-Anne,Doubs,France; Tel:+33(0)3 81 86 55 41; +33(0)6 68 47 25 81; Email:geerebox2001@yahoo. co.uk; Price:C; Note:Will collect and deposit pilgrims anywhere between Besançon and Jougne. 20€ per night per person including breakfast and collection and delivery, ; PR

Francis Geere,11 rue du Chateau,25330 Nans-Sous-Sainte-Anne,Doubs,France; Tel:+33(0)3 81 86 55 41; +33(0)6 68 47 25 81; Email:geerebox2001@yahoo. co.uk; Price:C; Note:Will collect and deposit pilgrims anywhere between Besançon and Jougne. 20€ per night per person including breakfast and collection and delivery, ; PR

Auberge de Jeunesse,21 rue Marpaud,25300 Pontarlier,Doubs,France; Tel:+33(0)3 81 39 06 57; Email:pontarlier@fuaj.org; Web-site:www.auberge-pontarlier.com; Price:B

Maison Familiale Rurale,20 rue des Granges,25300 Pontarlier,Doubs,France; Tel:+33(0)3 81 39 17 04; Email:mfr.pontarlier@mfr.asso.fr; Web-site:www.mfr-pontarlier.com; Price:C

Chambres d'Hôtes - la Ferme du Château,2 rue du Château,25520 Aubonne,Doubs,France; Tel:+33(0)3 81 69 90 56; Price:B

Apartment,(Famille Tyrode),7 rue de Rapaille,25520 Ouhans,Doubs,France; Tel:+33(0)3 81 69 96 15; +33(0)6 42 24 07 36; Email:sandrine.tyrode@orange.fr; Price:B

Ferme Hôtel de la Vrine,RN57,,25300 Vuillecin,Doubs,France; Tel:+33(0)3 81 39 47 74; Web-site:www.ferme-hotel-vrine.fr; Price:B

Chambres d'Hôtes - le Chant du Coq,4 rue du Chant du Coq,25300 Dommartin,Doubs,France; Tel:+33(0)3 81 69 36 75; +33(0)6 04 09 51 92; Email:phroy25300@orange.fr ; Web-site:www.le-chant-du-coq.com ; Price:B

Hotel F1 Pontarlier,Combe Sourchet, Zi rue Eiffel,25300 Pontarlier,Doubs,France; Tel:+33(0)8 91 70 53 58; Web-site:www.hotelf1.com; Price:C

Hotel Saint Pierre,3 place Saint-Pierre,25300 Pontarlier,Doubs,France; Tel:+33(0)3 81 46 50 80; Email:stpierrehotel@aol.com; Web-site:www.hotel-st-pierre-pontarlier.fr; Price:B

Hôtel Restaurant de Morteau,26 rue Jeanne d'Arc,25300 Pontarlier,Doubs,France; Tel:+33(0)3 81 39 14 83; Email:hoteldemorteau@wanadoo.fr; Web-site:www.hoteldemorteau.com; Price:B

Chambre d'Hôte - la Maison d'À Côté,11 rue Jules Mathez,25300 Pontarlier,Doubs,France; Tel:+33(0)3 81 38 47 18; Email:bienvenue@lamaison-da-cote.fr; Web-site:www.lamaison-da-cote.fr; Price:A

Camping le Larmont,2 rue du Toulombief,25300 Pontarlier,Doubs,France; Tel:+33(0)3 81 46 23 33; Web-site:www.camping-pontarlier.fr; Price:C; Note:Chalets also available,

Elevage de Cercour,(Aurore & Sébastien Bichet),Lieu Dit le Cercour,25520 Ouhans,Doubs,France; +33(0)6 79 82 17 92; +33(0)6 77 96 04 01

Leroy Christian,20 rue Clarines,25520 Sombacour,Doubs,France; Tel:+33(0)3 81 38 27 55

Les Ecuries de la Plaine,Rue Aérodrome,25300 Houtaud,Doubs,France; Tel:+33(0)3 81 38 80 79

Poney Club du Larmont Crins de Lune,Rue Toulombief,25300 Pontarlier,Doubs,France; Tel:+33(0)3 81 46 71 67

Office de Tourisme,14 Bis rue de la Gare,25300 Pontarlier,Doubs,France; Tel:+33(0)3 81 46 48 33; Web-site:www.haut-doubs.org

$ Crédit Agricole,33 rue Salins,25300 Pontarlier,Doubs,France;
Tel:+33(0)3 81 46 54 50

$ CIC,31 Faubourg Saint Pierre,25300 Pontarlier,Doubs,France;
Tel:+33(0)3 81 46 93 80

$ Crédit Mutuel,17 rue Salins,25300 Pontarlier,Doubs,France;
Tel:+33(0)8 20 04 39 74

$ LCL,31 rue de la République,25300 Pontarlier,Doubs,France;
Tel:+33(0)3 81 46 22 61

$ Société Générale,2 rue Tissot,25300 Pontarlier,Doubs,France;
Tel:+33(0)3 81 46 84 83

🛲 Gare SNCF,Place Villingen Schweningen,25300 Pontarlier,Doubs,France;
Tel:+33(0)8 92 33 53 35; Web-site:www.sncf.fr

H Centre Hospitalier,2 Faubourg Saint-Etienne,25300 Pontarlier,Doubs,France;
Tel:+33(0)3 81 39 96 02

➕ Scanner du Larmont,2 Faubourg Saint Etienne,25300 Pontarlier,Doubs,France;
Tel:+33(0)3 81 46 43 33

🐾 Cabinet Vétérinaire Sauret,12 rue Pontarlier,25300 Vuillecin,Doubs,France;
Tel:+33(0)3 81 46 42 02

🚶 Intersport,Les Grands Planchants, 4 rue Edgar Fauré,25300
Pontarlier,Doubs,France; Tel:+33(0)3 81 39 47 03

🚲 Pernet Cycles,23 rue République,25300 Pontarlier,Doubs,France;
Tel:+33(0)3 81 46 48 00

☎ Lp Taxi,61 rue de Salins,25300 Pontarlier,Doubs,France;
Tel:+33(0)3 81 46 54 17

☎ Taxis Defrasne Nicole,81 Grande rue,25520 Goux-les-Usiers,Doubs,France;
Tel:+33(0)3 81 38 21 45

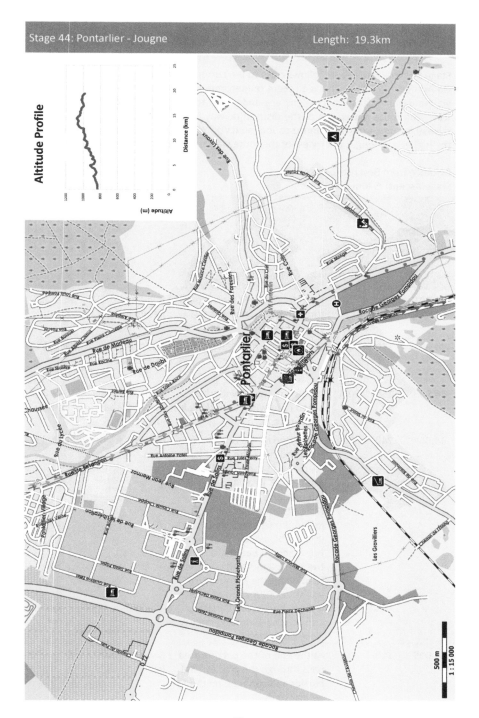

Stage Summary: the route follows close to the current view of the route taken by Sigeric via Antifern - Jougne. This is a recent reinterpretation and so as yet the route has few via Francigena signs - discussions are under-way to rectify this and confirm rights of way. The route makes use of the disused railway and then a track beside the tourist railway for much of the distance to Jougne (LVI). You may come across signs following the higher and longer prior view of the route via Sainte Croix and Yverdon-les-Bains.

Distance from Besançon: 66km   Distance to Vercelli: 369km
Stage Ascent: 576m   Stage Descent: 424m

Waypoint	Distance between waypoints	Total km	Directions	Verification Point	Compass	Altitude m
44.001	0	0.0	From the Porte St Pierre, pass through the archway and continue straight ahead	Rue de la République	SE	829
44.002	250	0.3	Turn right on rue de la Gare	Direction Maison de Tourisme	SW	833
44.003	150	0.4	At the crossroads with the broad road with car parking in the centre, turn left	Tourist Office ahead at the junction	SE	833
44.004	240	0.6	At the end of the road, turn right and cross the main road beside the traffic lights, climb the 3 steps and turn left on rue le Fauconnière. Note:- the pathway ahead includes a very narrow section impassable by horses. Horse-riders should bear right at the traffic lights and take the road under the railway, turn left at the T-junction and bear left on chemin des Carrières and continue with the railway close on the left	Beside parking area	SE	831
44.005	110	0.7	At the end of the parking area pass through the green metal barrier and continue on the tarmac path	River on your left	S	831

Waypoint	Distance between waypoints	Total km	Directions	Verification Point	Compass	Altitude m
44.006	800	1.5	With great care pass through the gate and cross the railway track	Pass through a second gate	SW	841
44.007	30	1.5	Bear left on the grass track	Railway line close on your left	S	844
44.008	230	1.7	At the T-junction with the gravel track, continue straight ahead	Close to the railway	S	852
44.009	240	2.0	At the T-junction beside the railway bridge, turn right uphill	Direction le Pont des Rosiers	S	856
44.010	80	2.1	Take the left fork	Narrow track close to the railway	S	856
44.011	900	2.9	At the T-junction with the main road, turn left, cross the bridge and immediately turn right on the pathway	Blue and yellow signs, direction Fort de Joux	SE	860
44.012	300	3.2	At the T-junction with a narrow track, turn right	Blue and yellow sign	SE	849
44.013	600	3.8	At the T-junction with a road and with a level crossing on your left, turn right	Remain on the road passing the château de Joux on your left	S	856
44.014	900	4.8	Bear right into the parking area	Sign "P1"	SE	913

Waypoint	Distance between waypoints	Total km	Directions	Verification Point	Compass	Altitude m
44.015	100	4.9	Bear left, keeping the picnic tables on your left, to the T-junction with the road. Turn right towards the brow of the hill, then turn right again on the path between the trees. Note:- the path is extremely difficult for cyclists and at the time of writing was partially blocked by a fallen tree and is impassable for horses. To avoid the obstacles - remain on the road and descend to the main road, cross the road with care and proceed to the right. Take the right turn, direction Oye et Pallet and rejoin the route where the path emerges from the right	Steeply descending path, GR sign	S	917
44.016	500	5.4	At the T-junction with the road, turn right	GR sign	SW	867
44.017	90	5.5	Turn left and then take the second turning on the right, towards 2 wooden sheds	Direction le Hameau du Moulin	S	867
44.018	110	5.6	Continue straight ahead	Disused railway track	S	860
44.019	800	6.3	At the T-junction with the tarmac road, continue straight ahead on the narrow path and climb the embankment back onto the old railway		S	883
44.020	400	6.7	At the T-junction with a broader track, continue straight ahead on the broad track into the trees	House with 3 garages on the left	S	887
44.021	110	6.8	In the clearing, continue straight ahead on the railway track	Weir on your left	S	897

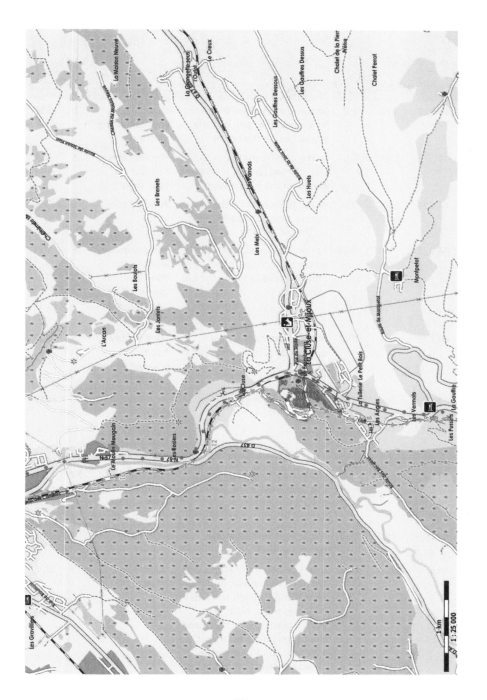

Waypoint	Distance between waypoints	Total km	Directions	Verification Point	Compass	Altitude m
44.022	220	7.0	At the junction take the right fork, avoid the path directly ahead beside the ponds	Sawmill on your left at the junction	S	907
44.023	1000	8.0	At the crossroads with the tarmac road, continue straight ahead on the old railway	Former railway building on your right	S	931
44.024	1000	9.0	At the junction with the road, again continue straight ahead on the old railway	Pond on your left	S	959
44.025	600	9.6	At the crossroads, continue straight ahead and mount the embankment to rejoin the old railway	The crossroad leads to the main road on the left and into the woods on the right	S	952
44.026	600	10.2	At the crossroads with a tarmac road, turn right on the tarmac	Former railway building on your left at the junction	S	985
44.027	260	10.5	Fork left on the gravel track	Pass beside the scenic railway (le Coni'Fer) station and bar	S	984
44.028	400	10.9	Continue straight ahead on the track beside the scenic railway	Pass the Fontaine Ronde below on your left	SW	978
44.029	190	11.1	At the junction, continue straight ahead	Beside the railway	SW	980
44.030	900	12.0	Bear right on the track, between the railway and the woods and turn left towards the main road. Note:- the track ahead is quite steep and can be very muddy, cyclists may wish to remain by the railway to the terminus in les Hôpitaux Neufs	Under the bridge	S	998

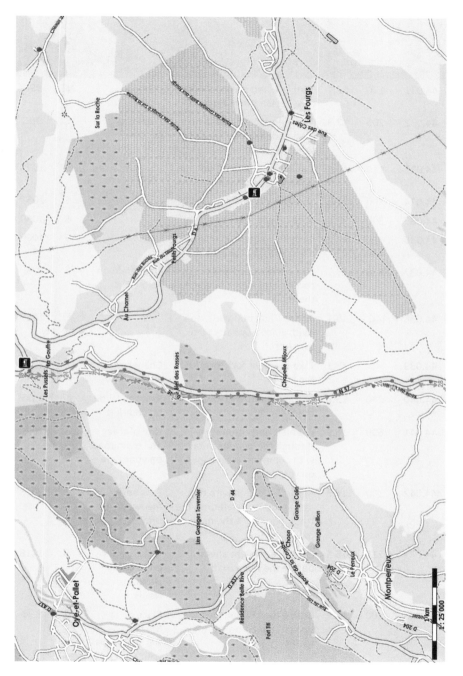

Waypoint	Distance between waypoints	Total km	Directions	Verification Point	Compass	Altitude m
44.031	120	12.1	Turn left and proceed with care beside the main road		NE	996
44.032	200	12.3	Turn right at 90° to the main road and take the left-hand forest track uphill to the left	From the lay-by	E	991
44.033	110	12.4	Turn right and continue uphill through the woods		S	1021
44.034	500	12.8	Take the left fork		S	1051
44.035	200	13.0	At the T-junction, turn right		S	1060
44.036	160	13.2	At the T-junction, turn right on the broad stony track		S	1066
44.037	500	13.7	Leave the woods and continue straight ahead on the track	Open field on your right	S	1057
44.038	1400	15.1	At the T-junction with the road, in les Hôpitaux Vieux, turn left		E	1037
44.039	40	15.1	Take the right fork towards the Mairie	Chapel ahead	E	1038
44.040	240	15.3	At the mini- roundabout take the first exit	Pass the lavoir on your left	S	1035
44.041	600	15.9	Bear left and continue through the parking area with commercial buildings on your left	Line of trees and main road on your right	S	1025
44.042	300	16.2	At the T-junction with the main road, turn left onto the track, parallel to the main road	Pass under highway bridge	S	1023
44.043	210	16.5	Continue straight ahead beside the main road	Towards the entry to les Hôpitaux Neufs	S	1018
44.044	400	16.9	Beside the church, continue straight ahead on the main street	Place de la Mairie, pass the Mairie on your right	SE	994

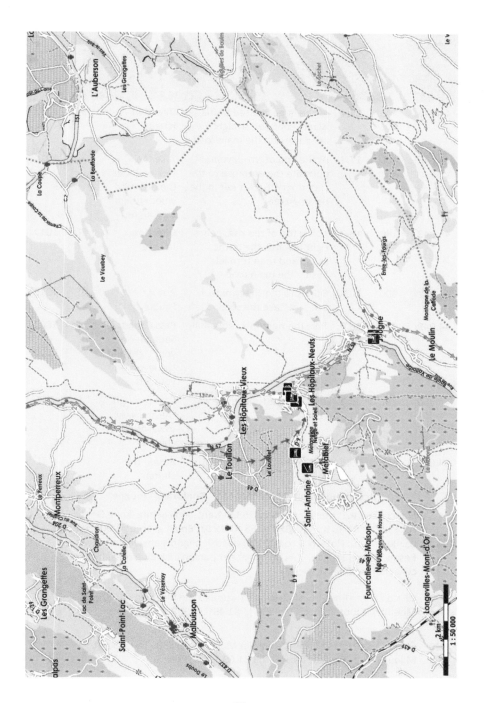

Waypoint	Distance between waypoints	Total km	Directions	Verification Point	Compass	Altitude m
44.045	500	17.4	At the large grassed traffic island, continue straight ahead beside the main road	Direction Jougne	SE	1002
44.046	400	17.8	At the end of the pavement, opposite the entrance to the supermarket, bear left in the parking area	Take the tunnel under the highway, wooden sign for Jougne	SE	1014
44.047	180	18.0	At the top of the rise, bear right towards the traffic island and then turn left beside the main road	Direction Jougne	SE	1017
44.048	300	18.3	Opposite the supermarket car park, take the second left	Rue de Faubourg	SE	1015
44.049	600	18.9	Take the right fork, downhill	Pass Chalet Saonoin on your right and the lavoir on your left	S	1007
44.050	260	19.2	Take the left fork on rue de l'Eglise	Pass through the archway towards the church	S	994
44.051	120	19.3	Arrive at Jougne (LVI) centre	Beside the church		981

Accommodation & Facilities .... Pontarlier - Jougne

Francis Geere,11 rue du Chateau,25330 Nans-Sous-Sainte-Anne,Doubs,France; Tel:+33(0)3 81 86 55 41; +33(0)6 68 47 25 81; Email:geerebox2001@yahoo. co.uk; Price:C; Note:Will collect and deposit pilgrims anywhere between Besançon and Jougne. 20€ per night per person including breakfast and collection and delivery, ; PR

Gîte d'Étape - Chez Cousin,(André Cousin),25 rue du Village,25370 Métabief,Doubs,France; Tel:+33(0)3 81 49 23 99; Price:C

Chambres d'Hôtes - Liliane Marguier,Montpetot,25300 La-Cluse-et-Mijoux,Doubs,France; Tel:+33(0)3 81 69 42 50; Price:B

Hostellerie de la Fontaine Ronde,9 Lieu-Dit Gauffre,25300 La-Cluse-et-Mijoux,Doubs,France; Tel:+33(0)3 81 69 46 57; Price:B

Maison d'Hôtes -le Montagnon,20 Grande rue,25300 Les-Fourgs,Doubs,France; Tel:+33(0)3 81 69 44 03; +33(0)6 07 98 34 24; Email:contact@lemontagnon.com; Web-site:www.lemontagnon.com; Price:B

Hotel Robbe,5 route de la Poste,25370 Les-Hôpitaux-Neufs,Doubs,France; Tel:+33(0)3 81 49 11 05; Price:B

Hôtel Étoile des Neiges,4 rue du Village,25370 Métabief,Doubs,France; Tel:+33(0)3 81 49 11 21; Email:contact@hoteletoiledesneiges.fr; Web-site:www.hoteletoiledesneiges.fr; Price:B

La Couronne,6 rue de l'Église,25370 Jougne,Doubs,France; Tel:+33(0)3 81 49 10 50; Email: courriel@hotel-couronne-jougne.com ; Web-site:www.hotel-couronne-jougne.com; Price:A

Hôtel de la Poste,9 route des Alpes,25370 Jougne,Doubs,France; Tel:+33(0)3 81 49 27 24; Web-site:www.hotel-restaurant-delaposte.fr; Price:B

Chambres d'Hôtes des 4 Monts,1 rue du Réservoir ,25370 Jougne,Doubs,France; +33(0)6 08 58 94 75; Email:les4monts@orange.fr; Web-site:www.maisondhotesdes4monts.com; Price:A

Hôtel-Restaurant Croix d'Or,Place du Château 1,1338 Ballaigues,VD,Switzerland; Tel:+41(0)21 843 26 09; Email:clauderecordon@hotmail.com ; Web-site:www.lacroixdor.ch; Price:A

B&B - la Pitchounette,6 Chez Barrat,1338 Ballaigues,VD,Switzerland; Tel:+41(0)21 843 07 67; +41(0)76 423 71 43; Email:contact@la-pitchounette.ch; Web-site:www.la-pitchounette.ch; Price:B

Camping le Miroir,Route de la Poste,25370 Les-Hopitaux-Neufs,Doubs,France; Tel:+33(0)3 81 49 10 64; +33(0)6 32 70 77 50; Email:contact@camping-lemiroir.com; Web-site:www.camping-lemiroir.com; Price:C

Tissot Andrée,Zone Artisanale,25300 La-Cluse-et-Mijoux,Doubs,France; Tel:+33(0)3 81 69 41 60

Office du Tourisme,1 place de la Mairie,25370 Les-Hôpitaux-Neufs,Doubs,France; Tel:+33(0)3 81 49 13 81

Crédit Agricole Franche-Comté,7 place Mairie,25370 Les-Hôpitaux-Neufs,Doubs,France; Tel:+33(0)3 81 49 13 44

Banque Populaire Bourgogne Franche-Com,7 route Lausanne,25370 Les-Hopitaux-Neufs,Doubs,France; Tel:+33(0)3 81 49 44 40

Ats Taxi,4 avenue des Grands Champs,25370 Métabief,Doubs,France; Tel:+33(0)3 81 46 81 33

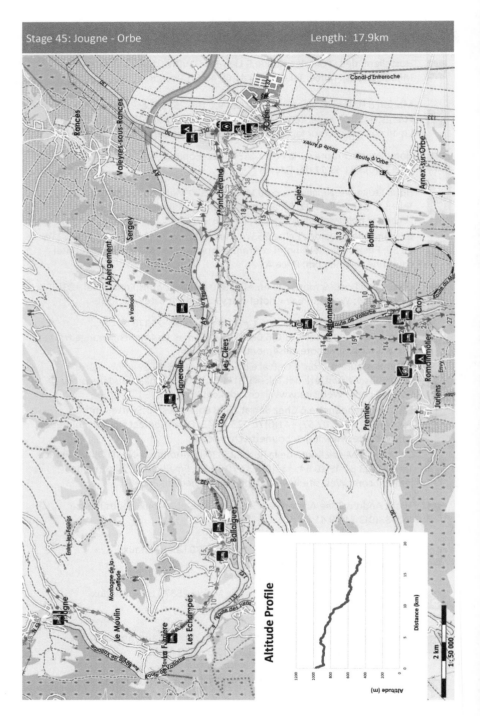

Altitude Profile

1 : 50 000

Stage Summary: the descent to Orbe (LV) passes the vestiges of a Roman road before taking to footpaths beside the dramatic river gorge. Alternate Routes allow a visit to the ancient abbey of Romainmôtier either returning to the more direct Main Route in Orbe (LV) or following close to Swiss Route 70 on a dog-leg route via Saint Sulpice.

Distance from Besançon: 85km

Distance to Vercelli: 350km

Stage Ascent: 371m

Stage Descent: 864m

Waypoint	Distance between waypoints	Total km	Directions	Verification Point	Compass	Altitude m
45.001	0	0.0	From the church in Jougne, proceed downhill	Towards the war memorial	SW	975
45.002	40	0.0	In front of the war memorial, turn left and downhill, in the direction of la Ferrière	Pass the post office on your right	E	970
45.003	90	0.1	Fork right onto the second of the two tracks steeply downhill	VF arrow, track just to the right of the sign for rock falls	S	966
45.004	400	0.6	Pass the Chapelle St-Maurice with its 9th century crypt, on your left and cross the road ahead	Blue and yellow signs, pass over bridge	S	877
45.005	210	0.8	At the T-junction with the tarmac road, bear right onto the road		SW	888
45.006	1700	2.5	Continue straight ahead	Rue Jules César	SE	881
45.007	700	3.2	At the end of the tarmac, continue straight ahead on the gravel track	Pass gîte on your left	SE	875
45.008	260	3.4	Continue straight ahead across the France-Switzerland frontier	Sentier Jougnena Table 6 – 15 mins.	SE	871
45.009	250	3.7	Continue straight ahead at the junction, avoiding the road to the right	Tourisme Pédestre sign	SE	883

Waypoint	Distance between waypoints	Total km	Directions	Verification Point	Compass	Altitude m
45.010	280	4.0	At the junction, continue straight ahead	Cycle Route 6	SE	910
45.011	500	4.4	At the left turn for Le Friand, briefly continue straight ahead and then fork left onto a grass track	Stone pillar on your left	E	909
45.012	270	4.7	At the crossroads in the track, continue straight ahead	Sentier de la Jougnena	E	916
45.013	90	4.7	Take the right fork, then bear left avoiding the second right fork	Sentier de la Jougnena, pass vestiges of the Roman road	E	914
45.014	200	4.9	At the T-junction at the end of the track, turn left	Sentier de la Jougnena	NE	895
45.015	290	5.2	At the T-junction turn right	Commercial building on your right	SE	883
45.016	400	5.6	At the T-junction in Ballaigues, turn left	Pass the bus stop on your left, Grande Rue	E	869
45.017	600	6.2	Fork left on Vieille Route	Pass a water trough on your right	E	865
45.018	900	7.1	At the Stop sign, turn left and proceed beside the road	Elevated highway in the valley on your right	NE	832
45.019	1000	8.0	Just before the road passes under the motorway and shortly after passing a Spanish Galleon in a garden to your right, fork left onto a small tarmac road, bear right in front of the house and continue on the road	Woods close on your left	E	804

Waypoint	Distance between waypoints	Total km	Directions	Verification Point	Compass	Altitude m
45.020	800	8.8	As the road approaches the motorway bridge, bear right on the path with the metal handrail. At the junction with the road below, cross over and take the small road straight ahead	Pass under the motorway	E	780
45.021	250	9.1	Take the right fork on to the concrete road	Only for farm and forest vehicles	E	770
45.022	1100	10.1	Continue straight ahead on the concrete road and avoid the turning to the left	Towards the valley bottom and the village of Les Clées	SE	669
45.023	600	10.8	At the crossroads in Les Clées turn sharp left with the more major road on your right. Note:- to visit the Abbey of Romainmôtier, turn right and follow the Alternate Route	Auberge de la Croix Blanche ahead at the junction	E	603
45.024	170	10.9	Just before reaching the cemetery, bear left on the grassy path uphill	Tourisme Pédestre sign ahead	E	601
45.025	160	11.1	Continue straight ahead on the path	Avoid the turning to the right	SE	613
45.026	80	11.2	At the T-junction with a broader track, turn right	Embankment on your left, trees on your right	SE	617
45.027	1000	12.2	Continue straight ahead, avoiding the left turn	Yellow diamond sign, river below on your right	E	588

Waypoint	Distance between waypoints	Total km	Directions	Verification Point	Compass	Altitude m
45.028	900	13.1	Shortly after joining a tarmac section, on the crown of the bend to the left, bear right on a gravel track downhill. Note:- horse-riders should continue on the tarmac track to the T-junction, then turn right. At the main road turn left and immediately right to continue, tending right, through Montcherand and down to the main road where they should turn left and continue down to Orbe	Sentier Pédestre sign	E	586
45.029	700	13.8	At the crossroads after crossing the long wooden bridge, continue straight ahead	Orbe 1 hour 10 min.	E	569
45.030	800	14.6	At the crossroads, turn right downhill	Yellow diamond	E	561
45.031	110	14.7	Take the left fork	Yellow diamond	E	555
45.032	110	14.8	In the parking area, turn right onto the small path	Beside the water pipeline	E	559
45.033	230	15.1	Bear left on the bridge over the pipeline, then bear right	Keep the pipeline on your right	E	532
45.034	400	15.5	At the T-junction with the road, turn right	Hydro-Electric station on your right	SE	510
45.035	270	15.8	Turn sharp right and then sharp left	Towards the river	SW	493
45.036	150	15.9	Take the foot-bridge over the river and then turn left		S	492
45.037	110	16.0	Turn left over a further foot-bridge. Note:- the Alternate Route from Romainmôtier joins from the track ahead	Route 70 sign, Orbe – 30 min.	E	503

Waypoint	Distance between waypoints	Total km	Directions	Verification Point	Compass	Altitude m
45.038	170	16.2	Continue downhill	Avoid the turning to the right	NE	499
45.039	50	16.2	Take the left fork	Yellow diamond	NE	497
45.040	400	16.6	At the T-junction approaching an open area with metal railings, turn left	70 sign	NE	479
45.041	90	16.7	Turn left on the narrow track	Tourisme Pédestre sign	NE	471
45.042	40	16.7	At the crossroads, continue straight ahead, down the wooden steps	Deer fencing on your right	E	469
45.043	280	17.0	At the T-junction, turn left	Tourisme Pédestre sign	NE	464
45.044	250	17.2	Bear right on the tarmac	Pass football pitch on the left	SE	457
45.045	210	17.4	Turn left over the river bridge	Orbe Gare 10 min.	SE	451
45.046	70	17.5	After crossing the bridge, continue up the hill on the tarmac		S	458
45.047	140	17.7	With the station ahead on your right, bear left up the ramp	Towards the main road	E	473
45.048	20	17.7	At the top of the ramp, turn right on the road		S	475
45.049	170	17.8	Beside the Casino turn left	Rue de la Poste	E	482
45.050	30	17.9	At the T-junction, turn left and immediately right	Narrow street	E	482
45.051	50	17.9	Arrive at Orbe (LV) centre	Place du Marché		482

Alternate Route #45.A1				Length: 46.6km		

Stage Summary: long route via the famous Cluinc abbey of Romainmôtier to Lausanne. The route comprises small roads and forest tracks and will in part follow Swissmobility route 70. Accommodation is available at a number of points along the route.

Stage Ascent: 799m				Stage Descent: 1017m		

Waypoint	Distance between waypoints	Total km	Directions	Verification Point	Compass	Altitude m
45A1.001	0	0.0	At the crossroads in Les Clées, turn right	Pass the restaurant la Croix Blanche on your left	W	602
45A1.002	30	0.0	Take the left fork, steeply downhill	Le Tillot	SW	602
45A1.003	120	0.1	At the T-junction at the bottom of the hill, turn right and immediately left	Across the old river bridge	SW	591
45A1.004	90	0.2	At the T-junction at the end of the old bridge, turn left	Direction Bretonnières and Romainmôtier	S	583
45A1.005	70	0.3	At the top of the slope, continue briefly ahead on the road and then fork right onto the uphill, gravel track. Note:- the route ahead will be difficult for cyclists who may wish to remain on the road to Bretonnières	River bridge on your left	S	593
45A1.006	270	0.6	At the crossroads with a concrete road, continue up the hill on the gravel track		E	638
45A1.007	250	0.8	At the next crossroads with a concrete road, cross over and continue up the hill	Tourisme Pédestre	SE	649

Waypoint	Distance between waypoints	Total km	Directions	Verification Point	Compass	Altitude m
45A1.008	900	1.7	At the T-junction with a tarmac road, turn right up the hill. Note:- cyclists rejoin from the left	Cycle Route sign on your right	SE	684
45A1.009	90	1.8	At the top of the hill just, before reaching the main road, bear left on the narrow tarmac track	Cycle Route n° 487	S	684
45A1.010	1000	2.8	At the T-junction with chemin de Chenevière, turn right under the bridges	Direction Romainmôtier, Route n° 70	SW	662
45A1.011	170	3.0	At the T-junction beside the auberge l'Ecusson Vaudois, bear left to the crossroads and continue straight ahead up the hill	Route 70 - Romainmôtier	SW	670
45A1.012	160	3.1	At the T-junction, turn left	Route de Premier	SW	687
45A1.013	140	3.3	Shortly after leaving Bretonniéres, take the left fork	Chemin des Bois de Forel	SW	696
45A1.014	230	3.5	Take the right fork	Line of trees on the right side of the road	S	702
45A1.015	700	4.2	At the end of the tarmac, continue straight ahead on the gravel track	Enter the woods	S	711
45A1.016	700	4.9	At the junction in the tracks, bear left	Follow Mountain Bike Route N° 991	S	727
45A1.017	70	4.9	Continue straight ahead down the hill on the broad gravel track	Mountain Bike Route n° 991	SW	724

Waypoint	Distance between waypoints	Total km	Directions	Verification Point	Compass	Altitude m
45A1.018	800	5.7	At the crossroads at the end of the track, continue straight ahead on the road downhill towards the centre of Romainmôtier	"Site Clunisien"	W	686
45A1.019	220	5.9	Opposite the Hôtel St Romain turn sharp left and pass through the archway	Tourist office on right of archway entrance	E	664
45A1.020	30	5.9	Bear left and pass the abbey on your right	Abbey bookshop on your left	SE	665
45A1.021	220	6.1	At the junction, continue straight ahead, pass the equestrian centre on your right	Tourisme Pédestre , parallel to the river on the left	E	659
45A1.022	600	6.7	Beside the bridge on your left, continue straight ahead uphill on the concrete track. Note :- to return to the Main Route in Orbe (LV) take the Aternate Route to the left	Direction Ferreyres	SE	647
45A1.023	80	6.8	At the entrance to the woods continue straight ahead on the concrete track, avoiding the tarmac road to the right	Yellow diamond	E	657
45A1.024	300	7.1	Take the left fork on the stony forest track, avoid the 90° turn to the left	Yellow arrow	SE	683
45A1.025	80	7.2	At the T-junction in the track, turn right uphill	Parallel to the edge of the forest	S	682

Waypoint	Distance between waypoints	Total km	Directions	Verification Point	Compass	Altitude m
45A1.026	190	7.4	Take the left fork on the broader track	Yellow arrow	S	684
45A1.027	600	8.0	Continue straight ahead on the more definite track	Pierre Gravé - 150m	S	682
45A1.028	200	8.2	Take the right fork on the more definite track	Large stone beside the track	SW	685
45A1.029	600	8.7	At the T-junction in the large open space, turn left on the broad gravel track	Route 70 - Ferreyres	S	710
45A1.030	110	8.8	Take the central track	Towards the yellow diamond	SE	710
45A1.031	500	9.3	Continue straight ahead on the gravel track downhill, avoid the track to the right	Towards the fenced field	SE	661
45A1.032	600	9.8	Continue straight ahead on the main track	Four à Fer on your right	S	628
45A1.033	500	10.3	Continue straight ahead on the gravel track	Sign Carrière Jaune on your left	S	614
45A1.034	300	10.6	At the T-junction with the tarmac road, turn left	Pass parking area on your left	SE	611
45A1.035	150	10.7	Continue straight ahead on the tarmac, towards Ferreyres	Route 70 leaves to the left	S	613
45A1.036	400	11.2	Continue straight ahead on the tarmac in the direction of Cossonay Gare	Pass garden centre on your right	SE	589
45A1.037	500	11.7	At the crossroads in the centre of Ferreyres, continue straight ahead on rue des Fontaines	Cossonay Gare -2 hours and 20 mins.	S	561

Waypoint	Distance between waypoints	Total km	Directions	Verification Point	Compass	Altitude m
45A1.038	70	11.7	Shortly after the 2nd fountain, bear left downhill on the tarmac	Ancienne Route. Pass the Chemin des Amoureux	E	557
45A1.039	400	12.1	At the T-junction with a more major road, turn right down the hill	Towards the restaurant	E	539
45A1.040	400	12.4	Beside the restaurant, turn sharp right down the hill	Route de la Tine	SW	527
45A1.041	400	12.8	After crossing the bridge and beginning to climb the hill, turn left into the parking area and left again on the well defined stony track	Keep the field close on your right, Dizy – 50 mins.	NE	526
45A1.042	140	12.9	At the bottom of the hill bear sharp right	Pass the viewpoint on your left	S	518
45A1.043	70	13.0	Turn left	Cross the metal bridge	NE	518
45A1.044	20	13.0	After crossing the bridge turn right	Up the steps	E	521
45A1.045	140	13.2	Facing a wooden fence, bear right on the narrow track up hill	Junction, beside the gorge	E	529
45A1.046	150	13.3	At the junction in the tracks, turn right		S	534
45A1.047	130	13.4	At the crossroads in the tracks, continue straight	Yellow diamond	S	548
45A1.048	400	13.8	At the junction with the broad track, continue straight ahead	Yellow diamond	S	555

Waypoint	Distance between waypoints	Total km	Directions	Verification Point	Compass	Altitude m
45A1.049	400	14.2	At the T-junction with the tarmac road, turn right	Towards the farm buildings	SW	557
45A1.050	300	14.4	After passing through the farm, continue straight ahead on the gravel track	Towards the woods	S	553
45A1.051	1000	15.4	At the T-junction with the tarmac road, turn left	Towards the village of Dizy	SE	574
45A1.052	700	16.1	At the mini-roundabout in the village at the top of the hill, turn right	Route de la Chaux, towards the woods	S	582
45A1.053	400	16.5	At the crossroads on the edge of the woods, continue straight ahead towards the woods and then immediately take the right fork	Dechéterie beside the junction	S	588
45A1.054	200	16.7	Take the left fork on the more define track		S	609
45A1.055	260	17.0	At the junction in the tracks, continue straight ahead on the main track	Avoid the turning to the right	SE	607
45A1.056	200	17.2	At the crossroads, turn left on the tarmac road with the field on your left and the trees on your right	Yellow arrow points to the right	SE	602
45A1.057	180	17.3	At the crossroads, turn right on the tarmac road	Between fields	S	578
45A1.058	1000	18.3	Beside the house, Les Clarines, bear left	Chemin Prés du Dimanche	E	580

Waypoint	Distance between waypoints	Total km	Directions	Verification Point	Compass	Altitude m
45A1.059	500	18.8	At the crossroads, turn right and immediately bear left	Towards the clock towers	S	555
45A1.060	140	18.9	Beside the café, take the left fork on rue du Four	Keep the first clock tower on your right	E	557
45A1.061	90	19.0	At the top of the hill, turn right	Around the first clock tower	SW	560
45A1.062	30	19.1	Bear left	Towards Maison de Ville	SW	562
45A1.063	50	19.1	Pass the rear of the church of St Peter and St Paul and continue straight ahead with the Maison du Ville on your right	Rue du Temple	SW	563
45A1.064	90	19.2	At the mini-roundabout, turn left and cross onto the right hand side of the road	Direction Lausanne	SE	564
45A1.065	260	19.5	At the end of the long wall on your left, cross the road with care and turn left into the woods	Yellow footpath sign	N	548
45A1.066	90	19.6	Turn sharp right downhill	Parking area	SE	546
45A1.067	130	19.7	Continue straight ahead	Avoid the track on the left	SE	527
45A1.068	400	20.1	At the T-junction overlooking the factory, turn right	Chemin de Randonée Pédestre	SE	475
45A1.069	130	20.2	At the junction in the tracks, turn left downhill on the gravel track	Keep disused funicular track to your right	SE	485

Waypoint	Distance between waypoints	Total km	Directions	Verification Point	Compass	Altitude m
45A1.070	400	20.7	Continue straight ahead, downhill on the tarmac		E	450
45A1.071	110	20.8	At the road junction at the foot of the hill, continue straight ahead on the main road	Cross railway bridge	E	437
45A1.072	250	21.0	At the mini-roundabout, turn right	Direction Lausanne	SE	432
45A1.073	210	21.2	Continue straight ahead beside the main road	Ignore the turning to the right, route de Lausanne	SE	443
45A1.074	60	21.3	Immediately before the petrol station, turn right	Direction Zone Artisanal	SE	444
45A1.075	400	21.6	At the T-junction, turn right	Pass under the height restriction barrier, yellow diamond	S	431
45A1.076	300	21.9	At the start of the woods, turn left on the track	Car park and sports-field on your right	SE	427
45A1.077	400	22.3	At the crossroads with the tarmac road, continue straight ahead on the concrete road	Direction Vufflens la Ville	S	422
45A1.078	150	22.5	Bear left on the concrete road	Avoid the turning to the right into the woods	SE	422
45A1.079	90	22.6	Turn right, keeping the woods close on your right	Yellow arrow	S	421
45A1.080	400	22.9	At the end of the concrete road, continue on the narrow footpath	Keep the field on your left and woods on your right	SE	422

Waypoint	Distance between waypoints	Total km	Directions	Verification Point	Compass	Altitude m
45A1.081	140	23.1	Enter the woods from the corner of the field on the narrow pathway	Yellow arrow	S	427
45A1.082	500	23.5	After crossing the stream, re-enter the woods and take the left fork on the gravel track uphill	Yellow arrow	S	441
45A1.083	160	23.7	At the T-junction at the top of the rise, turn left	Yellow arrow	SW	454
45A1.084	30	23.7	Take the left fork onto the smaller track	Yellow diamond	SW	457
45A1.085	400	24.1	At the T-junction with a tarmac track, turn left down the hill and at the T-junction with the road turn left with care on the road	Pass fields on your right, woods on your left	SE	452
45A1.086	1100	25.1	At the T-junction beside house n° 11, turn right towards the centre of Vufflens la Ville	Tourisme Pédestre	S	474
45A1.087	190	25.3	At the crossroads in the centre of the town, continue straight ahead	Direction Lausanne	S	475
45A1.088	220	25.5	Beside the church, continue straight ahead	Pass the Auberge de la Venoge on your right	S	478
45A1.089	100	25.6	Keep left towards the orchard	Tourisme Pédestre	SE	476
45A1.090	130	25.8	At the crossroads, after passing the orchard, turn right	Chemin des Bois	S	471

Waypoint	Distance between waypoints	Total km	Directions	Verification Point	Compass	Altitude m
45A1.091	600	26.3	Continue straight ahead down the hill	Towards the woods	SW	467
45A1.092	800	27.1	With the refuge to your right, continue straight ahead on the tarmac road	Yellow diamond	S	423
45A1.093	140	27.2	Continue straight ahead on the tarmac road	Avoid tracks to the left and right	SE	424
45A1.094	60	27.3	At the crossroads, continue straight ahead on the gravel track	Yellow diamond	SE	430
45A1.095	400	27.7	Turn right	Large yellow arrow	SE	447
45A1.096	170	27.9	Keep right on the tarmac track and then turn left at the T-junction with the road	Avoid the turning on the left, back into the woods. Yellow arrow	SE	445
45A1.097	400	28.3	continue straight ahead on the road	Pass a parking area on your left	E	448
45A1.098	70	28.4	At the end of the first parking area, turn right	Direction Bussigny - 25mins	S	445
45A1.099	110	28.5	At the junction continue straight ahead on the gravel track	Field on your right, poplar trees on your left	S	445
45A1.100	400	28.8	With magnificent views of the lake and the Alps ahead, continue straight ahead at the junction	Avoid the left turn towards the motorway	SE	439
45A1.101	700	29.5	At the Stop sign in Bussigny, turn left on rue Saint Germain	Lavoir ahead at the junction	E	413

Waypoint	Distance between waypoints	Total km	Directions	Verification Point	Compass	Altitude m
45A1.102	240	29.7	At the T-junction beside the Hôtel de Ville in Bussigny, turn right towards the train station	Tourisme Pédestre	SE	415
45A1.103	170	29.9	At the mini-roundabout, bear right	Towards the station entrance	SW	410
45A1.104	170	30.1	Bear right into the station parking area and take the subway under the railway	Metal barriers	S	408
45A1.105	90	30.1	At the exit from the subway, turn right on chemin du Bosquet and then immediately left	Towards poplar trees	SW	403
45A1.106	170	30.3	Take the right fork on the road	Pass under the highway	SW	398
45A1.107	90	30.4	Bear left and then right to the end of the road	Between the highway and the woods	S	396
45A1.108	250	30.7	At the end of the road, turn left on the path before the river bridge. Note:- the route ahead includes a very low bridge and narrow paths that are impassable by horses and very difficult for cyclists. To avoid these obstacles take the footbridge, and skirt the factory to join route de la Chocolatière.	Footbridge ahead at the junction	S	390

Waypoint	Distance between waypoints	Total km	Directions	Verification Point	Compass	Altitude m
45A1.108	250	30.7	**CONTINUED** Then follow the signed Swiss cycle route N° 5 all the way to the junction with the main Lausanne-Morges road. Turn left and rejoin the route at the next traffic lights.	Footbridge ahead at the junction	S	390
45A1.109	700	31.4	Walkers should continue straight ahead by the river and pass under the very low road bridge		SW	388
45A1.110	150	31.5	At the crossroads in the track, turn left on the gravel track	Wooden footbridge to your right at the junction	SE	387
45A1.111	230	31.8	Bear right on the path, close to the river		SW	389
45A1.112	1300	33.1	Continue on the main track, beside the river		S	383
45A1.113	120	33.2	Take the left fork	Towards the wooden fencing	SW	383
45A1.114	400	33.6	With metal bridges on both sides of the track, turn left over the smaller bridge and continue on the track		SE	381
45A1.115	180	33.7	On emerging from the woods on a small tarmac road, immediately turn right on a grass track	Between the field and the woods	S	383
45A1.116	700	34.4	After returning to the woods, continue on the broad track		S	382
45A1.117	250	34.6	Continue straight ahead on the track	Pass the equestrian centre on your right	S	381

Waypoint	Distance between waypoints	Total km	Directions	Verification Point	Compass	Altitude m
45A1.118	400	35.0	At the T-junction with the main road, turn right and continue straight ahead at the traffic lights. Pedestrians use the subway. Cyclists on Route n° 5 join from the right	Rue du Centre, towards the bus shelters	SE	394
45A1.119	1200	36.2	Just after passing the clock tower on your right, turn right and continue downhill towards the church	Chemin du Crêt	SE	395
45A1.120	230	36.4	After passing the church of St Sulpice, turn left	Avenue Léman	NE	374
45A1.121	1000	37.4	Beside the house with the spire on your left, turn right on the pathway	Towards the lake-shore	S	375
45A1.122	50	37.5	Turn left and continue on the path by the lake-shore		E	374
45A1.123	5100	42.6	Beside the marina in Ouchy, continue straight ahead by the lake-shore	Tourist Office and metro station to your left	E	375
45A1.124	1900	44.4	Beside the stone tower, la Tour Haldimand, follow the road inland and at the T-junction turn right on Avenue Général Guisan	Direction Pully Centre	E	374
45A1.125	2200	46.6	At the crossroads with chemin de la Damataire, continue straight ahead to rejoin the Main Route to Vevey			384

Alternate Route #45.A2				Length: 6.3km		
Stage Summary: link from Romainmôtier to rejoin the Main Route in Orbe (LV)						
Stage Ascent: 41m				Stage Descent: 184m		

Waypoint	Distance between waypoints	Total km	Directions	Verification Point	Compass	Altitude m
45A2.001	0	0.0	Turn left over the small bridge and immediately right, direction Croy Gare. Note:- horse and bike riders should remain on the road and bear right and rejoin this route at the bridge over the railway beside the Croy station. There are frequent trains from Croy to Lausanne.	Beside the water channel	NE	646
45A2.002	300	0.3	At the T-junction, turn left and then immediately right	Water channel on your left	E	641
45A2.003	300	0.6	At the T-junction, turn sharp left uphill	Croy - 5mins	N	637
45A2.004	80	0.7	At the top of the rise, bear left and then turn right towards the Croy station	Pass house n° 31 on your right	E	641
45A2.005	60	0.8	With the farmhouse on your right, turn left on La Riette	Towards the station	N	642
45A2.006	130	0.9	At the crossroads with the railway station directly ahead, turn right	Cross the railway bridge	E	642
45A2.007	200	1.1	Take the right fork	Direction Orbe	N	646
45A2.008	400	1.5	On the crown of the bend to the right, turn left onto the tarmac road, downhill towards the woods	The road quickly bears right	NE	642
45A2.009	210	1.7	Take the right fork	Towards the main road	E	645
45A2.010	160	1.8	At the crossroads with the main road, continue straight ahead on the concrete road	Downhill towards the village	NE	643

Waypoint	Distance between waypoints	Total km	Directions	Verification Point	Compass	Altitude m
45A2.011	1100	2.9	On reaching Bofflens, turn right and then turn left beside the lavoir	Pass an ivy covered house on your left	E	582
45A2.012	120	3.0	At the T-junction with the main road, turn right and follow route d'Orbe	Pass the bus stop - Laiterie Bofflens - on your right	E	575
45A2.013	400	3.4	Fork left on to the concrete track, beside the barn	Pass the sign Agiez Orbe 4km on your right	N	563
45A2.014	1200	4.6	Turn left downhill and then turn left again	Prés des Ruz	N	527
45A2.015	600	5.2	At the T-junction in Agiez, after passing Le Normand, turn left and then immediately right	Rue du Château	N	527
45A2.016	80	5.3	Turn right on le Coin and then turn left at the T-junction	Pass a fontaine on your right	NE	529
45A2.017	90	5.4	Take the left fork and continue straight ahead at the end of the tarmac	Pass large conifer on your right	N	527
45A2.018	300	5.7	At the junction in the tracks, continue straight ahead downhill on the stony track	Tourisme Pédestre	NE	533
45A2.019	130	5.8	At the crossroads continue straight ahead	Balade viticole des Côtes-de-l'Orbe	E	526
45A2.020	120	5.9	At the T-junction, turn right, downhill		SE	518
45A2.021	50	6.0	At the T-junction, turn sharp left into the woods	Vines on your right at the junction, Tourisme Pédestre	NE	515
45A2.022	110	6.1	Fork right down the hill	Yellow arrow	NE	514

Waypoint	Distance between waypoints	Total km	Directions	Verification Point	Compass	Altitude m
45A2.023	70	6.2	At the crossroads in the tracks, continue straight ahead	Yellow arrow	E	513
45A2.024	30	6.2	At the T-junction, turn left on the narrow path	Water below on your right	NE	510
45A2.025	100	6.3	At the junction turn right over the footbridge and rejoin the Main Route to Orbe			503

Accommodation & Facilities .... Jougne - Orbe

Paroisse Catholique,Chemin de la Dame 1,1350 Orbe,VD,Switzerland; Tel:+41(0)24 441 32 90; Price:D

Pully Latifa,Chemin des Fleurs de Lys 33B,1350 Orbe,VD,Switzerland; Tel:+41(0)24 441 72 15; Email:latifahousni@aol.fr; Price:C

Martin Arlette,Chemin de l'Epignau 40,1373 Chavornay,VD,Switzerland; Tel:+41(0)24 441 33 14; +41(0)79 731 42 40; Email:arlettemartin@bluewin.ch; Note:Sofa and inflatable mattress,

Daisy Nicolet,Chemin du Vieux-Moulin 9,1373 Chavornay,VD,Switzerland; Tel:+41(0)24 441 49 92; Email:daisynicolet@bluewin.ch

Françoise Golay,Route de Vaulion 40,1323 Romainmôtier-Envy,VD,Switzerland; Tel:+41(0)24 453 16 31; +41(0)78 885 86 60; Email:fc.golay@bluewin.ch; Price:C

Auberge Pour Tous,Rue du Simplon 11,1337 Vallorbe,VD,Switzerland; Tel:+41(0)21 843 13 49; +41(0)78 898 86 72; Web-site:www.aubergepourtous.ch; Price:B

Le Dortoir de l'Ermitage,Rue du Bourg 9,1323 Romainmôtier-Envy,VD,Switzerland; Tel:+41(0)24 453 14 65; +41(0)79 535 88 04; Email:ermitage.Romainmotier@gmail.com; Price:B

Apartment,(Brigitte Lambercy),Le Fochau 1,1357 Lignerolle,VD,Switzerland; Tel:+41(0)24 441 92 92; +41(0)77 422 92 17; Email:brigittelambercy@gmail.com; Price:B

Studio,(Lise Mandry),La Russille,1356 Les-Clées,VD,Switzerland; Tel:+41(0)24 441 56 42; +41(0)79 743 06 24; Email:elaime@bluewin.ch; Price:B

Hôtel des Mosaïques SA,Montchoisi 5,1350 Orbe,VD,Switzerland; Tel:+41(0)24 441 62 61; Web-site:www.hoteldesmosaiques.ch; Price:A

Hôtel Restaurant du Chasseur,Rue Sainte-Claire 2,1350 Orbe,VD,Switzerland; Tel:+41(0)24 441 67 80; Email:info@hotel-au-chasseur.com; Web-site:www.hotel-au-chasseur.com; Price:A

Hôtel des Deux-Poissons,Rue du Grand-Pont 2,1350 Orbe,VD,Switzerland; Tel:+41(0)24 441 20 01; +41(0)24 441 32 95; Price:B

Chambre d'Hôtes - Savoy,(Firmin and Josette Savoy),Route d'Agiez 1,1329 Bretonnières,VD,Switzerland; Tel:+41(0)24 453 15 90; +41(0)79 227 13 33; Web-site:www.1329.ch/Pernelle.html; Price:B

Hôtel de la Gare,Rue de l'Industri,1373 Chavornay,VD,Switzerland; Tel:+41(0)24 441 41 13; Email:info@hoteldelagarechavornay.ch; Web-site:www.hoteldelagarechavornay.ch; Price:A

gîte du Charron,(Yvan et Tania Benoît),Grand'rue 69,1373 Chavornay,VD,Switzerland; Tel:+41(0)24 441 09 43; Email:site@hotes.ch; Web-site:www.hotes.ch; Price:B

B&B,Rue des Fontaines 15,1322 Croy,VD,Switzerland; Tel:+41(0)24 453 16 21; +41(0)79 298 36 71; Email:arlaubscher@bluewin.ch ; Price:A

Chalet les Troènes,(Mme Gachet),Champs des Barres 1,1322 Romainmôtier-Envy,VD,Switzerland; Tel:+41(0)76 393 04 90; Email:fleurdusphinx@hotmail.com; Price:C; Note:Garden chalet, available May to October,

Maison du Lieutenant Baillival,Rue du Bourg 17,1323 Romainmôtier,VD,Switzerland; Tel:+41(0)24 453 22 77; Email:alb@baillival.ch; Web-site:www.baillival.ch; Price:A

Chez Rappaz,Chemin de la Foule 16,1322 Croy,VD,Switzerland; Tel:+41(0)24 453 10 74; Email:veronique.rappaz@gmail.com; Price:A

B&B la Butineuse,(Lucette Rochat),Le Pont de l'Etang 7,1322 Croy,VD,Switzerland; Tel:+41(0)24 453 16 38; +41(0)79 259 29 80; Email:lucetterochat@hotmail.com ; Price:A

Tcs Camping Orbe,Route du Signal,1350 Orbe,VD,Switzerland; Tel:+41(0)24 441 38 57; Email:camping.orbe@tcs.ch; Web-site:www.campingtcs.ch; Price:C

Camping - le Nozon,Route du Signal 2,1323 Romainmôtier-Envy,VD,Switzerland; Tel:+41(0)24 453 13 70; Email:caravanes@camping-romainmotier.ch; Web-site:www.camping-romainmotier.ch; Price:C; Note:"Tipi" available for rent,

Office du Tourisme,Grand-rue 1,1350 Orbe,VD,Switzerland; Tel:+41(0)24 442 92 37

Banque Raiffeisen,Grand-rue 39,1350 Orbe,VD,Switzerland; Tel:+41(0)24 442 88 20

BCV,Place du Marché 9,1350 Orbe,VD,Switzerland; Tel:+41(0)24 442 82 50

Raiffeisen Orbe,Grand-rue 9,1337 Vallorbe,VD,Switzerland; Tel:+41(0)21 843 99 99

Raiffeisen Schweiz,Grand'rue 87,1373 Chavornay,VD,Switzerland; Tel:+41(0)24 441 73 43

Gare - CFF,Rue de la Gare,1350 Orbe,VD,Switzerland; Tel:+41(0)90 030 03 00; Web-site:www.CFF.ch

Hôpital Orbe,Chemin de la Magnenette 2,1350 Orbe,VD,Switzerland; Tel:+41(0)24 442 61 11

Médecin Généraliste de Vevey Pierre,Rue de Sadaz 5,1373 Chavornay,VD,Switzerland; Tel:+41(0)24 441 41 49

Didier Schläfli,1443 Champvent,VD,Switzerland; Tel:+41(0)79 447 26 75

Benoît Kramer,Promenade des Pins 3,1400 Yverdon-les-Bains,VD,Switzerland; Ttel:+41(0)78 742 03 75

Marechal Ferrant Joseph Scordo,7 rue de l Étang,39260 Crenans,Jura,France; Tel:+33(0)6 33 50 52 50

Taxi d'Orbe, Denise Vaney,Chemin des Covets 17,1350 Orbe,VD,Switzerland; Tel:+41(0)24 441 22 41

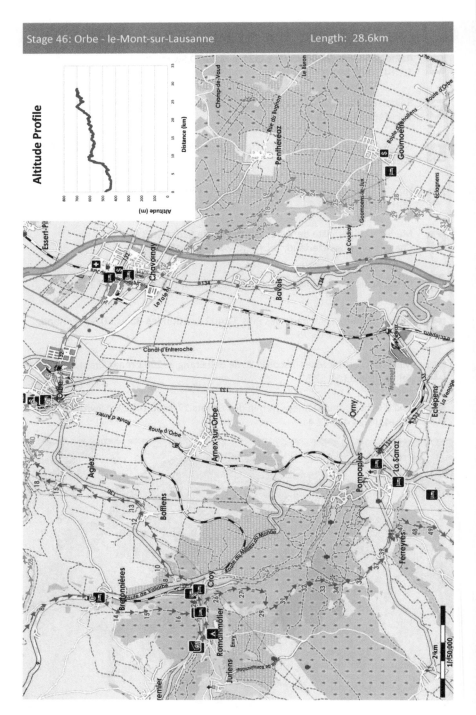

Stage Summary: after leaving Orbe the route follows minor roads, farm and woodland tracks to le-Mont-sur-Lausanne on the hills overlooking lake Geneva.

Distance from Besançon: 103km
Stage Ascent: 688m

Distance to Vercelli: 332km
Stage Descent: 471m

Waypoint	Distance between waypoints	Total km	Directions	Verification Point	Compass	Altitude m
46.001	0	0.0	From place du Marché, beside the restaurant du Chasseur, bear right on rue Centrale	No Entry sign	S	481
46.002	130	0.1	Take the right fork, direction Cossonay on rue du Grand Pont	Pass le ancien couvent des Clarisses	SW	476
46.003	80	0.2	At the crossroads, continue straight ahead	Cross the river bridge	SW	473
46.004	170	0.4	After crossing the bridge turn left	Route de Saint-Eloi, direction Chavornay	E	471
46.005	700	1.1	At the roundabout, turn right direction Chavornay and join cycle track on the left side of road	Pass the Nestlé factory on left	SE	440
46.006	2500	3.6	On the entry to Chavornay turn right to cross over the main road following the cycle path and pass in front of the hotel and railway station	Industrial buildings to the right	S	448
46.007	600	4.2	Turn left	Under the railway bridge	E	444
46.008	70	4.3	Fork left on the larger road	Rue du Château	NE	446
46.009	70	4.4	At the junction, turn right	Rue du Château	E	447
46.010	130	4.5	At the T-junction with the major road, turn right	Boulangerie ahead at the junction	S	453

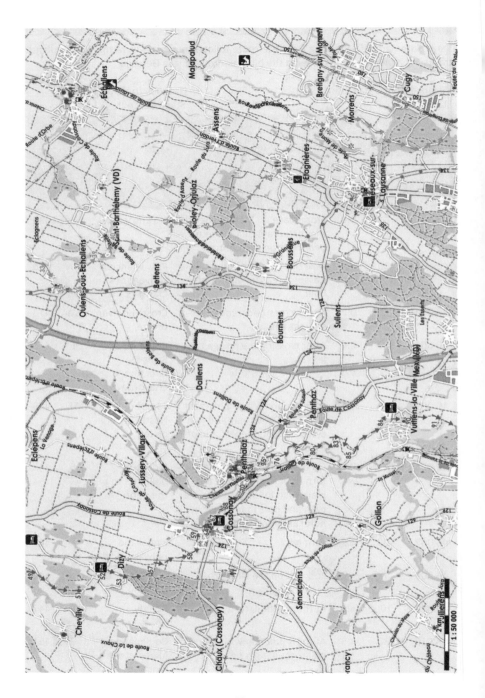

Waypoint	Distance between waypoints	Total km	Directions	Verification Point	Compass	Altitude m
46.011	400	4.9	Bear left onto rue de Collège	Café on your left	SE	456
46.012	160	5.0	On the apex of the bend to the left, turn right	Tourisme Pédestre sign	SE	468
46.013	400	5.4	Take the right fork, tarmac gives way to unmade road	Tourisme Pédestre sign	SE	469
46.014	600	6.0	At the junction, after passing under motorway, turn right down the hill	Tourisme Pédestre sign	W	470
46.015	100	6.1	Turn left, just in front of a large white house, pass through the courtyard and continue with woods to the right	Tourisme Pédestre sign	SE	454
46.016	1800	7.8	Fork left	Tourisme Pédestre sign	SE	495
46.017	40	7.9	Turn left up the hill	Tourisme Pédestre sign	E	499
46.018	400	8.2	Turn right at the top of the steep hill	Tourisme Pédestre sign	SE	560
46.019	500	8.7	Fork right up the hill	Tourisme Pédestre sign	SE	591
46.020	400	9.1	Cross the concrete road and continue on the track	Towards the tower	SE	605
46.021	260	9.3	Turn right at the crossroads in the track	Tourisme Pédestre sign	W	604
46.022	230	9.5	Turn left direction Etagnières	Tourisme Pédestre sign	S	602
46.023	180	9.7	The track emerges onto a concrete road, turn right down the hill	Tourisme Pédestre sign	S	611
46.024	180	9.9	Bear left down the hill beside "Golf du domaine du Brésil"	Tourisme Pédestre sign	S	596
46.025	900	10.8	At the T-junction, turn right down the hill	Sign for the golf club	SW	587
46.026	140	10.9	Turn left just after passing the house - Goumens-le-Jux	Tourisme Pédestre sign	SE	586

Waypoint	Distance between waypoints	Total km	Directions	Verification Point	Compass	Altitude m
46.027	400	11.3	Bear right at fork	Tourisme Pédestre sign	S	589
46.028	700	12.0	Turn right direction Etagniérs	Tourisme Pédestre sign	SW	583
46.029	700	12.6	Turn left onto Chemin du Talent, slightly up the hill and towards church spire	Tourisme Pédestre sign	SE	567
46.030	200	12.8	Fork right onto the concrete road	Tourisme Pédestre sign	S	575
46.031	140	12.9	Bear right between trees	Tourisme Pédestre sign	W	577
46.032	300	13.3	The track emerges onto a concrete road, turn left	Pass a water treatment plant on right	S	565
46.033	1000	14.2	At the crossroads, continue straight ahead on route d'Eclagnens	Towards Oulens-sous-Echallens	W	573
46.034	400	14.6	Bear left into village	Route du Centre	S	588
46.035	260	14.9	At the T-junction, turn left	Direction Echallens	S	587
46.036	140	15.0	Turn left on the gravel track, towards woods	Junction opposite "Antiques"	E	585
46.037	600	15.6	Turn right in front of woods	Keep trees on left	SE	583
46.038	250	15.9	Take the left fork, towards the river	Tourisme Pédestre sign	SE	575
46.039	220	16.1	After crossing the river, turn right keeping the farm buildings on your left	Tourisme Pédestre sign	E	572
46.040	700	16.8	At T-junction with major road turn right and immediately bear left beside trees	Tourisme Pédestre sign	S	586
46.041	1100	17.9	At the T-junction, turn left direction Bioley-Orjulaz	Large factory at the bottom of the hill on left	SE	593

Waypoint	Distance between waypoints	Total km	Directions	Verification Point	Compass	Altitude m
46.042	600	18.5	At the junction, continue straight ahead	Direction Assens	E	591
46.043	240	18.7	At the crossroads, just before reaching the village of Bioley-Orjulaz, turn right onto Cycle Route n° 22	Direction Lausanne	S	606
46.044	270	19.0	At the crossroads, continue straight ahead following the Cycle Route	Towards woods	S	614
46.045	600	19.6	Fork left and then bear right on chemin de la Forêt	Avoid the gravel track beside the woods to the left	SE	602
46.046	1700	21.3	Bear right	Into Etagnières	S	611
46.047	270	21.6	Continue straight ahead towards the village centre	Cycle Route n° 22, direction Lausanne	SE	623
46.048	220	21.8	At the T-junction with the main road, turn right and immediately left, Cycle Route n° 22	Junction opposite railway station	SE	628
46.049	2100	23.9	Pass through Morrens and bear right on Chemin de la Mèbre	Cycle Route n° 22, direction Lausanne	S	695
46.050	4100	28.0	At the T-junction, in le-Mont-sur-Lausanne turn left	Leave Cycle Route n° 22	NE	696
46.051	90	28.1	At the roundabout, turn right	Direction Lausanne	S	703
46.052	500	28.6	Arrive at le-Mont-sur-Lausanne centre. Note:- if you wish to reach the wider facilities of Lausanne, then bus n° 8 will take you from the bus stop near the roundabout to the centre of the city	Beside roundabout, hotel on the left		699

Paroisee Protestante,Route de la Blécherette,1052 Le-Mont-sur-Lausanne,VD,Switzerland; Tel:+41(0)21 652 21 47; Price:D

Hôtel de la Croix-Blanche,Grand rue,1315 La-Sarraz,VD,Switzerland; Tel:+41(0)21 866 71 54; Email:croixblanche@bluemail.ch; Web-site:www.hotelcroixblanche.ch; Price:A

B&B - Adam,(Yoko & Michel Adam),Route d'Eclagnens 14,1376 Goumoens-la-Ville,VD,Switzerland; Tel:+41(0)76 411 37 76; Price:B

Hôtel O Sole Mio,Route de la Foule,1315 La-Sarraz,VD,Switzerland; Tel:+41(0)21 866 71 39; Email:hotel@o-sole-mio.org; Web-site:www.o-sole-mio.org; Price:A

B&B - Christina de Raad-Iseli,Route de Dizy,1315 La-Sarraz,VD,Switzerland; +41(0)79 762 87 11; Email:de_raad_iseli@bluewin.ch; Web-site:www.ferme-iseli.ch; Price:A

La Ferme la Lizerne - Chambres d'Hôtes,(Francois-Philippe Devenoge),Rue du Village 16,1304 Dizy,VD,Switzerland; Tel:+41(0)21 861 38 52; +41(0)79 253 17 70; Email:fphd@worldcom.ch ; Web-site:www.tourisme-rural.ch; Price:B

Hôtel le Funi,(Michel & Marianne Tanniger),Avenue du Funiculaire 11,1304 Cossonay-Ville,VD,Switzerland; Tel:+41(0)21 863 63 40; Email:info@lefuni.ch; Web-site:www.lefuni.ch; Price:A

Galion's Pub & Hôtel,Route de Genève 1,1033 Chéseaux-sur-Lausanne,VD,Switzerland; Tel:+41(0)21 732 16 28; Email:info@galions.ch; Web-site:www.galions.ch; Price:A

B&B - Chez Vullioud,Rue Grande Vigne 7,1302 Vufflens-la-Ville,VD,Switzerland; Tel:+41(0)21 550 38 44; Email:pa@inetis.ch; Price:A

Hôtel Central,Place de Coppoz 4,1052 Mont-sur-Lausanne,VD,Switzerland; Tel:+41(0)21 652 01 46; Price:B

Hotel Ibis Budget,Rue de l'Industrie 67,1030 Lausanne-Bussigny,VD,Switzerland; Tel:+41(0)21 706 53 53; Web-site:www.ibis.com; Price:A

Hôtel Pont de la Venoge,Chemin du Tennis 4,1026 Echandens,VD,Switzerland; Tel:+41(0)21 701 50 55; Email:info@pontdelavenoge.ch; Web-site:pontdelavenoge.ch; Price:A

B&B - Deillon,Route des Flumeaux 10,1008 Prilly,VD,Switzerland; Tel:+41(0)21 625 76 80; +41(0)79 689 45 41; Email:deillon@2wire.ch; Web-site:www.bnb-prilly.ch; Price:A

Hôtel du Marché,Rue Pré-du-Marché 42,1004 Lausanne,VD,Switzerland; Tel:+41(0)21 647 99 00; Email:info@hoteldumarche-lausanne.ch; Web-site:www.hoteldumarche-lausanne.ch; Price:A

Ecurie des Planches,Chemin des Planches 3,1040 Echallens,VD,Switzerland; Tel:+41(0)21 881 62 68; Web-site:www.cheval-loisir.ch/ecuriedesplanches/

Centre Equestre,Chemin du Caudoz 4,1053 Bretigny-sur-Morrens,VD,Switzerland; Tel:+41(0)21 731 47 87

Manége du Mont,Chemin des Buchilles 30,1052 Mont-sur-Lausanne,VD,Switzerland; Tel:+41(0)21 652 99 11; Web-site:www.manege-du-mont.ch/

Manége du Mont,Chemin des Buchilles 30,1052 Mont-sur-Lausanne,VD,Switzerland; Tel:+41(0)21 652 99 11; Web-site:www.manege-du-mont.ch/

Raiffeisen Schweiz,Rue du Château 4 ,1376 Goumoens-la-Ville,VD,Switzerland; Tel:+41(0)21 886 02 02

Raiffeisen Schweiz,Route de Coppoz 22 ,1052 Le-Mont-sur-Lausanne,VD,Switzerland; Tel:+41(0)21 886 20 40

Postomat,Route de Lausanne 14,1052 Le-Mont-sur-Lausanne,VD,Switzerland; Tel:+41(0)84 888 87 10

Centre Hospitalier Universitaire Vaudois,Rue du Bugnon 21,1011 Lausanne,VD,Switzerland; Tel:+41(0)21 314 11 11

Vétérinaire Girard Pierre-Joël,Pré Verly,1374 Corcelles-sur-Chavornay,VD,Switzerland; Tel:+41(0)24 441 46 86

B & W Sports et Loisirs - Bantam & Wankmüller SA,Route en Rambuz 1,1037 Etagnières,VD,Switzerland; Tel:+41(0)21 731 91 91

Taxis Modernes S.A.,Chemin d'Entre-Bois 21,1018 Lausanne,VD,Switzerland; Tel:+41(0)21 648 41 18

Taxi Bleu,Route de Praz Palud 5,1040 Echallens,VD,Switzerland; Tel:+41(0)21 881 57 57

Daniel Services, Taxi Mais Pas Seulement,Chemin du Levant 25,1315 La-Sarraz,VD,Switzerland; Tel:+41(0)79 911 31 43

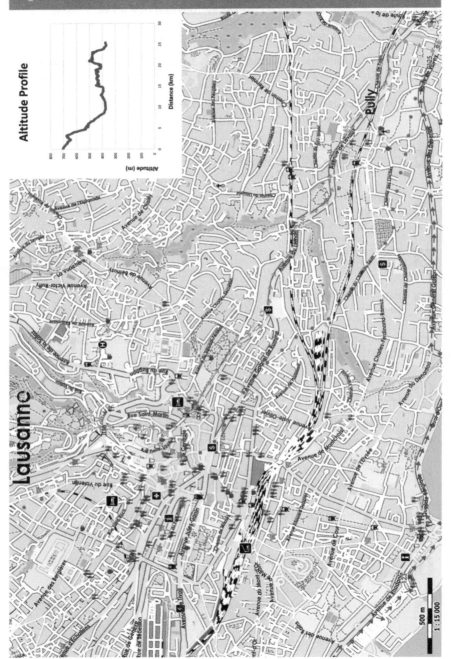

Stage Summary: the route takes small roads and pathways through woodland and parks and briefly joins the Via Jacobi (a further tributary of the St James Way) before passing beside the Lausanne Cathedral. The exit from the city follows pavements beside busy highways before rejoining Route 70 by the lake-shore. The section then climbs into the vineyard terraces with beautiful views of the lake and mountains, finally returning to the lake-side in Vevey. Cyclists may wish to avoid the climb into the vineyards and remain on the lake-side road. For those wishing for some relief from the tracks and roads and a change of scene, the lake steamers leave from Lausanne-Ouchy and visit Vevey, Montreux, Villeneuve and Le Bouveret. Details can be found at http://www.cgn.ch

Distance from Besançon: 132km   Distance to Vercelli: 303km
Stage Ascent: 568m   Stage Descent: 896m

Waypoint	Distance between waypoints	Total km	Directions	Verification Point	Compass	Altitude m
47.001	0	0.0	From beside Hôtel Central on place de Coppoz, continue straight ahead on the left side of the road and the join the pathway in the park that separates the 2 roads	Towards the church steeple, keep line of trees on your left	S	703
47.002	210	0.2	Pass the church on your left side and continue straight ahead	Between two lines of trees	S	703
47.003	240	0.5	At the end of the avenue of trees, return to the pavement on the right of the road and continue straight ahead	Open grassed area to your right	S	700
47.004	180	0.6	At the crossroads, beside the Auberge Communale le Mont, turn left and then bear left	Chemin du Pré-d'Ogue, pass No Through Road sign on your right	SE	694
47.005	50	0.7	Take the right fork, downhill	Chemin du Vallon, Tourisme Pédestre	SE	694

94

Waypoint	Distance between waypoints	Total km	Directions	Verification Point	Compass	Altitude m
47.006	140	0.8	At the end of the tarmac road, continue straight ahead and follow the track across the field	Two garages on your right	SE	687
47.007	500	1.3	At the T-junction with road, cross the road and turn right	Pass parking area close on your left	S	674
47.008	90	1.4	At the end of the parking area, go down the 3 steps and turn left to enter the fenced area around the sawmill. Curiously the path passes between the mill buildings.	Pass the yellow tower and adjacent wooden building, close on your right, yellow diamond on the wooden building	SE	669
47.009	250	1.6	Fork right downhill on the gravel track	St Jacques route n° 4	S	668
47.010	190	1.8	Turn right, down the hill on the wooden steps	Direction lac de Sauvabelin	SW	666
47.011	100	1.9	Turn right over the wooden foot-bridge and then immediately left	Keep the stream close on your left	S	657
47.012	250	2.2	Beside the highway bridge, turn right	Enter parking Vivarium	SW	648
47.013	70	2.3	Turn sharp right and climb the concrete steps. Note:- to avoid the steps, remain on the road to the T-junction with the main road and then turn right into the woods on the broad track to the crossroads with the Main Route where you should turn left	Under the highway bridge, beside the Buvette	W	643
47.014	70	2.3	At the top of the steps, bear left then right	Keep the highway on your right	W	645

Waypoint	Distance between waypoints	Total km	Directions	Verification Point	Compass	Altitude m
47.015	150	2.5	Shortly before reaching the bridge over the highway, turn left into the woods	Tourisme Pédestre	S	658
47.016	160	2.6	At the crossroads with the tarmac track, continue straight ahead		SW	658
47.017	80	2.7	At the junction with the main road, cross over and turn left and then bear right on chemin des Celtes	Towards parking area, yellow hiking route sign	S	663
47.018	220	2.9	Beside the bus stop for Lac de Sauvabelin, keep right on the road	Towards the Auberge du Lac de Sauvabelin	S	669
47.019	90	3.0	At the end of the buildings on the right, take the middle of the three paths	Towards la Tour	S	669
47.020	170	3.2	With la Tour directly ahead, take the left fork	Pass the tower on your right	S	677
47.021	150	3.3	At the T-junction after passing the tower, turn left on the tarmac	Views of lake Geneva through the trees	SE	669
47.022	90	3.4	At the crossroads, turn right	Yellow footpath signs	S	665
47.023	110	3.5	At the T-junction with the car park directly ahead, turn left		SE	649
47.024	60	3.6	At the T-junction with the road, take the pedestrian crossing and turn right	Beside the old funicular station	S	646
47.025	40	3.6	At the end of the funicular station, bear left diagonally across the car park and take the footpath	Pass the house with the red and white shutters on your right	S	643
47.026	220	3.9	At the viewpoint over the entire length of the lake, bear right and then turn left	Follow the yellow footpath sign	W	630

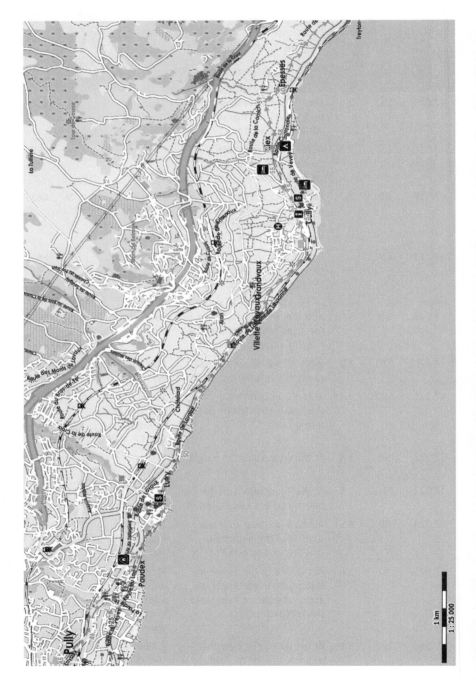

Waypoint	Distance between waypoints	Total km	Directions	Verification Point	Compass	Altitude m
47.027	130	4.0	At the T-junction, turn left and then left again	Follow the n° 4 footpath sign	S	622
47.028	30	4.0	Turn left on the track, following the n° 4 sign	Modern low rise office building on your right	SE	618
47.029	70	4.1	At the T-junction in the tracks, turn right	Grass on your right, trees on your left	SW	615
47.030	250	4.3	At the foot of the track, bear left around the circle and then turn left following the Tourisme Pédestre sign	Pass Fondation de l'Hermitage on your right	S	583
47.031	80	4.4	As the pathway starts to turn sharply to the right, turn left through the trees	Tourisme Pédestre sign	S	572
47.032	150	4.6	At the crossroads in the tracks, continue straight ahead downhill	Yellow arrow	SW	551
47.033	130	4.7	At the T-junction with the main road, rue de la Barre, turn left	Towards the mini-roundabout	S	533
47.034	50	4.7	At the mini-roundabout, continue straight ahead, then bear left in the direction of the cathedral	Pass Château Saint-Marie on your right	S	529
47.035	110	4.8	Cross the place du Château and then bear left into rue de Cité Derrier	Initially towards the Préfecture	S	531
47.036	190	5.0	At the junction with rue Charles-Vuilermet, bear left	Under the archway	S	533
47.037	40	5.1	At the junction with place de la Cathédrale, continue straight ahead and skirt the cathedral	Cathedral walls on the right	SW	527

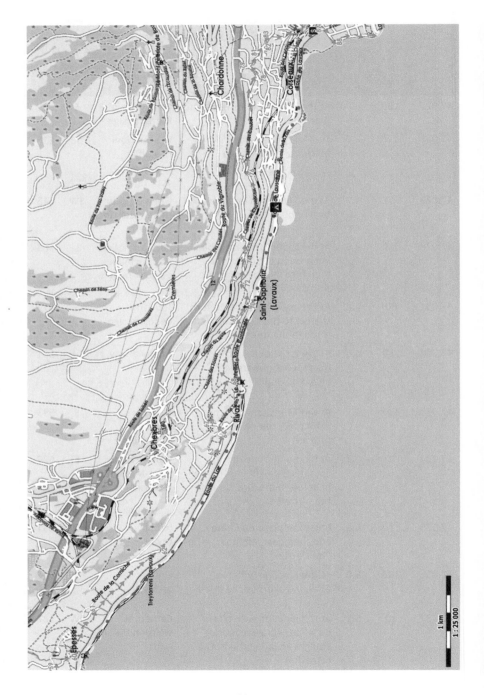

Waypoint	Distance between waypoints	Total km	Directions	Verification Point	Compass	Altitude m
47.038	80	5.1	From the side entrance to the cathedral, bear left and downhill	Pass MUDAC - Musée de Design et d'Arts Appliqués Contemporains on the right	SE	523
47.039	70	5.2	At the T-junction, turn left	Pass between the stone pillars and cross the road bridge	SE	514
47.040	150	5.4	At the traffic lights, continue straight ahead, direction Vevey	Beside the metro station	SE	520
47.041	170	5.5	At the traffic lights continue straight ahead	Pass Parc de Mon-Repos on the left	SE	519
47.042	400	6.0	Shortly after passing the steps on the left, bear right at the traffic lights	Avenue du Léman	SE	512
47.043	290	6.3	Bear left on Avenue du Léman	Direction Vevey, pass a park on the right	E	498
47.044	700	6.9	At the roundabout, continue straight ahead on Avenue du Léman	Enter Pully and pass a further roundabout	SE	463
47.045	800	7.8	At the major crossroads, continue straight ahead	Towards the lake	SE	430
47.046	300	8.1	At the roundabout, after passing under the railway, continue straight ahead	Trees in the centre of the road	E	415
47.047	400	8.4	At the traffic lights, after passing the arched railway bridge on the left, turn right	Chemin de la Damataire	S	396

Waypoint	Distance between waypoints	Total km	Directions	Verification Point	Compass	Altitude m
47.048	260	8.7	At the traffic lights, turn left;Note:- the AlternateRoute from Romainmôtier joins from the right	Direction Vevey Montreux, Cycle Route n° 7	E	383
47.049	700	9.4	Bear right through the car park towards the boat dock and follow the lake-side	Water immediately on the right	E	378
47.050	1300	10.7	Turn left and then right to rejoin the main road	Route de Lavaux, beside pedestrian subway	SE	375
47.051	1200	11.8	Beside the Villettes railway station, cross the road, descend the ramp, pass under the railway and bear right, parallel to the railway and into the vineyards	Direction Villette Bourg	SE	384
47.052	2000	13.8	On reaching the Cully railway station, bear right on the small road	Close to the railway, Café la Gare on the left	NE	390
47.053	120	14.0	At the crossroads beside the railway bridge, continue straight ahead	Pass winery on the left, chemin de Vigny	NE	391
47.054	300	14.3	Take the right fork, close to the railway	Pass a cemetery on the left	E	395
47.055	160	14.4	Take the left fork	Elevated highway on your right	E	392
47.056	140	14.6	Gently bear left up the hill	Between the vines	E	391
47.057	100	14.7	Keep right	Parallel to lake-shore	E	394
47.058	190	14.9	Bear left on chemin de Plan-Pérey	Continuing to climb the hill	E	400

Waypoint	Distance between waypoints	Total km	Directions	Verification Point	Compass	Altitude m
47.059	400	15.3	At the T-junction, on the outskirts of the village of Epesses turn right	Chemin de l'Ouchette	SE	449
47.060	170	15.4	Bear left in the hamlet	Chemin du Calamin, parallel to lake-shore	SE	428
47.061	700	16.1	At the junction, continue straight ahead		SE	433
47.062	900	17.0	At the junction, continue straight ahead	Winery on the right at the junction	SE	438
47.063	1300	18.3	At the crossroads, turn right, downhill on the tarmac road	Viewpoint on the right at the junction	E	443
47.064	220	18.5	On the outskirts of the village of Rivaz turn right and right again	Cross the bridge	SE	436
47.065	60	18.6	Turn left left on rue du Collége	Beside the covered water trough	NE	432
47.066	80	18.7	Turn left on route des Bons Voisins	House with large clock ahead	N	443
47.067	50	18.7	Turn right on chemin des Paleyres	Continue in the vineyards parallel to the lake-shore	E	451
47.068	500	19.2	At the crossroads, continue straight ahead, chemin de la Vigne-a-Gilles	Château on the lake-side below	E	417
47.069	800	20.0	At the T-junction, turn right	Towards the village	SE	426
47.070	170	20.2	In front of the bell tower in Saint-Saphorin bear left up the hill	Sentier des Rondes	E	411
47.071	200	20.4	At the crossroads continue straight ahead up the hill	Sentier des Rondes	NE	437

Waypoint	Distance between waypoints	Total km	Directions	Verification Point	Compass	Altitude m
47.072	80	20.5	At the junction, bear left up the hill		E	449
47.073	60	20.5	At the T-junction with the road turn right and then bear left uphill on the narrow road	Route 70 sign, keep wall close on the left	E	462
47.074	220	20.8	At the fork bear left on chemin du Burignon	Towards and under railway	E	470
47.075	290	21.1	On the bend to the right bear right on the lower road	Parallel to the railway, Chemin de Chavonchin	E	502
47.076	800	21.9	At the fork, bear right on chemin des Combes		E	485
47.077	170	22.0	At the junction, keep left	Chemin des Combes	E	477
47.078	900	22.9	On the crown of the bend to the right, turn sharp left	Chemin du Grand Pin	NE	464
47.079	180	23.1	At the crossroads, turn sharp right and go downhill on chemin des Rochettes	Towards Corseaux	SE	479
47.080	170	23.3	At the T-junction in Corseaux, turn left on rue du Village	Vinicole Corseaux	E	449
47.081	40	23.3	At the junction, bear right downhill	Rue du Village, boulangerie on the left	SE	449
47.082	80	23.4	At the T-junction, turn left	Hotel on the left	SE	445
47.083	170	23.6	Shortly before crossing the funicular track, turn right down the steps on chemin de la Crausaz. Note:- to avoid the steps continue straight ahead on the cyclists and riders Alternate Route	Parallel to the funicular	SW	430
47.084	160	23.7	At the T-junction, turn left	Chemin du Marguery	SE	404

Waypoint	Distance between waypoints	Total km	Directions	Verification Point	Compass	Altitude m
47.085	180	23.9	At the T-junction, turn left on rue des Cerisiers and then bear right under the railway bridges	Funicular station on the left	S	391
47.086	210	24.1	At the roundabout continue straight ahead on avenue Nestlé	Direction Vielle Ville	S	385
47.087	130	24.3	Turn right on avenue de Savoie	Beside Nestlé offices	SW	385
47.088	170	24.4	Turn left and proceed along the lake-shore	Quai Ernest Ansermet	SE	379
47.089	1100	25.5	Arrive at Vevey (LIII)	Grande Place on the left		375

Alternate Route #47.A1		Length: 0.8km				
Stage Summary: avoiding steps.						
Stage Ascent: 2m		Stage Descent: 41m				
47A1.001	0	0.0	Continue straight ahead	Cross the funicular track	E	428
47A1.002	400	0.4	At the traffic lights turn right	Pass petrol station on the left	SW	419
47A1.003	500	0.8	Rejoin the Main Route and continue straight ahead	Under railway bridge		390

Paroisse Lutry,Route de Lavaux 17,1095 Lutry,VD,Switzerland; Tel:+41(0)21 791 25 49; Email:paroisse.lutry@cath-vd.ch; Price:D

Paroisse de Notre Dame,Rue des Chenevières 4,1800 Vevey,VD,Switzerland; Tel:+41(0)21 944 14 14; Price:D

Auberge de Jeunesse Jeunotel,Chemin du Bois-de-Vaux 36,1007 Lausanne,VD,Switzerland; Tel:+41(0)21 626 02 22; Email:lausanne@ youthhostel.ch; Web-site:www.youthhostel.ch/lausanne; Price:B

Lausanne Backpacker Hôtel,Chemin des Epinettes 4,1007 Lausanne,VD,Switzerland; Tel:+41(0)21 601 80 00; Email:info@lausanne-guesthouse.ch; Web-site:www.lausanne-guesthouse.ch; Price:B

Riviera Lodge Backpacker Hostel,Place du Marché 5,1800 Vevey,VD,Switzerland; +41(0)79 318 75 93; Email:info@rivieralodge.ch; Web-site:www.rivieralodge.ch; Price:B

Pension Bon-Séjour,Rue Caroline 10,1003 Lausanne,VD,Switzerland; Tel:+41(0)21 323 59 52

Motel des Pierrettes,Route Cantonale 19,1025 Saint-Sulpice,VD,Switzerland; Tel:+41(0)21 691 25 25; Email:info@motel-lausanne.com ; Web-site:motel-lausanne.com; Price:A

Starling Hotel,Route Cantonale 31,1025 Saint-Sulpice,VD,Switzerland; Tel:+41(0)21 694 85 85; Email:contact@shlausanne.ch; Web-site:www.shlausanne.com; Price:A

Hôtel Bellerive,Avenue de Cour 99,1007 Lausanne,VD,Switzerland; Tel:+41(0)21 614 90 00; Web-site:hotelbellerive.ch; Price:A

B&B - le Vigny,Chemin du Vigny 10,1096 Cully,VD,Switzerland; Tel:+41(0)21 799 38 12; +41(0)79 764 69 24; Email:bnb@levigny.ch; Web-site:www.levigny.ch; Price:B

Hôtel-Restaurant au Major-Davel,Place d'Armes 8,1096 Cully,VD,Switzerland; Tel:+41(0)21 799 94 94; Web-site:www.hotelaumajordavel.ch; Price:A

B&B - Nabel,(Jean-Pierre & Elisabeth Narbel),Chemin des Arquebusiers 20,1800 Vevey,VD,Switzerland; Tel:+41(0)21 921 52 10; +41(0)79 643 00 34; Web-site:www.bnb.ch; Price:B

Pension Burgle,Rue Louis-Meyer 16,1800 Vevey,VD,Switzerland; Tel:+41(0)21 921 40 23; Web-site:www.burgle.ch; Price:B

Camping de Vidy,Chemin du Camping 3,1007 Lausanne,VD,Switzerland; Tel:+41(0)21 622 50 00; Email:info@campinglausannevidy.ch; Web-site:www. campinglausannevidy.ch; Price:C; Note:Bungalows also available,

Camping de Moratel,Route de Moratel 2 ,1096 Cully,VD,Switzerland; Tel:+41(0)21 799 19 14; Email:camping.moratel@bluewin.ch; Web-site:www.cvmc.ch/index.php/moratel/camping.html; Price:C

Camping de la Pichette,Chemin de la Paix 37,1802 Corseaux,VD,Switzerland; Tel:+41(0)21 921 09 97; Email:gerances@vevey.ch; Web-site:www.vevey.ch/N1134/camping-de-la-pichette.html; Price:C

Manége du Chalet-À-Gobet,Route de Berne 304,1000 Chalet-À-Gobet,VD,Switzerland; Tel:+41(0)21 784 14 34; Web-site:www.manege-chalet-a-gobet.ch/

ℹ Lausanne Tourisme,Avenue de Rhodanie 2,1007 Lausanne,VD,Switzerland; Tel:+41(0)21 613 73 73

ℹ Office du Tourisme,Place de la Gare 4,1096 Cully,VD,Switzerland; Tel:+41(0)84 886 84 84; Web-site:www.lavaux.com

ℹ Office du Tourisme,Grande place 29,1800 Vevey,VD,Switzerland; Tel:+41(0)84 886 84 84; Web-site:www.montreux-vevey.com/

$ BCV,Place Saint-François 14,1003 Lausanne,VD,Switzerland; Tel:+41(0)84 422 82 28

$ BSI,Avenue de Rumine 3,1005 Lausanne,VD,Switzerland; Tel:+41(0)58 809 41 41

$ LGT Bank,Avenue Ramuz 43,1009 Pully,VD,Switzerland; Tel:+41(0)21 711 87 00

$ Raiffeisen Schweiz,Grand-rue 38 ,1095 Lutry,VD,Switzerland; Tel:+41(0)21 796 65 25; Web-site:www.raiffeisen.ch

$ Raiffeisen Schweiz,Place du Temple 18,1096 Cully,VD,Switzerland; Tel:+41(0)21 799 30 93

$ Banca COOP,Avenue Général-Guisan 15,1800 Vevey,VD,Switzerland; Tel:+41(0)61 286 21 21

$ Banque COOP,Avenue Général- Guisan 15,1800 Vevey,VD,Switzerland; Tel:+41(0)21 925 93 20

$ Banque Migros,Rue de Lausanne 17,1800 Vevey,VD,Switzerland; Tel:+41(0)21 923 34 34

$ UBS,Rue de Lausanne,1800 Vevey,VD,Switzerland; Tel:+41(0)21 925 97 11

🚉 Gare - CFF,Place de la Gare,1003 Lausanne,VD,Switzerland; Tel:+41(0)90 030 03 00; Web-site:www.CFF.ch

🚉 Gare - CFF,Place de la Gare,1800 Vevey,VD,Switzerland; Tel:+41(0)90 030 03 00; Web-site:www.CFF.ch

ℍ Hôpital de Lavaux,Ch.de Colombaires 31,1096 Cully,VD,Switzerland; Tel:+41(0)21 799 01 11; Web-site:www.hopitaldelavaux.ch

ℍ Hôpital la Providence,Avenue de la Prairie 3,1800 Vevey,VD,Switzerland; Tel:+41(0)21 977 55 55; Web-site:www.hopital-riviera.ch

✚ Dr.Laurent Föllmi,Rue Haldimand 14,1003 Lausanne,VD,Switzerland; Tel:+41(0)21 320 07 67

🚶 Sports Discount,Rue de Genève 17,1003 Lausanne,VD,Switzerland; Tel:+41(0)21 311 00 74

🚲 Bicycles Shop Sàrl,Avenue de Tivoli 7,1007 Lausanne,VD,Switzerland; Tel:+41(0)21 320 10 80

🚲 Le Cyclocampeur,Rue d'Italie 26,1800 Vevey,VD,Switzerland; Tel:+41(0)21 922 04 90

🚗 Michel Bertschy,Maréchal Ferrant,Route de la Comba 11,1680 Romont,VD,Switzerland; Tel:+41(0)26 652 14 13

🚕 Taxis Sans Frontières Sàrl,Rue de Fribourg 28,1800 Vevey,VD,Switzerland; Tel:+41(0)21 923 50 50

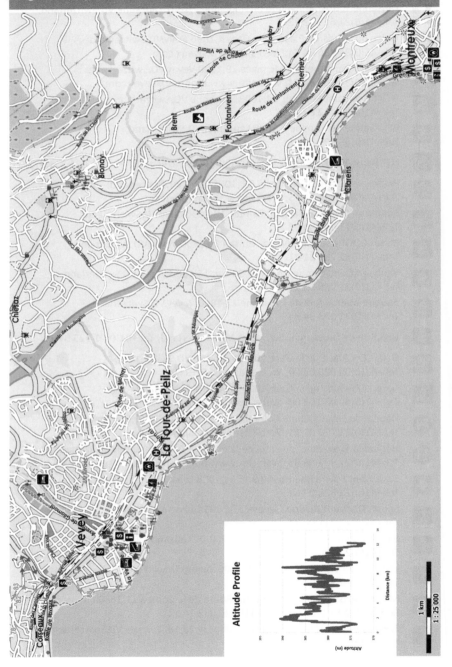

Altitude Profile

Altitude (m)

Distance (km)

1 km

1 : 25 000

Stage Summary: this short section continues almost entirely on the lake-side paths and roadways generally following Swiss cycle route n° 1. There is the opportunity to break the journey in Montreux.

Distance from Besançon: 157km
Stage Ascent: 186m

Distance to Vercelli: 277km
Stage Descent: 187m

Waypoint	Distance between waypoints	Total km	Directions	Verification Point	Compass	Altitude m
48.001	0	0.0	From the Grande Place, continue straight ahead along the lake-shore	Boat dock on the right	SE	376
48.002	1400	1.4	In la Tour-de-Peilz, shortly after the lake-side road turns inland on rue du Château turn right on rue du Bourg-Dessous	Cycle Route n° 1	SE	382
48.003	160	1.6	Turn left on the Cycle Route towards the main road	Pass water fountain on the right	NE	382
48.004	70	1.6	At the T-junction with the main road, turn right	Cycle Route n° 1, towards Montreux	SE	387
48.005	3200	4.9	At the traffic lights, after passing the bus garage on the left, turn right on rue du Torrent to return to lake-side and then turn left	Quai de Clarens	SE	384
48.006	2000	6.8	Beside the Tourist Office in Montreux continue straight ahead	Quai de la Rouvenaz	S	381
48.007	4700	11.5	On entry to Villeneuve, bear right to remain close to the water	Leaving Cycle Route n° 1	S	378
48.008	700	12.2	Arrive at Villeneuve	Beside the steamer jetty		375

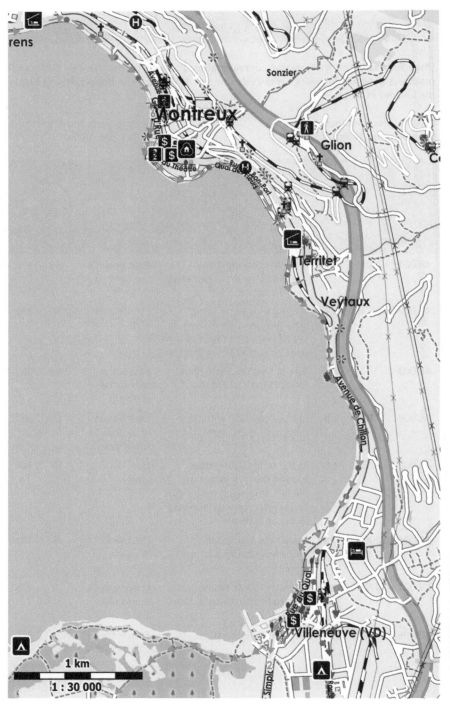

rens

Sonzier

H

Montreux

Glion

S
S S

du Théâtre
Quai de Fleurs
Rue Bon-Port

Territet

Veytaux

Avenue de Chillon

Villeneuve (VD)

S

S

1 km

1 : 30 000

Paroisse Catholique de Montreux,Avenue des Planches 27,1820 Montreux,VD,Switzerland; Tel:+41(0)21 963 37 08; Email:paroisse.montreux@cath-vd.ch; Price:D

Montreux Lake-Side (B&B,Hostel),Rue du Lac 46,1815 Clarens,VD,Switzerland; Tel:+41(0)76 340 33 50; Web-site:www.montreux-bnb.com; Price:B

Auberge de Jeunesse Montreux-Territet,Passage de l'Auberge 8,1820 Montreux,VD,Switzerland; Tel:+41(0)21 963 49 34; Email:montreux@ youthhostel.ch; Web-site:www.youthhostel.ch/montreux; Price:B

B&B - Marzio,(Rita Marzio),Route de Longefan 21,1844 Villeneuve,VD,Switzerland; Tel:+41(0)12 196 02 71 7; +41(0)76 397 27 17; Price:B

Auberge de la Truite,Ruelle de la Truite 3,1845 Noville,VD,Switzerland; Tel:+41(0)21 960 10 91; Price:B

Motel de Rennaz,Route de Praz-Riond 27,1847 Rennaz,VD,Switzerland; Tel:+41(0)21 960 40 41; Email:reservations@motelderennaz.ch; Web-site:www.motelderennaz.ch; Price:A

Hôtel l'Ecusson Vaudois,Route du Village,1847 Rennaz,VD,Switzerland; Tel:+41(0)21 960 10 85; Price:A

Hôtel Edirol,Rue de la Praise 32,1896 Vouvry,VS,Switzerland; Tel:+41(0)24 481 14 16; Email:info@hotel-edirol.ch; Web-site:www.hotel-edirol.ch; Price:A

Camping - les Grangettes,Route des Grangettes,1845 Noville,VD,Switzerland; Tel:+41(0)21 960 15 03; Email:noville@treyvaud.com; Web-site:www.les-grangettes.ch; Price:C

Camping les Bouleaux,Route de la Tronchenaz 5,1844 Villeneuve,VD,Switzerland; Tel:+41(0)21 960 16 30; Email:info@les-bouleaux.ch; Web-site:www.les-bouleaux.ch

Camping des Ravers,Route des Ravers 25,1894 Port-Valais,VS,Switzerland; Tel:+41(0)26 918 50 02; Price:C

Centre Équestre les Neyex,Chemin de Pionnex 13,1817 Brent,VD,Switzerland; Tel:+41(0)21 981 12 85

Centre Équestre les Neyex,Chemin de Pionnex 13,1817 Brent,VD,Switzerland; Tel:+41(0)21 981 12 85

Manège de Rennaz,1847 Rennaz,VD,Switzerland; Tel:+41(0)21 960 22 65; Web-site:www.handicheval.ch/

Tourist Office,Rue du Théâtre 11,1820 Montreux,VD,Switzerland; Tel:+41(0)84 886 84 84

Office du Tourisme,Rue du Théâtre 11,1820 Montreux,VD,Switzerland; Tel:+41(0)21 966 08 00; Web-site:www.montreux-vevey.com

Office du Tourisme le Bouveret,Case Postale 25,1897 Bouveret,VD,Switzerland; Tel:+41(0)24 481 51 21

Credit Suisse,Rue de la Paix 1,1820 Montreux,VD,Switzerland; Tel:+41(0)21 962 76 11

UBS,Avenue du Casino 41,1820 Montreux,VD,Switzerland; Tel:+41(0)21 966 78 11

$ UBS,Avenue du Casino 41,1820 Montreux,VD,Switzerland;
Tel:+41(0)21 966 78 11

$ Banque Cantonale Vaudoise,Grand rue 1,1844 Villeneuve,VD,Switzerland;
Tel:+41(0)21 967 31 69

$ Raiffeisen Schweiz,Grand rue 49,1844 Villeneuve,VD,Switzerland;
Tel:+41(0)21 921 32 88

⚶ Gare - CFF,Rue de la Gare,1820 Montreux,VD,Switzerland;
Tel:+41(0)90 030 03 00; Web-site:www.CFF.ch

H Hôpital Riviera,Avenue de Belmont 25,1820 Montreux,VD,Switzerland;
Tel:+41(0)21 966 66 66

H Clinique Bon Port,Rue de Bon-Port 27,1820 Territet,VD,Switzerland;
Tel:+41(0)21 966 57 57; Web-site:www.biotonus.ch

+ Dr.Raymond Dufour,Avenue du Casino 40,1820 Montreux,VD,Switzerland;
Tel:+41(0)21 963 23 01

🐕 Dr.Natacha Schmid Vétérinaire,Rue de l'Eglise Catholique 14,1820
Montreux,VD,Switzerland; Tel:+41(0)21 963 80 80

🥾 Muller Sports,Route de Bugnon 2,1823 Glion,VD,Switzerland;
Tel:+41(0)21 963 17 26

🚲 Cyclosport,Avenue des Alpes 64,1820 Montreux,VD,Switzerland;
Tel:+41(0)21 963 59 09

🏠 Maréchal Ferrant,Rue du Centre 33,1637 Charmey,VD,Switzerland;
Tel:+41(0)26 927 11 20

☎ Abaco Taxi,Grand rue 18,1844 Villeneuve,VD,Switzerland;
Tel:+41(0)21 965 20 20

☎ Swiss Executive Limousines Services Sàrl,Avenue de Chillon 37,1820
Veytaux,VD,Switzerland; Tel:+41(0)21 961 10 10

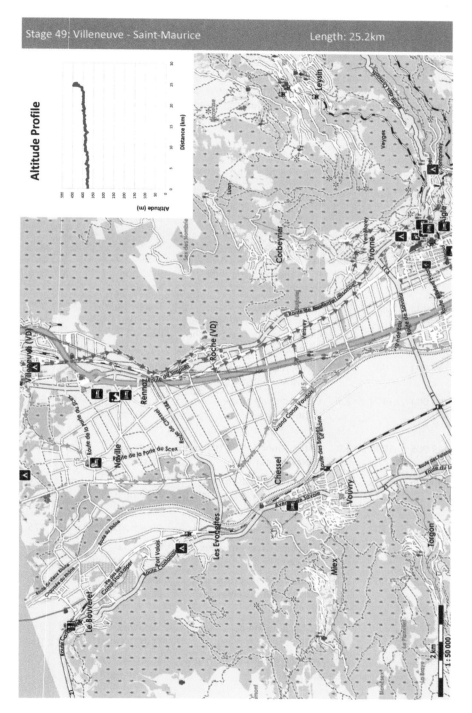

Stage Summary: this section follows pleasant pathways on the side of le Grand Canal and then on the banks of the Rhône. Route 70 diverges in Villeneuve and hugs the base of the hills first on the east and then the western side of the valley adding distance and unnecessary climbing. Route 70 will rejoin our route on the banks of the Rhône before reaching St Maurice.

Distance from Besançon: 169km   Distance to Vercelli: 265km
Stage Ascent: 319m   Stage Descent: 266m

Waypoint	Distance between waypoints	Total km	Directions	Verification Point	Compass	Altitude m
49.001	0	0.0	From the jetty, continue straight ahead	Direction Noville	SW	376
49.002	600	0.6	Turn right and leave the main road immediately after crossing the bridge over the waterway	Towards the lake, Cycle Route n°7	NW	375
49.003	90	0.7	Turn left to follow the Tourisme Pédestre sign	Keep the lake to the right	W	375
49.004	1400	2.1	Proceed straight ahead on route des Saviez	Equestrian centre on the right	SW	380
49.005	1000	3.0	At the T-junction, at the entry to Noville, turn left	Chemin du Battoir	S	374
49.006	220	3.2	At the crossroads in the centre of Noville bear right on the more major road	Rue des Anciennes Postes	S	374
49.007	70	3.3	Take right fork on the road	Direction Evian	S	375
49.008	40	3.3	Turn right on chemin des Bousses	House, la Belette, on left	S	376
49.009	90	3.4	At the T-junction turn right remaining on chemin des Bousses	Tourisme Pédestre sign	SW	376
49.010	120	3.5	At the junction bear left	Tourisme Pédestre sign	SW	374
49.011	400	3.9	Join the canal-side path and turn left	Keep the canal on your right	S	373

113

Waypoint	Distance between waypoints	Total km	Directions	Verification Point	Compass	Altitude m
49.012	1600	5.5	As the tarmac becomes an unmade track, go straight ahead remaining beside the canal	Canal on right	S	374
49.013	1100	6.6	At the junction with the main road, cross over to continue on the track beside the Grand Canal	Chessel is to the right where drinking water can be obtained	SE	380
49.014	1200	7.8	Bear right over canal bridge and turn left to continue on the canal-side path	Now, keep canal on left	SE	377
49.015	1300	9.1	Turn right and pass through the trees towards the river, then turn left to follow the path beside the Rhône. Note:- those wishing to visit the named Sigeric village of Versvey (LII) should take the canal bridge and continue straight ahead for 1200 metres. There is some controversy over whether this low lying modern village is an appropriate interpretation of the name Burbulei from Sigeric's chronicle. The village is to the left. Rejoin the route by retracing your steps to this point	Shortly before the next bridge	SE	386
49.016	2000	11.1	Continue straight ahead over the bridge	Tourisme Pédestre signs to Aigle Centre	SE	387
49.017	8500	19.6	Continue straight ahead beside the river. Note:- Swiss Route 70 joins from the left		SE	397
49.018	1900	21.5	Pass under the highway and continue straight ahead alongside the Rhône	Equestrian Centre ahead on left	S	398

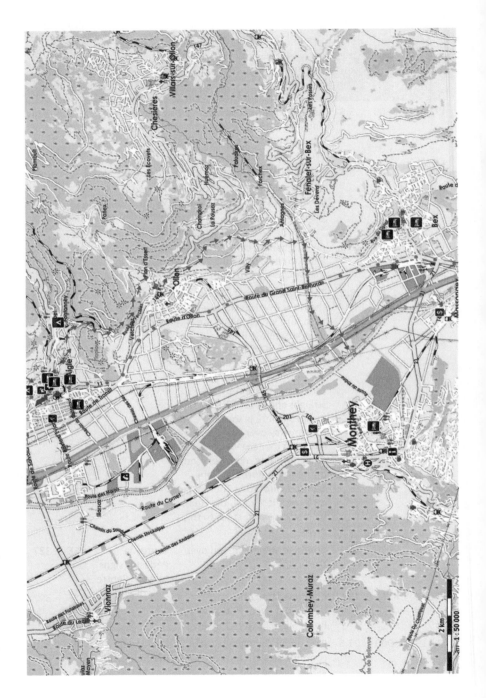

Waypoint	Distance between waypoints	Total km	Directions	Verification Point	Compass	Altitude m
49.019	500	21.9	Turn left onto road beside pedestrian river bridge. Note:- Route 70 will cross the footbridge and pass through Massongex before turning left to follow the railway towards Saint-Maurice	Holiday Camp on left	NE	398
49.020	90	22.0	Turn right following the Tourisme Pédestre sign for St Maurice	Pass through trees and rejoin river-side path	SE	401
49.021	2600	24.6	At the junction with main road, cross over the road and turn right down the ramp		SE	427
49.022	140	24.7	Turn right under the road bridge and across the river bridge	The château of Saint Maurice is straight ahead	SW	441
49.023	100	24.8	Turn left in front of the château	Route 70 via Francigena sign	S	423
49.024	300	25.1	On entering St Maurice (LI) fork right on avenue d'Agaune and proceed through the town. Note:- Route 70 takes the left fork before turning right towards the station and left in the station forecourt. The route then crosses the railway bridge and proceeds on the far side of the tracks before rejoining our route	Direction Martigny	S	435
49.025	120	25.2	Arrive at Saint-Maurice (LI) centre	Abbaye de Saint Maurice to the right		430

Hôtellerie Foyer Franciscain,Antoine de Quartery 1,1890 Saint-Maurice,VS,Switzerland; Tel:+41(0)24 486 11 11; Email:foyer-reception@capucins.ch; Web-site:www.hotellerie-franciscaine.ch; Price:B

Abbaye de Saint-Maurice,Avenue d'Agaune 15,1890 Saint-Maurice,VS,Switzerland; Tel:+41(0)24 486 04 04; Web-site:www.abbaye-stmaurice.ch

Paroisse Saint Sigismund,Avenue de la Gare,1890 Saint-Maurice,VS,Switzerland; Tel:+41(0)24 485 10 30; Price:D

Hôtel du Nord,Rue Colomb 2,1860 Aigle,VD,Switzerland; Tel:+41(0)24 468 10 55; Email:info@hoteldunord.ch; Web-site:www.hoteldunord.ch; Price:A

Hôtel des Messageries,Rue du Midi 19,1860 Aigle,VD,Switzerland; Tel:+41(0)24 466 20 60; Email:messageries@bluewin.ch; Price:A

B&B - Yves & Josette Jaccard,Rue de la Chapelle 23,1860 Aigle,VD,Switzerland; Tel:+41(0)24 466 72 41; +41(0)79 364 38 21 3; Email:y.jaccard@bluewin.ch; Web-site:www.bnb.ch; Price:A

B&B - Ausserladschiede,Chemin des Charmettes 18,1860 Aigle,VD,Switzerland; Tel:+41(0)12 446 79 58 0; +41(0)79 448 15 11; Price:B

Hôtel de la Gare,Avenue de la Gare 60,1870 Monthey,VD,Switzerland; Tel:+41(0)24 471 93 93; Email:info@hotelgaremonthey.com; Web-site:www.hotelgaremonthey.com; Price:A

B&B - Siegenthaler,(Rosemarie & Fritz Siegenthaler),Avenue de la Gare 22,1880 Bex,VD,Switzerland; Tel:+41(0)24 463 27 81; Price:A

Hôtel de Ville,Rue Centrale 8,1880 Bex,VD,Switzerland; Tel:+41(0)24 463 41 52; Email:info@bexhoteldeville.ch; Web-site:www.bexhoteldeville.ch; Price:B

Gîte de Vuarrens,(Myriam & André Berney Jaquerod),Chemin de Vuarrens 6,1880 Bex,VD,Switzerland; Tel:+41(0)24 466 95 25; +41(0)24 463 31 02; +41(0)79 476 24 38; Web-site:www.bexnbex.ch; Price:A

Hôtel la Dent-du-Midi,Avenue du Simplon 1,1890 Saint-Maurice,VS,Switzerland; Tel:+41(0)24 485 12 09; Email:dentdumidi@torrente.ch; Web-site:www.torrente.ch; Price:A

Camping de la Piscine,Avenue des Glariers,1860 Aigle,VD,Switzerland; Tel:+41(0)24 466 26 60; +41(0)79 813 66 92; Email:campingdelapiscine@bluewin.ch; Web-site:www.campingdelapiscine.ch; Price:C; Note:Pre-erected tents available,

Camping des Farettes,Chemin de l'Ecluse 39,1860 Aigle,VD,Switzerland; Tel:+41(0)24 466 56 90; Price:C

Camping du Bois Noir,Route Cantonale,1902 Evionnaz,VS,Switzerland; Tel:+41(0)27 767 12 52; +41(0)79 321 99 21; Web-site:campingduboisnoir.ch; Price:C

Office de Tourisme,Avenue de la Gare 24,1880 Bex,VD,Switzerland; Tel:+41(0)24 463 30 80; Web-site:www.bex-tourisme.ch/

Office de Tourisme,Place Centrale 3,1870 Monthey,VD,Switzerland; Tel:+41(0)24 475 79 63; Web-site:www.heureorange.ch/

ℹ️ Office de Tourisme,Avenue des Terreaux 1,1890 Saint-Maurice,VS,Switzerland; Tel:+41(0)24 485 40 40; Web-site:www.martolet.ch/

💲 Raiffeisen Schweiz,Rue des Colombes 15,1868 Collombey-Muraz,VD,Switzerland; Tel:+41(0)24 473 40 70

💲 BCV,Rue Centrale 5,1880 Bex,VD,Switzerland; Tel:+41(0)24 463 05 10

💲 Raiffeisen Schweiz,Route du Chablais 11,1869 Massongex,VS,Switzerland; Tel:+41(0)24 471 85 77

💲 Banque Raiffeisen,Grand-rue 48,1890 Saint-Maurice,VS,Switzerland; Tel:+41(0)24 485 27 79; Web-site:www.raiffeisen.ch

💲 Postomat,Place de la Gare 1,1890 Saint-Maurice,VS,Switzerland; Tel:+41(0)84 888 87 10

🄷 Centre Hospitalier du Chablais,Route de Morgins 10,1870 Monthey,VD,Switzerland; Tel:+41(0)24 473 33 33; Web-site:www.ichv.ch/fr/offresmedicales/chc

➕ Mrs.Isabelle Chappaz,Rue du Rhône 16,1860 Aigle,VD,Switzerland; Tel:+41(0)24 466 77 77

➕ Mr.Philippe Paratte,Avenue du Simplon 21,1890 Saint-Maurice,VS,Switzerland; Tel:+41(0)24 485 20 06

🐾 Cabinet Vétérinaire du Molage,Rue du Molage 34,1860 Aigle,VD,Switzerland; Tel:+41(0)24 466 56 76

🚶 Valaysport,Place Centrale 7,1870 Monthey,VD,Switzerland; Tel:+41(0)24 471 64 63

🚲 Dom Cycle,Chemin du Sillon 4,1860 Aigle,VD,Switzerland; Tel:+41(0)24 466 93 88

🚲 Athleticum Sportmarkets AG,Chemin des Fossaux,1868 Collombey-Muraz,VD,Switzerland; Tel:+41(0)24 473 47 60

🔧 D.Grandjean Maréchal Forgeron,Rte des Marais 17,1860 Aigle,VD,Switzerland; Tel:+41(0)79 688 13 46

🚕 Taxicity, Zelenovic,Route du Tonkin 16,1870 Monthey,VD,Switzerland; Tel:+41(0)24 471 11 11

🚕 Taxi du Soleil,Chemin de la Planchette 13,1860 Aigle,VD,Switzerland; Tel:+41(0)79 212 23 23

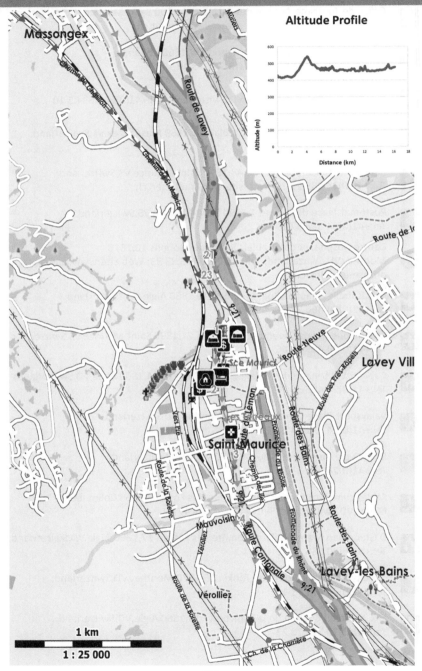

Altitude Profile

Stage Summary: the route follows the western side of the Rhône valley on a mix of woodland tracks and quiet roads

Distance from Besançon: 195km
Stage Ascent: 445m

Distance to Vercelli: 240km
Stage Descent: 396m

Waypoint	Distance between waypoints	Total km	Directions	Verification Point	Compass	Altitude m
50.001	0	0.0	From the Abbaye, continue straight ahead	Avenue d'Aguane	S	428
50.002	300	0.3	Bear left and then right on avenue du Simplon	Direction Martigny	S	419
50.003	600	0.9	At the T-junction with the main road, turn right	Direction Martigny	S	416
50.004	400	1.3	At the roundabout, turn right to pass under railway bridge and proceed with the railway on your left	Direction Vérolliez, Cycle Route n°1	SE	422
50.005	1100	2.3	Fork right and then bear left on route de la Cantine	Direction Bois Noir	SE	426
50.006	500	2.8	At the crossroads, proceed straight ahead	Chemin du Bois Noir	SE	456
50.007	300	3.1	Proceed straight ahead into woods on the unmade road. Note:- The path through the woods includes a narrow bridge which is impassable by horses. Horse riders should turn left here and pass under the motorway on the Alternate Route rejoining the Main Route at the approach to Evionnaz	Chemin du Bois Noir	S	476
50.008	500	3.6	Fork right		SW	510
50.009	10	3.6	Fork left		SW	510
50.010	200	3.8	At the T-junction turn left		SE	527
50.011	70	3.9	Straight ahead	Footbridge over gorge	SE	531

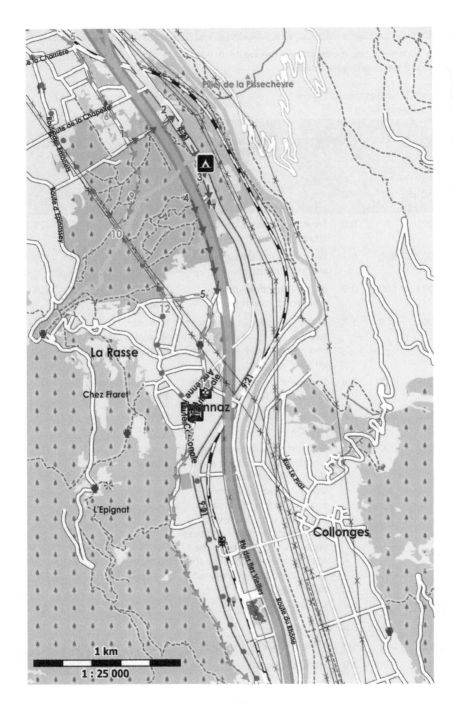

Waypoint	Distance between waypoints	Total km	Directions	Verification Point	Compass	Altitude m
50.012	600	4.5	At the T-junction with the road, turn left	Direction Evionnaz	E	516
50.013	400	4.8	Turn right to proceed parallel to the motorway. Note: the Alternate Route rejoins from the left	Pédestre sign	S	490
50.014	500	5.3	At the crossroads go straight ahead	Downhill	S	477
50.015	140	5.5	Bear right and continue down the main street of Evionnaz	Church on right, VF sign	S	470
50.016	300	5.8	At the T-junction turn left	Cycle Route n°1	S	465
50.017	60	5.9	Turn right onto a small road, towards the hill-side	VF and Martigny signs	S	463
50.018	2300	8.1	Turn right at T-junction on the edge of La Balmaz, staying close to the mountain-side on your right	VF and Martigny signs	SE	456
50.019	300	8.5	Turn right onto the main road beside the railway track	Cycle track towards rocky outcrop	S	457
50.020	1100	9.5	Turn right towards the Pisse Vache waterfalls, cross the railway track and keep the gulley as close as possible to your right. Note:- riders and cyclists may prefer to remain on the road and avoid the path which though passable has some narrow parts	VF sign, power plant on the right	S	455
50.021	600	10.1	Bear left to cross the railway track. The track bears right and recrosses the railway	VF sign	S	457
50.022	600	10.6	Turn left towards the road	VF sign	E	466
50.023	70	10.7	At the crossroads turn right onto the tarmac, after crossing the bridge	VF sign	SE	455

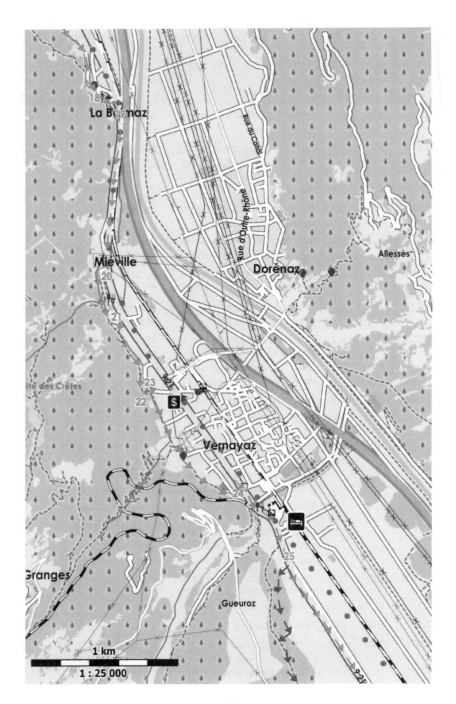

Waypoint	Distance between waypoints	Total km	Directions	Verification Point	Compass	Altitude m
50.024	1100	11.8	At the T-junction with the main road in Verayaz, turn right towards Martigny	Pass the Victoria bar	SE	455
50.025	700	12.5	Bear right onto the farm track running parallel to road. Note:- Route 70 turns further to the right and progresses between the orchards and the foot of the cliffs	Shortly after car sales area	SE	456
50.026	2300	14.8	The track bears right towards the mountain-side	Keep power plant on the right	S	462
50.027	160	14.9	The track bears left and joins a road, go straight ahead towards Martigny	Rue de la Bâtiaz	SE	470
50.028	500	15.5	At the T-junction, turn right and enter Martigny over the river bridge	Tower high on the hilltop to the right	SE	473
50.029	800	16.2	Arrive at Martigny centre in place Centrale	Tourist office to the left on rue de la Gare		477

Alternate Route #50.A1				Length: 1.8km		
Stage Summary: Bois Noir bypass for horse-riders and cyclists						
Stage Ascent: 37m				Stage Descent: 23m		
50A1.001	0	0.0	Proceed towards the motorway and pass under road bridge		NE	475
50A1.002	300	0.3	At the T-junction turn right on route Cantonale – 21	Motel ahead at the junction	SE	459
50A1.003	600	0.9	Shortly after passing a lay-by on the left and before a restaurant on the right, bear right down the ramp	Pass under motorway	SW	470

Paroisse Protestante,Rue d'Oche 3a,1920 Martigny,VS,Switzerland; Tel:+41(0)27 722 33 52; +41(0)27 722 32 20; Email:paroissep@bluewin.ch; Web-site:www.paroissep.ch; Price:D

Hôtel de la Gare,Route Cantonale,1902 Evionnaz,VS,Switzerland; Tel:+41(0)27 767 19 57; Price:B

Hotel Pont du Trient,La Verrerie,1904 Vernayaz,VS,Switzerland; Tel:+41(0)27 764 14 12; Web-site:www.dorenaz.ch; Price:B

Hotel Vieux Stand,Avenue du Grand-Saint-Bernard 41,1920 Martigny,VS,Switzerland; Tel:+41(0)27 722 15 06; Email:info@hoteldustand.ch; Web-site:www.hoteldustand.ch; Price:A

Hôtel du Forum,Avenue du Grand-Saint-Bernard 72,1920 Martigny,VS,Switzerland; Tel:+41(0)27 722 18 41; Web-site:www.hotel-forum.chl; Price:A

Hotel Beau-Site,Chemin,1927 Chemin,VS,Switzerland; Tel:+41(0)27 722 81 64; Email:info@chemin.ch; Web-site:www.chemin.ch; Price:A

Camping Tcs les Neuvilles,Rue du Levant 68,1920 Martigny,VS,Switzerland; Tel:+41(0)27 722 45 44; Email:camping.martigny@tcs.ch; Web-site:www. campingtcs.ch; Price:C; Note:3 dormitories available,

Manège des Ilôts,1920 Martigny,VS,Switzerland; Tel:+41(0)27 722 85 07; Web-site:www.les-maneges.com/

Office de Tourisme,Avenue de la Gare 6,1920 Martigny,VS,Switzerland; Tel:+41(0)27 720 49 49; Web-site:www.martigny.com/

Banque Raiffeisen du Salentin,Grand rue 103,1904 Vernayaz,VS,Switzerland; Tel:+41(0)27 763 19 19; Web-site:www.raiffeisen.ch

Credit Suisse,Avenue de la Gare 21,1920 Martigny,VS,Switzerland; Tel:+41(0)27 721 11 11; Web-site:www.credit-suisse.com/us

Banque Migros SA,Place Centrale 9B,1920 Martigny,VS,Switzerland; Tel:+41(0)84 884 54 00

Raiffeisen Schweiz,Rue Principale 117,1932 Bovernier,VS,Switzerland; Tel:+41(0)27 723 16 73

Gare - CFF,Avenue de la Gare,1920 Martigny,VS,Switzerland; Tel:+41(0)90 030 03 00; Web-site:www.CFF.ch

Hôpital Régional,Avenue du Grand-Champsec 80,1951 Sion,VS,Switzerland; Tel:+41(0)27 603 40 00

Hôpital du Valais,Avenue de la Fusion 27,1920 Martigny,VS,Switzerland; Tel:+41(0)27 603 90 00

Josy-Philippe Cornut,Rue Principale,1902 Evionnaz,VS,Switzerland; Tel:+41(0)27 767 14 00

Dr.Marcel Moillen,Avenue de la Gare 10,1920 Martigny,VS,Switzerland; Tel:+41(0)27 723 25 50

Ochsner Sport,Avenue a la Gare 25,1920 Martigny,VS,Switzerland; Tel:+41(0)27 723 28 69

Garage Pro-Bike Vélo Accessoires,Avenue de Fully 33,1920 Martigny,VS,Switzerland; Tel:+41(0)27 722 39 26

Altitude Profile

Stage Summary: after leaving Martigny the route takes to a narrow track on the precipitous hill-sides high above the river. The track is prohibited to horses and cyclists and is disliked by some walkers. Cyclists may wish to remain on the main road. However the road passes through a very noisy gallery and there is little protection from the traffic. If you chose to follow the main road, consider a very early start to minimise the level of traffic. An Alternate Route via Vens is available to bypass the narrow track and the main road, but involves a stiff climb of 800m much of which is given up as you approach Sembrancher. After Sembrancher there is the choice of Route 70 on the right side of the valley or the very quiet roads and tracks we prefer on the left. A short section of main road is followed prior to the entry into Orsières. A bus service (133) and train service are available from Martigny to Bovernier, Sembrancher and Orsières. The road over the Grand St Bernard Pass is normally open from early June to late September. In the event that the pass is closed, 2 buses per day run from Martigny, via Sembrancher, Orsières, Bourg St Pierre and the road tunnel to Etroubles and Aosta.

Distance from Besançon: 211km
Stage Ascent: 1269m

Distance to Vercelli: 224km
Stage Descent: 853m

Waypoint	Distance between waypoints	Total km	Directions	Verification Point	Compass	Altitude m
51.001	0	0.0	Proceed through place Centrale between the rows of trees	Follow signs for the Col Grand St Bernard	SW	476
51.002	280	0.3	At the roundabout, continue straight ahead, direction Grand St Bernard	Sculpture in middle of roundabout	SW	479
51.003	1000	1.2	At the roundabout, take the third exit	Direction le Bourg	S	488
51.004	160	1.4	Continue straight ahead. Note:- the Alternate Route via Vens leaves to the left	Rue du Bourg	SW	494
51.005	400	1.8	At the roundabout, continue straight ahead direction Grand St Bernard. Note:- Horse-riders and those want a more gentle ascent on the Alternate Route via Vens should turn left on the road to Chemin sur Martigny	Church to the right just before roundabout	SW	499

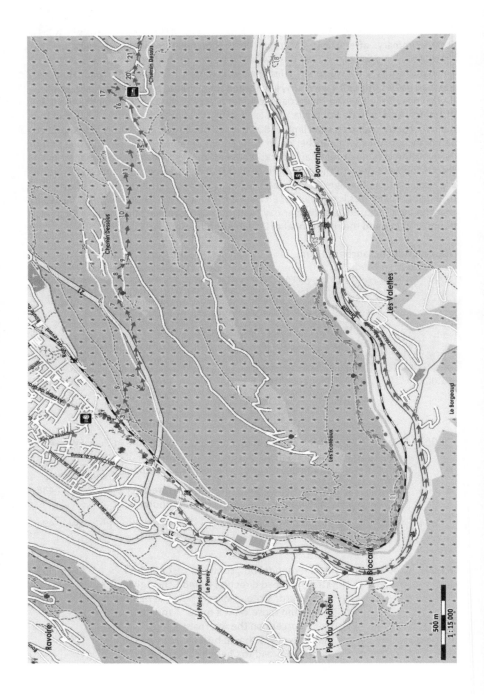

500 m

1 : 15 000

129

Waypoint	Distance between waypoints	Total km	Directions	Verification Point	Compass	Altitude m
51.006	270	2.1	Just before river bridge, turn left direction Orsières. Note:- the pathway ahead is prohibited to horses and cyclists and involves narrow stretches with exposed falls on the right side and is judged dangerous by a number of walkers. The Alternate Route remains on the road and crosses the bridge	VF sign, pass picnic area on the right and railway on the left	SW	502
51.007	130	2.2	Pass through the car park and turn left	Take the flight of steps	S	511
51.008	800	3.1	Cross the railway and turn right	VF sign	S	546
51.009	500	3.5	Turn left after passing under the railway	VF sign	N	562
51.010	50	3.6	Turn sharp right to go up a flight of steps	VF sign	SE	564
51.011	500	4.1	Take left fork	Pédestre sign	E	589
51.012	2200	6.3	Turn left and then sharp right over a small pedestrian bridge	River to the right, vines on left	SE	609
51.013	110	6.4	Continue straight ahead	Bridge on the right and river on the left	E	614
51.014	300	6.7	Turn right to go under the road bridge	Pédestre sign, rue Principale	NE	617
51.015	150	6.8	At the T-junction, turn left into Bovernier	Pédestre sign	NE	622
51.016	400	7.2	At the junction with main road turn right	Pédestre sign, Marbrerie on right	E	624
51.017	260	7.4	Just before the main road bends to the right, bear right on the small tarmac road	Pédestre sign, No Through Road	E	621
51.018	300	7.7	Turn right onto a grass track	Pédestre sign	E	636

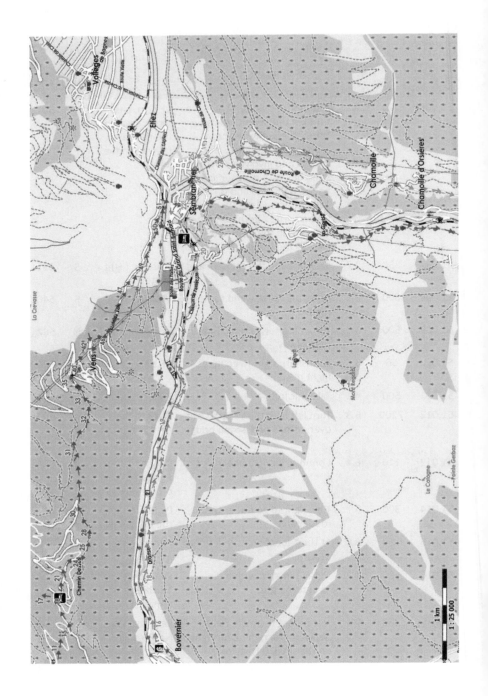

Waypoint	Distance between waypoints	Total km	Directions	Verification Point	Compass	Altitude m
42.019	900	10.3	ATurn right onto the main road beside the railway track	Cycle track towards rocky outcrop	SE	379
51.020	2200	11.9	Turn left over a railway bridge and then bear right on rue de la Gravenne	Pédestre sign	NE	726
51.021	600	12.4	Turn right at the crossroads in the centre of Sembrancher on rue Amédée IV	Pédestre sign	SE	714
51.022	100	12.5	At the T-junction, turn right direction Grand St Bernard	Route du Cleusuit, Pédestre sign	S	719
51.023	90	12.6	Turn left. Note:- Route 70 goes straight ahead keeping to the right side of the valley above and parallel to the railway rejoining our route at the entry to Orsières	Chemin Gaspard-Etienne Delasoie	E	723
51.024	290	12.9	Proceed straight head across the main road on route des Moulins	Pédestre sign, direction Chamoille	E	731
51.025	270	13.2	Turn right with the barn on the right	Pédestre sign	S	733
51.026	50	13.2	Turn right up the hill beside the barn	Pédestre sign	S	738
51.027	400	13.6	Cross over the minor road and continue on the track. Note:- for a more gentle ascent on tarmac bear right on the minor road to Chamoille d'Orsières	Pédestre sign	S	792
51.028	80	13.6	At the junction, keep right	Pédestre sign	S	795
51.029	1900	15.5	The track joins a minor road, bear right direction Orsières	Pédestre sign	SW	947
51.030	800	16.3	In Chamoille d'en Bas , turn left, direction Orsières, route des Prés Neufs	Pédestre sign	S	911

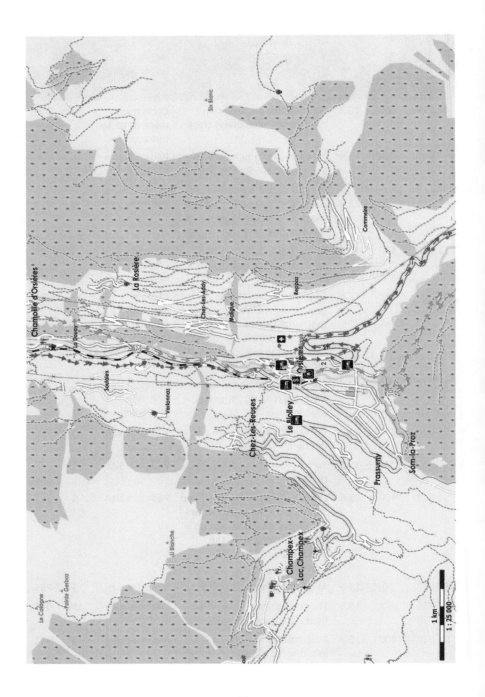

1 km

1 : 25 000

Waypoint	Distance between waypoints	Total km	Directions	Verification Point	Compass	Altitude m
51.031	700	17.0	In Chamoille d'Orsières fork left on the road		S	933
51.032	1700	18.7	Take the bridge over the main road and bear left down the ramp onto the main road	Direction Orsières, pass petrol stations	S	838
51.033	900	19.7	Turn right to leave main road	Direction Orsières	S	868
51.034	600	20.2	Fork left direct Grand St Bernard	Pass over the river bridge	S	881
51.035	240	20.4	Arrive at Orsières (L) centre - place Centrale	Restaurant les Alpes on the left		893

Alternate Route #51.A1   Length: 10.0km

Stage Summary: route via Vens avoiding the narrow path above the river Dranse and the main road. The initial section involves a number of steps and steep paths in the woods. These can be avoided by continuing on rue du Bourg and taking the road to Chemin sur Martigny This route is largely undertaken off-road on woodland tracks, but unfortunately requires a climb of some 800m before returning to the Dranse valley.

Stage Ascent: 1001m   Stage Descent: 781m

Waypoint	Distance between waypoints	Total km	Directions	Verification Point	Compass	Altitude m
51A1.001	0	0.0	Turn left on Ruelle du Mont-Chemin	Signs for Chemin-Dessous and Chemin-Dessus	E	499
51A1.002	30	0.0	At the road junction take the ramp and carefully cross the train lines before mounting the steps	Chemin Pédestre	SE	507
51A1.003	170	0.2	At the T-junction with the broad track, turn left		E	560
51A1.004	100	0.3	Fork right on to a narrow track	Yellow diamond on the rock ahead	E	571
51A1.005	140	0.4	Turn sharp right on the narrow track	Vertical yellow diamond	SE	602

134

Waypoint	Distance between waypoints	Total km	Directions	Verification Point	Compass	Altitude m
51A1.006	300	0.8	At the T-junction with the tarmac road, turn left and after 30m turn sharp right on the steeply climbing narrow path		E	686
51A1.007	600	1.4	At the T-junction with the road, turn left and immediately right onto the woodland track		E	812
51A1.008	230	1.6	At the junction with the road, turn left and then immediately right on the woodland track	Yellow signs	SE	856
51A1.009	130	1.7	At the crossroads with the small tarmac road, continue straight ahead. Note:- this is approximately the mid-point of the climb	Yellow signs	E	889
51A1.010	400	2.1	Continue straight ahead	Avoid the pathway that leads back to the road	E	943
51A1.011	300	2.4	At the crossroads with the tarmac road, continue straight ahead on the broad track		SE	1008
51A1.012	150	2.5	At the crossroads with the road, continue straight ahead on the track. Note:- there is a flight of steps ahead, to avoid these turn left on the road to the next waypoint	Steep winding path, yellow signs	SE	1042
51A1.013	110	2.6	At the top of the steps turn right on the road	Yellow signs	SW	1064
51A1.014	20	2.7	At the end of the exposed rock, turn left on track		SE	1061

Waypoint	Distance between waypoints	Total km	Directions	Verification Point	Compass	Altitude m
51A1.015	20	2.7	At the T-junction with the road, turn left and remain on the road		NE	1063
51A1.016	300	3.0	At the right hand hairpin, continue straight ahead	Yellow signs	NE	1104
51A1.017	140	3.2	Turn sharp right on the forest track	Direction Vens	S	1110
51A1.018	190	3.3	At the T-junction, with the hotel Beau-site on your right, turn left on the road	Vens 1hour	E	1124
51A1.019	90	3.4	Bear right beside the bus stop	Yellow sign	E	1132
51A1.020	40	3.5	At the T-junction with the road, turn right		E	1139
51A1.021	150	3.6	With the church on your left, turn right	Yellow sign, house Mon Plaisir on your right	SE	1158
51A1.022	90	3.7	Continue straight ahead on the road, avoid the turning to the left	Beside le Tieudray	SE	1163
51A1.023	130	3.8	At the crossroads, continue straight ahead	Chemin du Jouer	S	1156
51A1.024	70	3.9	At the T-junction in the tracks, turn left on the gravel track	Pass modern wooden chalets on your left	E	1150
51A1.025	210	4.1	At the end of the gravel, fork right	Pass the wooden bench on your right	E	1155
51A1.026	70	4.2	Turn sharp right to follow the more definite track uphill	Avoid the narrow track straight ahead	E	1155

Waypoint	Distance between waypoints	Total km	Directions	Verification Point	Compass	Altitude m
51A1.027	80	4.3	Take the left fork	Pass the wooden electricity poles on your right	E	1155
51A1.028	20	4.3	At the crossroads, continue straight ahead up the hill		NE	1155
51A1.029	280	4.6	At the crossroads in the tracks, continue straight ahead on the central steeply ascending track		NE	1250
51A1.030	40	4.6	At the T-junction with a broader track, turn right		E	1261
51A1.031	800	5.4	At the stile, continue straight ahead to follow the ancient sunken track. Note:- to avoid this and a further stile, turn left on to the broad definite track, turn right and at the junction with the tarmac road, turn right and follow the hairpins to Vens	Sign for Vens and Sembrancher	SE	1361
51A1.032	500	5.8	Pass through the stile and continue straight ahead		E	1272
51A1.033	270	6.1	At the T-junction with the road, turn right, downhill	Towards the centre of Vens	NE	1208
51A1.034	150	6.3	At the crossroads, continue straight ahead	Pass La Clef des Champs on your left	NE	1171
51A1.035	130	6.4	At the crossroads, continue straight ahead	Chemin du Four	SE	1152
51A1.036	50	6.4	At the next crossroads continue straight ahead downhill on chemin de la Chapelle	Pass the chapel on your right	SE	1136

Waypoint	Distance between waypoints	Total km	Directions	Verification Point	Compass	Altitude m
51A1.037	30	6.5	At the crossroads, continue straight ahead	Towards the café	SE	1127
51A1.038	50	6.5	At the T-junction with the road, cross over and continue on the grass track	Café	SE	1118
51A1.039	70	6.6	At the T-junction with the road, turn left	Towards the pylons	E	1103
51A1.040	20	6.6	Take the right fork on the tarmac	Pass the pylon on your right	NE	1101
51A1.041	50	6.7	Under the power lines take the right fork on the narrow grass track	Sembrancher ahead in the valley below	SE	1110
51A1.042	400	7.0	At the T-junction on the apex of the hairpin bend, turn left, downhill	Yellow signs	W	1064
51A1.043	120	7.1	Under the power lines, turn sharp left on the grass track	Yellow signs	SE	1025
51A1.044	300	7.5	At the T-junction on the hairpin bend, turn left, downhill		W	950
51A1.045	80	7.5	Turn sharp left, downhill on the grassy track	Yellow sign	SE	959
51A1.046	210	7.7	At the T-junction with the road, turn left and cross the bridge over the torrent	Yellow signs	E	908
51A1.047	700	8.4	Shortly after crossing the second bridge, turn sharp right on the stony track	Chemin Pédestre	S	851
51A1.048	60	8.4	At the crossroads with a broad track, continue straight ahead and then bear right, downhill		SE	829
51A1.049	400	8.8	At the T-junction with a terrace track, turn left	Tourisme Pédestre	E	781

Waypoint	Distance between waypoints	Total km	Directions	Verification Point	Compass	Altitude m
51A1.050	600	9.5	Remain on the broad track as it passes under the railway		E	725
51A1.051	400	9.8	Turn right on the bridge over the river, cross the road and continue straight ahead towards the centre of Sembrancher	La Place	S	726
51A1.052	160	10.0	At the junction with rue Principale, continue straight ahead to rejoin the Main Route			719

Alternate Route #51.A2				Length: 4.6km		

Stage Summary: this Alternate Route takes the main road passing through enclosed galleries and should be followed with great care. An early start is recommended to avoid the worst of the traffic.

Stage Ascent: 205m   **Stage Descent: 83m**

Waypoint	Distance between waypoints	Total km	Directions	Verification Point	Compass	Altitude m
51A2.001	0	0.0	Continue straight ahead across the river bridge	Towards roundabout	W	501
51A2.002	50	0.1	Turn left on rue Principale	Direction Martigny-Croix	SW	499
51A2.003	500	0.5	At the junction with main road, cross over and turn left. Note:- take great care, heavy traffic and enclosed road galleries ahead	Pass vineyards on the right	SE	520
51A2.004	2700	3.2	Turn right on slip road and follow rue Principale parallel to main road	Direction Bovernier	E	617
51A2.005	1400	4.6	Rejoin Main Route and proceed straight ahead	Enter Bovernier		623

Paroisse Orsières,Place de l'Eglise,1937 Orsières,VS,Switzerland;
Tel:+41(0)27 783 11 44; Price:D

Hôtel de la Gare,Avenue de la Gare 28,1933 Sembrancher,VS,Switzerland;
Tel:+41(0)27 785 11 14; Email:hotelgaresembrancher-sg@hotmail.com; Price:B

Hôtel de l'Union,Rue de la Commune,1937 Orsières,VS,Switzerland;
Tel:+41(0)27 783 11 38; Email:info@chezjo.ch; Web-site:www.chezjo.ch;
Price:A

Hôtel Terminus,Route de la Gare,1937 Orsières,VS,Switzerland;
Tel:+41(0)27 783 20 40; Email:info@grosminus.ch;
Web-site:www.grosminus.ch/; Price:A

Gîte Serge,La Duay,1937 Orsières,VS,Switzerland; Tel:+41(0)27 783 12 30;
+41(0)79 552 56 60; Email:giteserge@netplus.ch;
Web-site:www.giteserge.ch; Price:A

B&B - Tornay,(Marie-Claude Tornay),Route de Seneire,1937
Orsières,VS,Switzerland; Tel:+41(0)27 783 10 12; +41(0)79 582 70 35; +41(0)79
259 19 25; Email:mtornay@drasnet.ch; Web-site:www.bnb.ch; Price:B

Office du Tourisme,Route de la Gare,1937 Orsières,VS,Switzerland;
Tel:+41(0)27 783 32 48; Web-site:www.bergfex.ch/sommer/saint-bernard/

Postomat,Route de la Gare 29,1937 Orsières,VS,Switzerland;
Tel:+41(0)84 888 87 10

Bernard Darbellay,La place,1937 Orsières,VS,Switzerland;
Tel:+41(0)27 783 13 14

Taxi Grand Saint-Bernard,1943 Praz-de-Fort,VS,Switzerland;
Tel:+41(0)79 217 08 27

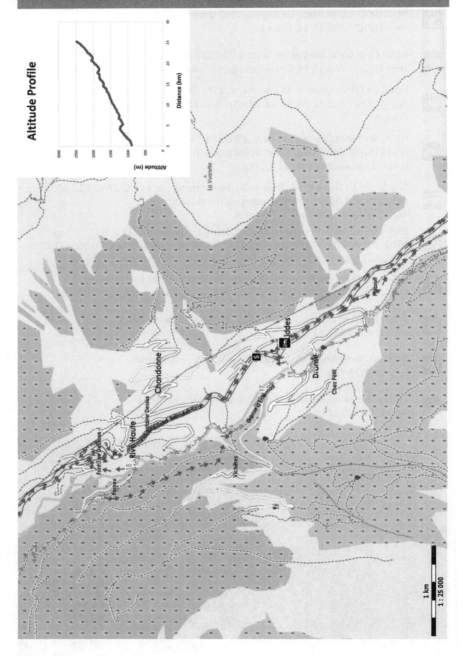

Stage Summary: the Main Route is generally off-road making a steady, but continuous climb to the summit with short steeper sections. The route bypasses the intermediate towns and so walkers need to be well prepared. It is essential to verify the weather conditions on the pass before leaving Orsières. Horse riders and mountain bikers can use parts of the route but will need to divert to avoid the steepest and narrowest sections. Options are available to divert to the main road and intermediate towns in the event of bad weather.

Distance from Besançon: 231km　　　　　　Distance to Vercelli: 203km
Stage Ascent: 2205m　　　　　　　　　　　Stage Descent: 621m

Waypoint	Distance between waypoints	Total km	Directions	Verification Point	Compass	Altitude m
52.001	0	0.0	From the place Centrale with the Restaurant des Alpes behind, bear right	Rue de la Commune	S	893
52.002	80	0.1	Bear right onto Charrière Challant	Avoid ruelle de la Montoz	SW	895
52.003	110	0.2	Turn left on route de Podemainge	VF sign	SE	893
52.004	50	0.2	Bear left and then immediately right on place de la Creuse	VF sign	SW	895
52.005	170	0.4	At a small crossroads, go straight ahead, direction Liddes	Route de la Podemainge	S	897
52.006	260	0.7	Stay on the tarmac road and bear right	Pedestrian sign	S	912
52.007	300	1.0	Fork left	VF sign, wier on the right	S	921
52.008	260	1.3	Turn right to cross over the bridge	VF sign and RP1993 on bridge	S	935
52.009	80	1.3	Bear right uphill	VF sign	W	950
52.010	260	1.6	Bear left uphill	Route 70 signs	SE	962

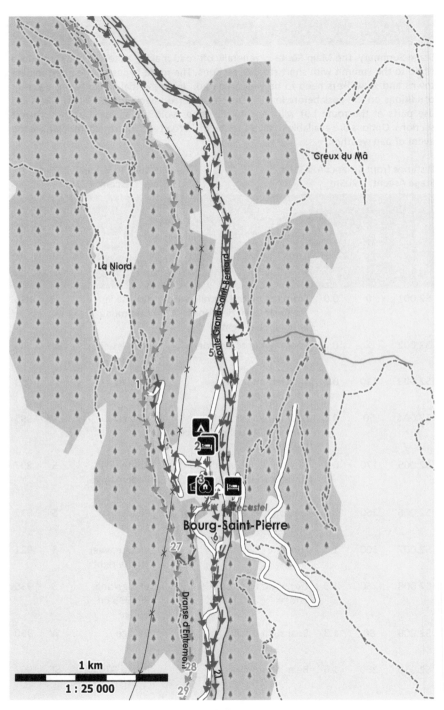

Creux du Mâ

La Niord

route Grand-Saint-Bernard

4

5

1

2

3

Au Châtelet

Bourg-Saint-Pierre

6

27

Dranse d'Entremont

28

29

21

1 km

1 : 25 000

143

Waypoint	Distance between waypoints	Total km	Directions	Verification Point	Compass	Altitude m
52.011	2800	4.4	At the fork above Fornex bear right. Note:- bike riders may prefer to bear left on the roadway for an easy descent to the river crossing	Towards village	SE	1221
52.012	110	4.5	Take the right fork	Pass between the houses in Fornex	SE	1209
52.013	240	4.8	Bear left down the hill towards the woods on a narrow track. Note:- Route 70 turns to the right and takes the higher path through the forest	Direction Les Moulins	SE	1218
52.014	400	5.2	As the track emerges onto the road turn right	Towards the river	E	1146
52.015	40	5.2	Cross the bridge, turn right direction Liddes. Note:- the track ahead is extremely difficult for horse and bike riders who should turn left and climb the hill to join the on-road route	Follow narrowing path with river on the right	SE	1139
52.016	1300	6.5	Narrow track intersects with broad track, turn right to cross river and then turn left on the track through woods. Route 70 rejoins from the right	Proceed with river on the left	SE	1229
52.017	800	7.3	At the junction with broad track turn left	Towards the village of Dranse	SE	1247
52.018	300	7.6	At the T-junction turn right. Note:- turn left on Route 70 to visit Liddes and follow a higher route to Bourg-Saint-Pierre or join the on-road route	Towards Dranse	SW	1256

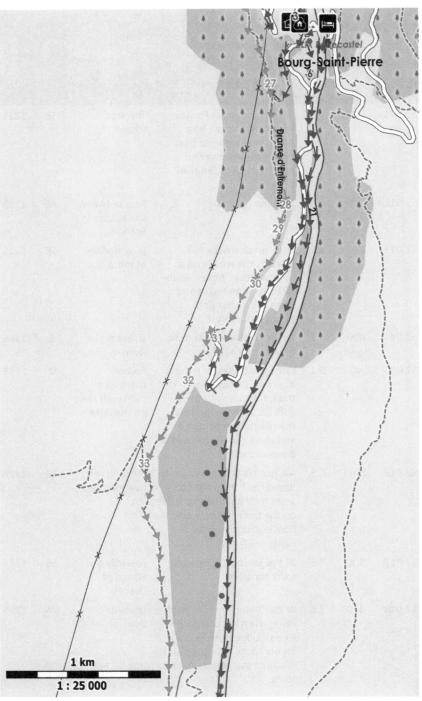

Bourg-Saint-Pierre

Dranse d'Entremont

27
28
29
30
31
32
33
6
21

1 km
1 : 25 000

Waypoint	Distance between waypoints	Total km	Directions	Verification Point	Compass	Altitude m
52.019	90	7.7	In Dranse bear left		SE	1261
52.020	140	7.8	At the junction, continue straight ahead	Track narrows with river to the left	SE	1271
52.021	900	8.7	Bear left	Skirt reservoir and water plant on your right	E	1329
52.022	170	8.9	Turn right	Continue around reservoir	SE	1334
52.023	160	9.0	Turn right	Across the bridge	SW	1343
52.024	50	9.1	After crossing bridge turn left to follow the river	River to the left	S	1348
52.025	3500	12.5	At the junction with the broad track turn sharp right. Note:- to visit Bourg-Saint-Pierre (XLIX) on the Alternate Route or rejoin the on-road route, turn left		N	1542
52.026	130	12.7	Turn left, direction Barrage des Toules	VF sign	S	1551
52.027	1300	14.0	Continue straight ahead direction Lac des Toules. The Alternate Route from Bourg-St-Pierre joins from the left	VF sign	S	1621
52.028	800	14.7	Bear left down the hill	VF sign	S	1704
52.029	300	15.0	Continue straight ahead with the river on the left	VF sign	SW	1691
52.030	300	15.3	Pass the house on your right and then pass through a small wicket gate onto a narrow grass track	VF sign	SW	1711
52.031	700	16.0	Approaching the face of the dam, turn right onto the gravel track	VF sign	SW	1763

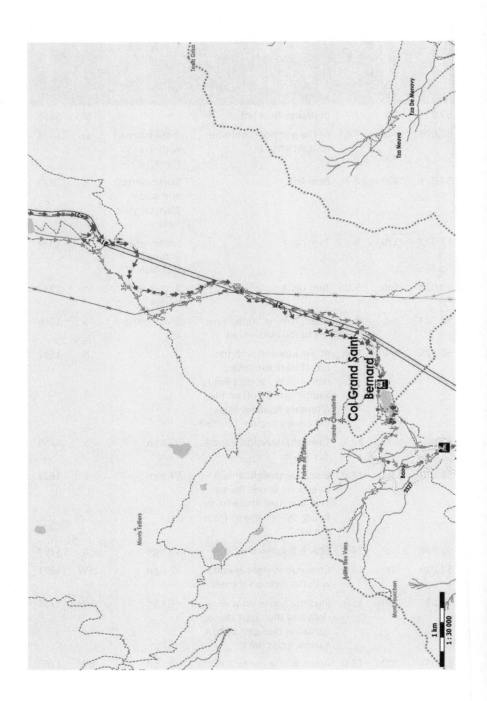

Col Grand Saint Bernard

1 km
1 : 30 000

147

Waypoint	Distance between waypoints	Total km	Directions	Verification Point	Compass	Altitude m
52.032	600	16.5	Fork left with the reservoir on the left	VF sign	SW	1823
52.033	800	17.3	Continue straight ahead on small track downhill towards the water	Avoid the track up the hill	S	1825
52.034	2300	19.6	Continue straight ahead, direction Col St Bernard. Note:- ahead the route is often blocked by cattle fencing. Horse riders can turn left here over the wooden bridge to regain the on-road route at the upper end of the avalanche gallery	VF and chemin Historique signs	SW	1904
52.035	800	20.3	Continue straight ahead	Direction Col St Bernard	SW	1990
52.036	400	20.7	Bear left	Towards farm buildings	SW	2054
52.037	190	20.9	Turn left beside the farm buildings	Towards the road	SE	2037
52.038	600	21.6	Turn sharp left towards the road		NE	2028
52.039	90	21.6	Turn sharp right onto a path running parallel to the road		S	2034
52.040	700	22.3	Cross over the road and continue straight ahead. Note:- even in summer there is often snow and ice on the pathway ahead. If in doubt turn right to follow the road to the summit	Tunnel air vent to the right	SW	2105
52.041	3000	25.3	Arrive at Col-Grand-St-Bernard summit	Hospice to the left		2477

Stage Summary: this Alternate Route takes the main road passing through enclosed galleries and should be approached with great care. An early start should be considered to minimise the amount of traffic that you will encounter. Traffic conditions normally improve above the tunnel entrance. The Alternate Route may be preferred in difficult weather conditions and has the advantage of easy access to more points of shelter.

Stage Ascent: 1925m   Stage Descent: 344m

Waypoint	Distance between waypoints	Total km	Directions	Verification Point	Compass	Altitude m
52A1.001	0	0.0	From the place Centrale with the Restaurant les Alpes behind, bear left on the main exit road towards the col Grand-Saint-Bernard	Rue de Grand-Saint-Bernard	S	897
52A1.002	600	0.6	Continue straight ahead and continue climbing	Under the road bridges	SE	931
52A1.003	4200	4.8	On the crown of the bend to the left, just after passing Fontaine-Dessous, continue straight ahead. Note:- walkers and riders join here from the Main Route	Road joins from the right	SE	1190
52A1.004	6400	11.2	Continue straight ahead. Note:- at the entrance to gallery, cyclists continue straight ahead, horse riders and walkers can bear right onto a small track and then bear left crossing over the gallery and rejoining the road beyond the gallery end		S	1530

Waypoint	Distance between waypoints	Total km	Directions	Verification Point	Compass	Altitude m
52A1.005	1500	12.6	For the summit cyclists will need to continue straight ahead on the road. Note:- to visit Bourg Saint Pierre (XLIX) or for horse riders and walkers to avoid the 4km gallery ahead bear right into the town and join the Alternate Route leading to the barrage and rejoining the Main Route		S	1606
52A1.006	1300	13.9	Continue straight ahead	Entry to avalanche gallery	S	1691
52A1.007	5200	19.0	Bear right to leave gallery	Before the tunnel entrance	S	1915
52A1.008	2600	21.6	The Main Route crosses from the right, continue straight ahead	Towards tunnel air vent	SW	2103
52A1.009	4100	25.7	Rejoin the Main Route at the summit of the Col-Grand-Saint-Bernard	Hospice to the left		2478

Waypoint	Distance between waypoints	Total km	Directions	Verification Point	Compass	Altitude m
			Alternate Route #52.A2	**Length: 2.5km**		
			Stage Summary: link to Bourg-Saint-Pierre			
			Stage Ascent: 152m	**Stage Descent: 79m**		
52A2.001	0	0.0	Turn left, cross the valley bottom and climb the hill towards the town	Tarmac road	SE	1544
52A2.002	1500	1.5	At the T-junction, turn right into the town		S	1622
52A2.003	230	1.7	In the centre of Bourg-Saint-Pierre (XLIX), bear right on route Principale. Note:- route 70 continues straight ahead	Close beside the church	S	1634
52A2.004	100	1.8	Bear right on the track	Towards the valley bottom	SW	1638
52A2.005	700	2.5	Rejoin the Main Route, climbing the hill	Towards the barrage		1617

Accommodation & Facilities .... Orsières - Col-Grand-St-Bernard

 Hospice du Grand-Saint-Bernard,Situated On The Col,1946 Bourg-Saint-Pierre,VS,Switzerland; Tel:+41(0)27 787 12 36; +41(0)79 221 16 89; Email:hospice@gsbernard.net; Web-site:www.gsbernard.net; Price:B

 Paroisse,Rue de l'Eglise,1946 Bourg-Saint-Pierre,VS,Switzerland; Tel:+41(0)27 787 11 72; +41(0)79 414 98 17; Price:D

 Maison Saint-Pierre,(Claude Lattion),1946 Bourg-Saint-Pierre,VS,Switzerland; Tel:+41(0)27 787 13 98; +41(0)79 221 16 89; Email:info@bivouac.ch; Web-site:www.maisonstpierre.ch; Price:C

 Hôtel du Grand Saint Bernard,1945 Liddes,VS,Switzerland; Tel:+41(0)27 783 13 02; Email:info@hotel-gd-st-bernard.ch; Web-site:www.hotel-gd-st-bernard.ch; Price:A

 Auberge les Charmettes,(Gilbert Tornare-Delasoie),1946 Bourg-Saint-Pierre,VS,Switzerland; Tel:+41(0)27 787 11 50; Email:gtornare@netplus.ch; Web-site:www.les-charmettes.ch; Price:A; Note:Price group B in dormitory,

Hôtel au Bivouac-de-Napoléon,Route du Grand-Saint-Bernard,1946 Bourg-Saint-Pierre,VS,Switzerland; Tel:+41(0)27 787 11 62; Email:bivouac.napoleon@bivouac.ch; Web-site:www.bivouac.ch; Price:A

Auberge au Petit Vélan,(Pascal Loubry),1946 Bourg-Saint-Pierre,VS,Switzerland; Tel:+41(0)27 787 11 41; Email:info@petit-velan.ch; Web-site:www.petit-velan.ch; Price:B; Note:Price group C in dormitory,

Hôtel de l'Hospice,Situated On The Col,1946 Bourg-Saint-Pierre,VS,Switzerland; Tel:+41(0)27 787 11 53; Email:ch.carrupt@bluewin.ch; Web-site:www.hotelhospice.ch; Price:A

Casa Don Angelo Carioni,Strada Statale 27 del Gran San Bernardo,11010 Saint-Rhemy-en-Bosses(AO),Italy; +39 3356 012847; +39 3333 114442; Email:fondazioneGSB@tiscali.it

Casa Vacanze,Località Saint Rhémy,11010 Saint-Rhémy-en-Bosses(AO),Italy; Tel:+39 0165 780601; +39 3336 816012; Price:C; Note:For groups of 6 or more people,

Camping du Grand-Saint-Bernard,1946 Bourg-Saint-Pierre,VS,Switzerland; Tel:+41(0)27 787 14 11; +41(0)79 370 98 22; Email:reservation@campinggrand-st-bernard.ch; Web-site:www.campinggrand-st-bernard.ch; Price:C

Raiffeisen Schweiz,Route Grand-Saint-Bernard,1945 Liddes,VS,Switzerland; Tel:+41(0)27 783 22 88

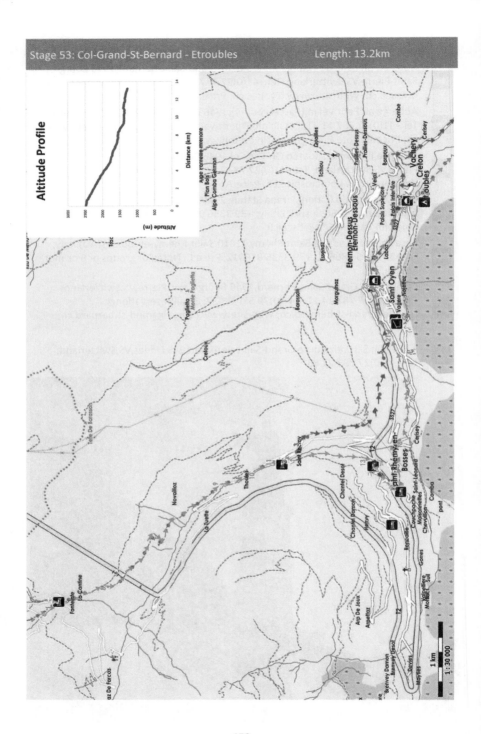

Stage Summary: the descent to Etroubles is generally gentle and progressive, largely on off-road tracks. There are a number of intersections with the main road where extra care is necessary. Cyclists may wish to take advantage of the easy road descent to Aosta. In Italy many groups have worked at signing their view of the best route to Rome and these views often conflict and so do not be surprised if you see via Francigena signs of many styles some of which will diverge from our route. We will primarily follow the route approved by the European Association of the via Francigena, but will offer alternatives where we feel there advantages.

Distance from Besançon: 257km   Distance to Vercelli: 178km
Stage Ascent: 197m   Stage Descent: 1397m

Waypoint	Distance between waypoints	Total km	Directions	Verification Point	Compass	Altitude m
53.001	0	0.0	With the hostel behind continue straight ahead on the road down the hill	Towards the border post	W	2473
53.002	500	0.5	At the Italian border post bear right on the path	Pass beside the hotel	W	2457
53.003	130	0.6	Go straight ahead	Beside the statue of Saint Bernard	W	2460
53.004	270	0.9	Just before the avalanche gallery cross the road to join a track at the foot of a stone slope	Yellow arrow	W	2409
53.005	400	1.2	Fork left	Yellow arrow	S	2361
53.006	700	1.9	Cross over the road and continue on the track	Yellow arrow	SE	2266
53.007	500	2.3	Cross over the road onto the grass track	Path n°13	S	2207
53.008	600	2.9	Fork right down the hill	Yellow arrow	SE	2127
53.009	2800	5.6	Turn left onto the road, SS27	Yellow arrow	S	1722
53.010	400	6.0	Turn right onto small track and then left in the direction of Saint-Rhemy	VF sign	SE	1704
53.011	500	6.5	Enter Saint-Rhemy-en-Bosses (XLVIII) and continue straight ahead on the road	Frazione Cerisey	S	1654

Waypoint	Distance between waypoints	Total km	Directions	Verification Point	Compass	Altitude m
53.012	180	6.6	At the fork at the end of the main street turn right over the bridge and then left. Note: the shorter Alternate Route initially continues straight ahead on the road	River on the left after the bridge	S	1621
53.013	1200	7.8	At the end of the track bear right on the road		W	1549
53.014	110	7.9	On entering San Leonardo keep left at the first junction		S	1556
53.015	130	8.0	At the crossroads go straight ahead down the hill	Frazione Predumaz Falcoz	SW	1542
53.016	280	8.3	Cross the main road and continue straight ahead down the hill		S	1542
53.017	80	8.4	Cross the road – Frazione Saint Leonard – and continue straight ahead	Chiesa di Saint Leonard	E	1524
53.018	700	9.1	At the T-junction with the road, turn right	Frazione Cerisey	SE	1409
53.019	230	9.4	At the exit from Cerisey turn left	Before the bridge	E	1377
53.020	600	9.9	Continue straight ahead	Through fields	E	1370
53.021	900	10.8	On approaching the quiet rue de la Montée bear left uphill on the track	Towards the main road	NE	1356
53.022	200	11.0	Turn right onto the SS27 via Roma into the village of Saint-Oyen. Note:- the Alernate Route joins from the left	Footpath sign for Martigny-Aosta	E	1390
53.023	600	11.6	Turn right off the main road onto via Verraz	Sign for Martigny-Aosta	S	1369
53.024	80	11.7	Turn left down the hill between houses	Sign for Martigny-Aosta	S	1359

Waypoint	Distance between waypoints	Total km	Directions	Verification Point	Compass	Altitude m
53.025	70	11.7	At the T-junction, turn left	Strada di Flassin	E	1346
53.026	400	12.1	At the junction with the main road, cross over and take the road straight ahead	Direction Prailles	E	1350
53.027	60	12.1	Turn right and continue on the track close to the main road	Wooden statue at the junction	SE	1351
53.028	800	12.9	On approaching Etroubles cross the minor road rue de Vachèry and follow the pathway towards the town centre	Shrine on the left	E	1293
53.029	120	13.1	Rejoin the main road and continue straight ahead on the pavement	Towards hairpin bend	SE	1283
53.030	90	13.1	On the apex of the hairpin bend to the right, bear left to follow the minor road into Etroubles	Pedestrian zone	SE	1279
53.031	60	13.2	Arrive at Etroubles Centre	Beside the crossroads in the pedestrian zone		1272

| Alternate Route #53.A1 | | | | | Length: 2.9km | |

Stage Summary: shorter route, saving 1.5km, bypassing Saint Leonard and following a narrow hill-side track

| Stage Ascent: 121m | | | | | Stage Descent: 349m | |

Waypoint	Distance between waypoints	Total km			Compass	Altitude m
53A1.001	0	0.0	Turn left up the hill to rejoin the SS27	Frazione Cerisey	SE	1620
53A1.002	40	0.0	At the intersection with SS27 turn left, uphill	Stone wall on the left	SE	1615
53A1.003	300	0.4	At the apex of a hairpin bend to the left, turn right on the track	Footpath sign, direction Aosta	S	1641
53A1.004	700	1.0	Fork right on the track		SE	1656
53A1.005	1600	2.6	Track intersects with SS27. Cross over and turn left on the track	Take steps from the lay-by	E	1415
53A1.006	300	2.9	Continue straight ahead beside the road, the "Official Route" via Saint Leonard joins from the right	Sign for Martigny-Aosta		1393

Accommodation & Facilities .... Col-Grand-St-Bernard - Etroubles

Casa Ospitaliera Chateau Verdun,Rue de Flassin,11014 Saint-Oyen(AO),Italy; Tel:+39 9016 578247; Email:casagsb@gsbernard.ch; Web-site:www.gsbernard.ch; Price:C

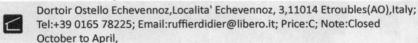

Dortoir Ostello Echevennoz,Localita' Echevennoz, 3,11014 Etroubles(AO),Italy; Tel:+39 0165 78225; Email:ruffierdidier@libero.it; Price:C; Note:Closed October to April,

Casa Ospitaliera Chateau Verdun,(Padre Louis Lamon),Rue de Flassin,11014 Saint-Oyen(AO),Italy; Tel:+39 0165 78247; Email:casagsb@gsbernard.ch; Price:C

Casa Alpina Sacro Cuore,Route Nationale du Gd.Saint.Bernard, 24,11014 Etroubles(AO),Italy; Tel:+39 0165 78126; +39 0141 964002; +39 3401 687873; Email:casalpinaetroubles@fmaipi.it; Price:C

Hotel le Relais du Pelerin,Frazione Predumaz Falcoz,11010 Saint-Rhémy-en-Bosses(AO),Italy; Tel:+39 0165 780007; Email:info@lerelaisdupelerin.com; Web-site:www.lerelaisdupelerin.com; Price:A

Hotel des Alpes,Località Cuchepache, 15,11010 Saint-Rhemy-en-Bosses(AO),Italy; Tel:+39 0165 780818; Email:info@desalpeshotel.com; Web-site:www.desalpeshotel.com; Price:A

B&B - la Vieille Cloche,Frazione Saint Leonard, 11,11010 Saint-Léonard(AO),Italy; Tel:+39 0165 780927; +39 3805 159554; Email:info@lavieillecloche.it; Web-site:www.casevacanzavalledaosta.it; Price:B

Camping del Mulino,Localita' Flassin, 3,11014 Saint-Oyen(AO),Italy; Tel:+39 0165 78119; Email:campeggiodelvecchiomulino@pec.it; Web-site:www.campingdelvecchiomulino.it; Price:C

Camping Tunnel,Rue Chevrieres, 4,11014 Etroubles(AO),Italy; Tel:+39 0165 78292; Email:info@campingtunnel.it; Web-site:www.campingtunnel.it; Price:C; Note:Open all year,

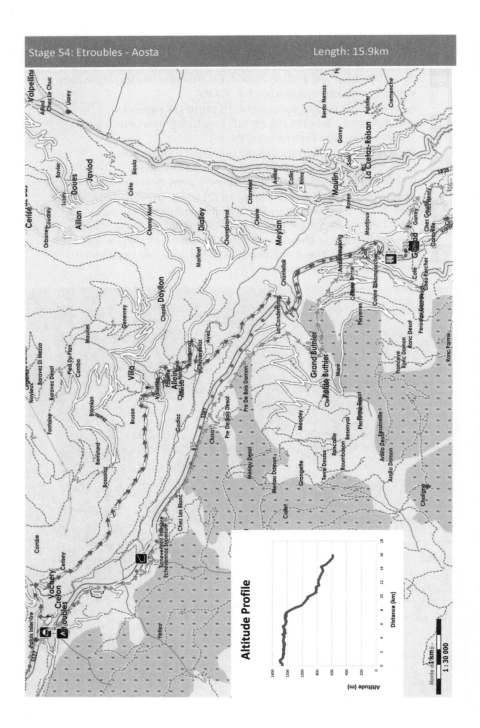

Altitude Profile

Altitude (m)

Distance [km]

1 : 30 000

Monte d.1km

Stage Summary: the "Official Route" continues to descend gently on small woodland paths and tracks above Gignod. Unfortunately some of these are not suitable for riders. The route then follows a series of very minor roads, before a section beside the SS27. The route passes through the outskirts of Aosta on sometimes steeply descending pathways and narrow roads, before finally crossing the very busy SS26 and entering the pedestrian zone of the old town.

Distance from Besançon: 270km   Distance to Vercelli: 165km
Stage Ascent: 515m   Stage Descent: 1200m

Waypoint	Distance between waypoints	Total km	Directions	Verification Point	Compass	Altitude m
54.001	0	0.0	From the crossroads in Etroubles turn right. Note:- parts of the route ahead are impassable for horses and difficult for cyclists, riders are advised to turn left and follow the Alternate Route to Gignod. Bike riders can take the main road after crossing the river	Rue du Mont Velan	SW	1272
54.002	130	0.1	Continue straight ahead	Cross the river bridge	S	1264
54.003	30	0.2	At the end of the bridge, cross the road and bear left	Climb the steps	S	1266
54.004	10	0.2	At the T-junction with the main road, bear right and cross the road with great care into the hotel car park and bear left	Towards the Hotel Beau Sejour	SW	1266
54.005	110	0.3	Bear left on rue Saint-Roch	Footpath sign for Martigny-Aosta,	E	1269
54.006	70	0.3	Turn right	Unmade road	SE	1272
54.007	800	1.1	At the T-junction, turn right onto the tarmac with the main road close on your left	VF sign	S	1261
54.008	400	1.5	Turn right onto a grassy track	VF sign	SE	1251

Waypoint	Distance between waypoints	Total km	Directions	Verification Point	Compass	Altitude m
54.009	400	1.9	Join a tarmac road and then turn right at the junction in Echevennoz Dessus	VF sign, farm on right	SE	1256
54.010	140	2.0	Beside the parking area, turn left onto the track	VF and Martigny-Aosta signs	E	1252
54.011	700	2.7	At the T-junction with the road, turn right	VF sign	E	1243
54.012	60	2.8	Turn right to proceed between two houses and then bear left on the track	VF sign	SE	1244
54.013	70	2.8	Bear left alongside the aqueduct	VF sign, concrete water trough	E	1251
54.014	1200	4.0	Fork left down the hill	VF sign	E	1243
54.015	50	4.1	Fork right back up the hill	VF sign	SE	1238
54.016	280	4.3	Fork left on the lower track	VF sign	SE	1244
54.017	1400	5.8	Turn right onto a road and then immediately left on the track slightly up the hill	VF sign	S	1244
54.018	800	6.6	Take the left fork	VF sign	SE	1223
54.019	1100	7.7	Turn left on the track	VF and Martigny-Aosta signs	SE	1209
54.020	230	7.9	Remain on grass track	Ignore the dirt track on the right	SE	1175
54.021	400	8.3	Cross over the road to continue down the hill on the grass track	VF sign, TAM Aoste – Martigny	SE	1099
54.022	50	8.4	Turn sharp left down the hill	VF sign	E	1084
54.023	100	8.5	Continue straight ahead on a long flight of steps		SE	1054
54.024	40	8.5	Turn right onto the road and immediately turn left on the grass track	VF sign	SE	1042

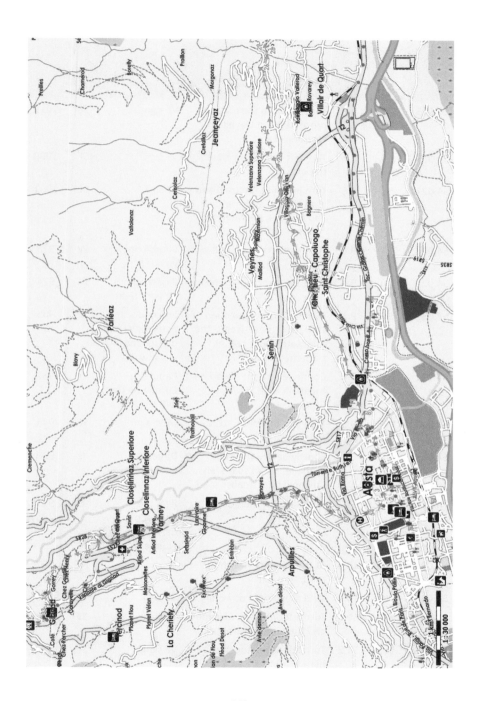

162

Waypoint	Distance between waypoints	Total km	Directions	Verification Point	Compass	Altitude m
54.025	110	8.6	Turn left onto the road to proceed down the hill on Frazione Lexert	VF sign	SE	1019
54.026	80	8.7	Turn left on a small grass track	VF sign	SE	1008
54.027	50	8.8	Turn left onto the road and then immediately right and first left, between the houses	VF sign	SE	1001
54.028	250	9.0	Turn right down the hill	Church on your left	W	978
54.029	70	9.1	Turn left to go down the hill	Pass a school on your right	SW	974
54.030	50	9.1	Turn right at the junction with main road. Note:- the Alternate Route rejoins from the left	Proceed between crash barrier and stone wall	S	965
54.031	220	9.4	Continue straight ahead on the main road	Camp site Europa on the left	S	952
54.032	120	9.5	Turn left, direction Aosta-Martigny	TAM sign	SE	944
54.033	400	9.8	Shortly before the bend to the left, turn sharp left downhill on a smaller road	Direction Caravex	E	930
54.034	100	9.9	Bear right on the track	Pass the hamlet of Caravex on your left	E	913
54.035	140	10.1	At the T-junction with the road, turn left		NE	887
54.036	70	10.1	Turn sharp right downhill	VF sign	SE	876
54.037	500	10.6	Turn left onto a tarmac road and then immediately right	VF sign	SE	818
54.038	500	11.2	Turn left at the top of the hill	VF sign	SE	817

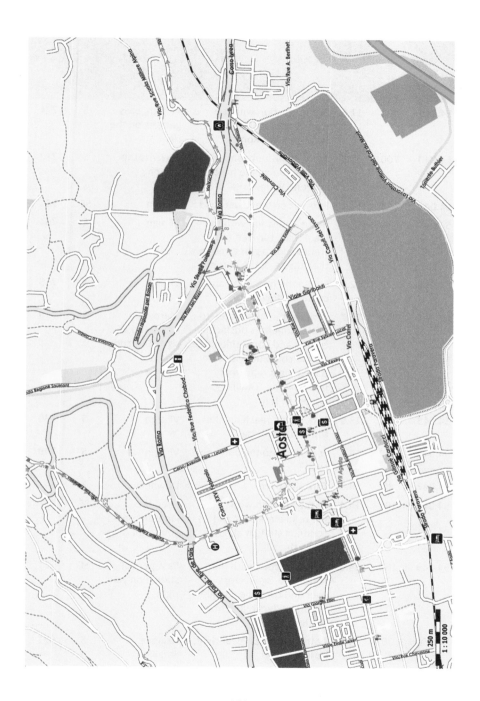

Waypoint	Distance between waypoints	Total km	Directions	Verification Point	Compass	Altitude m
54.039	400	11.6	At the junction with the main road, turn right on Frazione Chez Roncoz	VF sign, pass garages on the right	S	774
54.040	700	12.3	At the mini-roundabout bear left down the hill on Frazione Variney	Towards the church	S	782
54.041	100	12.4	Fork left on the lower road	VF sign	SE	781
54.042	400	12.7	At the T-junction with the main road, turn left and continue on a grass track on the outside of the barrier	VF sign	S	764
54.043	200	12.9	Rejoin the main road and continue downhill	VF sign	S	755
54.044	800	13.7	Fork right uphill. Note:- to avoid numerous obstacles, cyclists and horse-riders should continue with care on the main road until rejoining the "Official Route" in 1km	Martigny-Aosta and VF signs!Direction Grand Signayes	S	719
54.045	180	13.9	Fork left on reaching the top of a small rise	VF sign	S	730
54.046	300	14.2	Fork left onto the unmade road	VF sign	S	748
54.047	80	14.3	Turn sharp left	Downhill	E	741
54.048	100	14.4	At the junction with the road cross over and continue straight ahead down the hill	Keep the vineyard on your right	SE	715
54.049	180	14.6	At the junction with the main road, again cross over and continue straight ahead. Riders rejoin from the left	Pass pertrol station on your right	SE	681
54.050	70	14.7	At the T-junction bear right, downhill	Regione Saraillon	S	671

Waypoint	Distance between waypoints	Total km	Directions	Verification Point	Compass	Altitude m
54.051	60	14.7	At the junction with the main road, turn left and then right on the small road	Keep house n° 71 close on your left, via Edelweiss	SW	664
54.052	280		At the junction, continue straight ahead, downhill on via Edelweissl	VF sign	SW	635
54.053	500		At the roundabout take the pedestrian crossing and continue into the centre of Aosta	VF sign, hospital on the right	SE	595
54.054	220		At the traffic lights, proceed straight ahead	Into pedestrian zone	S	587
54.055	190		In Piazza Roncas turn left and immediately right into the narrow street	Towards the Cathedral	E	586
54.056	60		Turn right	Via Forum	SE	586
54.057	40		Arrive at Aosta (XLVII) centre	Piazza della Cattedrale		586

Alternate Route #54.A1   Length:10.9km

Stage Summary: this riders route avoids a narrow pathway trapped between an aqueduct and steep hillsides leading to steps that are impassable by horses. The route follows small roads on the east side of the river before crossing the valley floor and climbing to rejoin the "Official Route" on the entry to Gignod.

Stage Ascent: 348m   **Stage Descent: 660m**

Waypoint	Distance between waypoints	Total km	Directions	Verification Point	Compass	Altitude m
54A1.001	0	0.0	At the crossroads turn left	Rue du Mont Velan	NE	1274
54A1.002	30	0.0	Turn right	Ruelle Millet	SE	1279
54A1.003	80	0.1	Turn left	Rue du Bordonnet	NE	1279
54A1.004	160	0.3	At the T-junction turn right on rue de Vachèry	Direction Allein	SE	1312

Waypoint	Distance between waypoints	Total km	Directions	Verification Point	Compass	Altitude m
54A1.005	4100	4.3	On approaching Allein, turn right and follow the hairpin bends down the hill, direction Aosta	Frazione Clavel	SE	1250
54A1.006	500	4.8	At the junction continue straight ahead on the road down the hill	Frazione Frein	SE	1213
54A1.007	1000	5.7	At the junction, continue straight ahead on the road	Frazione Ayez	SE	1159
54A1.008	500	6.2	Keep right on the road	Direction Aosta	SE	1104
54A1.009	2900	9.1	At the T-junction turn left on the main road and proceed with great care into Gignod	Direction Aosta	SE	1077
54A1.010	1800	10.9	Rejoin the "Official Route" in Gignod and continue on the main road			962

Accommodation & Facilities .... Etroubles - Aosta

Monastero Mater Misericordiae,Villaggio Moulin, 1,11020 Quart(AO),Italy; Tel:+39 0165 765848; Price:D

Parrocchia Saint Ansemlo,Avenue d'Ivrea,11100 Aosta(AO),Italy; Tel:+39 0165 40627

Parrocchia Saint Martin,Avenue Saint-Martin-de-Corléans,11100 Aosta(AO),Italy; Tel:+39 0165 553373; +39 0165 555379; +39 3290 845757; Price:D

Hotel Bellevue,Frazione la Ressaz, 3,11010 Gignod(AO),Italy; Tel:+39 0165 56392; +39 3494 651655; Email:hotelbellevuegignod@tiscali.it ; Web-site:www.hotelbellevuegignod.com; Price:A

B&B Lo Chalet,(Gianfranco Salatiello),Frazione les Fiou,11010 Gignod(AO),Italy; Tel:+39 0165 56294; +39 3471 599705; Email:barnabo54@libero.it; Web-site:www.bedandbreakfastineurope.com/lochalet; Price:A

Hotel Papa Grand,Frazione Variney,11010 Gignod(AO),Italy; Tel:+39 0165 56076; Price:B

La Roche Hotel,Località Signayes,11100 Aosta(AO),Italy; Tel:+39 0165 262426; Email:info@laroche.it; Web-site:www.laroche.it ; Price:A

Hotel Ristorante la Belle Epoque,Via Claude d'Avise, 18,11100 Aosta(AO),Italy; Tel:+39 0165 262276; Email:info@hotelbellepoqueaosta.it; Price:B

B&B al Nabuisson,Via Aubert, 50,11100 Aosta(AO),Italy; Tel:+39 0165 363006; +39 3396 090332; Email:aostacentro@hotmail.com; Price:A; PR

Affittacamere Borrano,Chemin Voison, 9,11100 Aosta(AO),Italy; Tel:+39 1016 543224; Web-site:bed-and-breakfast.infretta.it; Price:B

Camping Europe,Frazione le Plan du Chateau, 5,11010 Gignod(AO),Italy; Tel:+39 0165 56444; Web-site:www.camping.it/english/valledaosta/aosta/; Price:C

Camping Monte Bianco,Frazione Saint Maurice, 15,11010 Sarre(AO),Italy; Tel:+39 0165 258514; +39 3405 201169; Email:info@campingmontebianco.it; Web-site:www.campingmontebianco.it; Price:C

Camping Arvier,Rue Chaussas, 17,11011 Arvier(AO),Italy; Tel:+39 0165 069006; Email:campingarvier@yahoo.it; Web-site:www.campingarvier.com; Price:C

Societa' Ippica Valdostana,Via Grand'Eyvia, 25,11100 Aosta(AO),Italy; Tel:+39 0165 551580

Societa' Ippica Valdostana,Via Grand'Eyvia, 25,11100 Aosta(AO),Italy; Tel:+39 0165 551580

Office Regional du Tourisme,Via Frédéric Chabod, 15,11100 Aosta(AO),Italy; Tel:+39 0165 548065

Banca Nazionale del Lavoro,Corso Saint-Martin-de-Corléans, 73,11100 Aosta(AO),Italy; Tel:+39 0165 235386

Banca Monte dei Paschi di Siena,Piazza Emile Chanoux, 51,11100 Aosta(AO),Italy; Tel:+39 0165 363813

Unicredit,Viale Conseil des Commis, 19,11100 Aosta(AO),Italy; Tel:+39 0165 262216

Banca d'Italia,Viale Conseil des Commis, 21,11100 Aosta(AO),Italy; Tel:+39 0165 238267

Ospedale Generale Regionale,Viale Ginevra, 3,11100 Aosta(AO),Italy; Tel:+39 0165 543292

Farcoz Rodolfo,Frazione Arliod,11010 Gignod(AO),Italy; Tel:+39 0165 56220

Salval Dr.Micky,Via Guido Rey, 1,11100 Aosta(AO),Italy; Tel:+39 0165 361196

Studio Medico Centre Ville,Via Monte Grappa,11100 Aosta(AO),Italy; Tel:+39 0165 369596

Veterinario Dr.Mosca,Corso Lancieri d'Aosta, 14,11100 Aosta(AO),Italy; Tel:+39 0165 364921

Joe Sport,Via Monte Pasubio, 3,11100 Aosta(AO),Italy; Tel:+39 0165 364155

Nellasport,Piazza Emile Chanoux, 37,11100 Aosta(AO),Italy; Tel:+39 0165 262200

Cicli Lucchini Srl,Corso Battaglione Aosta, 49,11100 Aosta(AO),Italy; Tel:+39 0165 32224

Atelier Boldrini di Roberto Boldrini,Frazione Borettaz, 11,11020 Gressan(AO),Italy; Tel:+39 3356 114906

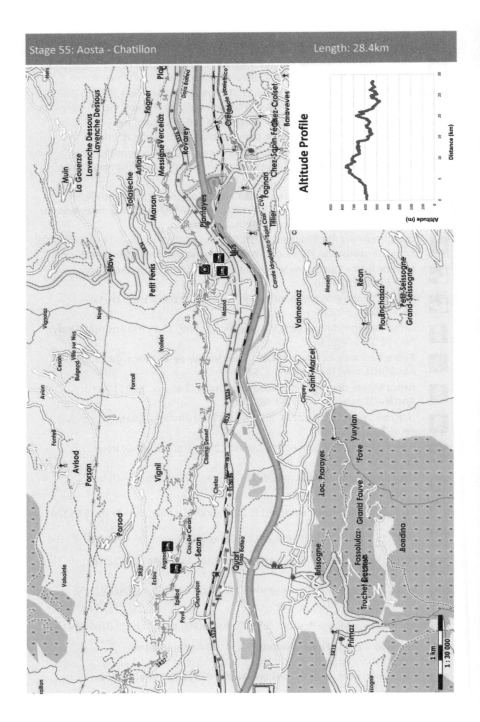

Altitude Profile

Stage Summary: this is a strenuous section, but with the opportunity to break the journey at Nus. After quitting Aosta the route follows quiet roads, farm tracks and hillside pathways through the vineyards, before entering the busy town of Chatillon.

Distance from Besançon: 286km

Distance to Vercelli: 149km

Stage Ascent: 1222m

Stage Descent: 1275m

Waypoint	Distance between waypoints	Total km	Directions	Verification Point	Compass	Altitude m
55.001	0	0.0	Cross piazza della Cattedrale		SE	586
55.002	30	0.0	Turn left	Via Monseigneur de Sales	E	585
55.003	120	0.2	Turn right	Rue de l'Hôtel des Etats	S	586
55.004	140	0.3	At the T-junction, turn left towards the Porta Pretoria	Pass Hôtel de Ville on your left	E	586
55.005	700	1.0	At the roundabout, at the end of the pedestrian zone, proceed straight ahead and cross the river bridge	Direction Torino	NE	584
55.006	130	1.1	At the traffic lights continue straight ahead. Note:- there is a flight of steps ahead – riders should turn left and follow via Mont-Velan, turn left on via Mont-Gelé, take the underpass under the busy ring-road and then turn right on via Scuola Militare Alpina	Follow signs for Hôpital Beauregard	E	582
55.007	80	1.2	Continue straight ahead	Via Mont-Zerbion	E	583
55.008	200	1.4	At the T-junction, turn right	Elevated road on your left	E	593
55.009	70	1.5	Turn left over the pedestrian crossing and mount the steps		N	592

Waypoint	Distance between waypoints	Total km	Directions	Verification Point	Compass	Altitude m
55.010	30	1.5	At the top of the steps turn right on the road, via Scuola Militare Alpina	Towards garages in the wall	E	596
55.011	100	1.6	Bear right on via Luigi Vaccari	Direction St Christophe, VF sign	NE	601
55.012	1800	3.4	Take the left fork	Località Chaussod, VF sign	E	598
55.013	170	3.6	Bear left on the track	Towards the church	NE	601
55.014	120	3.7	At the junction with the road, turn right and then bear left	Pass a cemetery and VF panel on your right	E	617
55.015	100	3.8	At the crossroads, continue straight ahead	Direction Bagnere	E	616
55.016	800	4.6	At the Stop sign in Bagnere, turn right	Pass water course on your left	SE	651
55.017	100	4.7	Take the left fork	Direction Creton	E	641
55.018	60	4.8	Keep left on the road	Modern house with balcony on your left	E	640
55.019	400	5.1	Bear left, up the hill remaining on the road	Sharp bend to the left	NW	660
55.020	300	5.4	Shortly before reaching the winery, turn sharp right	Towards the monastery	E	687
55.021	800	6.2	Turn sharp left	Towards the monastery	NW	711
55.022	160	6.3	Continue straight ahead	Pass the monastery on your right	N	725

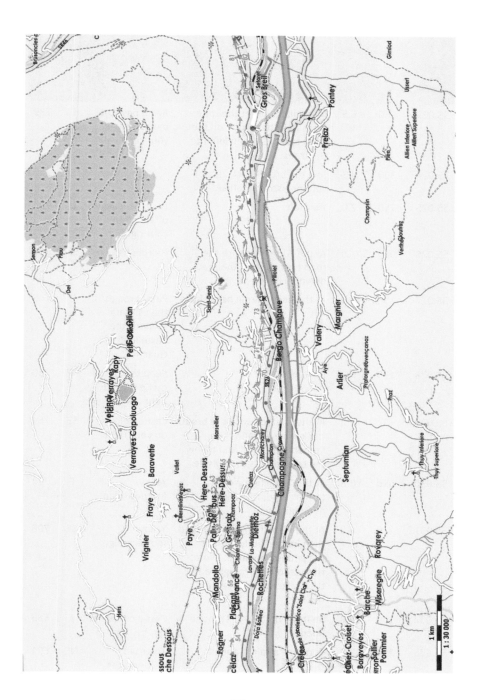

172

Waypoint	Distance between waypoints	Total km	Directions	Verification Point	Compass	Altitude m
55.023	130	6.5	Immediately after the road turns right bear right on the track and then keep left into the trees	Again pass the monastery on your right	E	739
55.024	300	6.8	Join the broad track and continue straight ahead		E	742
55.025	150	7.0	Turn left	Pass the village of Villair on your right	E	725
55.026	900	7.8	At the T-junction with the road turn right on the road, downhill	Hairpin bend	SE	767
55.027	150	8.0	At the next hairpin bend, bear left	Pass through the car park towards the Castello di Quart	E	745
55.028	130	8.1	Bear left	Keep the castle on your right	NE	750
55.029	70	8.2	At the junction with the broad track, turn left and then immediately right and follow the track across the hillside	Castle below on your right	SE	764
55.030	600	8.8	At the T-junction with the tarmac road, turn right, downhill	Yellow footpath sign	E	724
55.031	210	9.0	At the T-junction, turn left and then immediately right on the pedestrian ramp. Note:- riders should turn right and then take the first road on the left	Yellow footpath sign	SE	708
55.032	140	9.2	Bear left on the No Through Road	Pass a car park on the right	E	685
55.033	130	9.3	Continue straight ahead	The road deteriorates into a path	NE	691

Waypoint	Distance between waypoints	Total km	Directions	Verification Point	Compass	Altitude m
55.034	170	9.5	After a brief climb, at a junction with a tarmac road, bear right	Chantignan	SE	716
55.035	250	9.7	At the crossroads continue straight ahead on the road	Imperiau	SE	706
55.036	400	10.1	Continue straight ahead on the road	Enter Seran	E	704
55.037	1100	11.2	Take the left fork on the road	Towards Amerique	E	649
55.038	900	12.0	Just before the hairpin to the left, take the right fork	Pass the quarry on your right	E	665
55.039	600	12.7	At the end of the track take the faint pathway, downhill and bearing left	Parallel to the road and motorway below	E	659
55.040	270	12.9	Cross over a water-course	Remain parallel to the road	E	666
55.041	170	13.1	Continue straight ahead	Parallel to the road	E	663
55.042	300	13.4	Continue straight ahead	Avoid the right turn	E	659
55.043	700	14.0	At the fork take the path to the right	Steeply downhill	E	658
55.044	220	14.3	At end of steep path turn left on the road and cross bridge		SE	597
55.045	180	14.4	Keep left on the main road	Enter Nus	E	578
55.046	150	14.6	Fork left on via Pramatton	Pass conifers in the garden on your right	E	573
55.047	400	15.0	At the T-junction, bear left	Junction beside church	NE	570
55.048	150	15.2	After exiting Nus and beside the monument, turn right and then immediately left on the path	VF sign, pass vines on the left	E	581

Waypoint	Distance between waypoints	Total km	Directions	Verification Point	Compass	Altitude m
55.049	290	15.4	At the fork bear left	Downhill	NE	555
55.050	250	15.7	At the road junction turn right and then immediately left	Frazione Plantayes, towards Rovarey	NE	541
55.051	500	16.2	Continue straight ahead	Château on right	E	553
55.052	700	16.9	At the T-junction, turn left to proceed up the hill into Rovarey	Large white house on the left	NE	551
55.053	290	17.1	At the bend to the left, turn right on a small road		E	570
55.054	600	17.7	Bear right on the stony track	Downhill	E	593
55.055	800	18.5	At the road junction continue straight ahead	Parallel to the motorway	E	561
55.056	700	19.2	At the Stop sign turn left	Pass parking area on the right	E	573
55.057	260	19.5	Shortly after passing the church take the steep path to the right	Cemetery ahead at the junction	NE	595
55.058	80	19.5	Rejoin the tarmac road and bear right	Uphill	NE	610
55.059	50	19.6	At the T-junction, turn left	VF road sign on the right	NW	618
55.060	30	19.6	Turn right on the small road	Pass water channel on your left	E	622
55.061	400	20.0	After a steep climb continue straight ahead	Direction Chatillon	E	663
55.062	300	20.3	At the fork bear right downhill on the path	Beside two old buildings	E	661
55.063	190	20.5	Cross the bridge and turn right then left on the tarmac road		SE	627
55.064	300	20.8	Continue straight ahead on the road	Uphill	E	630

Waypoint	Distance between waypoints	Total km	Directions	Verification Point	Compass	Altitude m
55.065	240	21.0	In Grangeon beside an agriturismo turn right	Through vines	S	649
55.066	230	21.3	After a steep descent take the road to the left	Beside the hamlet	E	583
55.067	120	21.4	Join an tarmac road and bear right	Downhill	E	579
55.068	140	21.5	Go straight ahead, avoid the turning to the left	Road bends to the right and then left	SE	570
55.069	300	21.8	At the T-junction turn left	Direction Chambave	E	529
55.070	800	22.7	At the T-junction, turn right direction Torino	Enter Chambave	E	507
55.071	300	23.0	Turn left in front of the Café l'Arquebusier	Rue E. Chanoux	E	493
55.072	500	23.5	At the Stop sign bear left beside the main road		E	472
55.073	40	23.5	Take the left fork on the small road towards Chandianaz	Pass wooden crucifix on your right	E	470
55.074	900	24.3	Continue straight ahead	Pass through the hamlet of Chandianaz	E	534
55.075	900	25.2	Go straight ahead	Path passes through Beudegaz	E	491
55.076	270	25.5	Before entering the derelict hamlet take the faint path to the left	Skirt the hamlet	E	498
55.077	400	25.9	At the T-junction with a tarmac road, turn left on the road		E	505
55.078	180	26.0	At the next bend in the road, bear right on the small road		NE	519
55.079	270	26.3	Bear right on the path down the hill towards Chatillon	Beside clearing	E	554

Waypoint	Distance between waypoints	Total km	Directions	Verification Point	Compass	Altitude m
55.080	500	26.8	Continue straight ahead on the tarmac road	Beside fountain and over pipeline	E	525
55.081	500	27.3	At the T-junction, turn right		S	525
55.082	20	27.3	At the next T-junction, turn left		E	524
55.083	400	27.7	On reaching the Chatillon ring-road take the subway and continue straight ahead into the town	Via Menabreaz	E	534
55.084	500	28.2	In the centre of Chatillon turn left. Note:- caution travelling against the one-way system	Cross the bridge on via Emile Chanoux	E	525
55.085	160	28.4	Turn left	Via Gervasone	NE	527
55.086	30	28.4	Arrive at Chatillon centre	In front of the church of San Pietro		533

Accommodation & Facilities .... Aosta - Chatillon

Convento Cappuccini,Via Emile Chanoux, 130,11024 Châtillon(AO),Italy; Tel:+39 0166 61471; Price:D

Istituto Don Bosco,Via Tornafol, 7,11024 Châtillon(AO),Italy; Tel:+39 0166 560111; Web-site:www.istitutosalesianovda.it; Price:C

Parrocchia San Vincenzo,Piazza della Chiesa,11027 Saint-Vincent(AO),Italy; Tel:+39 0166 512350; Price:D

Parrocchia Sant'Ilario,Via Pramatton, 2,11020 Nus(AO),Italy; Tel:+39 0165 767901; +39 0335 686644; Email:parrocchianus@alice.it; Price:D

B&B le Rosier,Frazione Crotache, 1,11027 Saint-Vincent(AO),Italy; Tel:+39 0166 537726; +39 3391 273354; Email:omar@lerosier.it; Web-site:www.lerosier.it; Price:B

Hotel le Verger,Via Tour de Grange, 53,11024 Chatillon(AO),Italy; Tel:+39 0166 563066; Email:info@leverger.it; Web-site:www.leverger.it; Price:B

Hotel au Soleil,Via Marconi, 20,11027 Saint-Vincent(AO),Italy; Tel:+39 0166 512685; Email:info@hotelausoleil.it; Web-site:www.hotelausoleil.it; Price:A

Clair Matin - B&B,Via Tour de Grange, 40,11024 Châtillon(AO),Italy; Tel:+39 0166 61822; +39 3280 922916; Email:info@clairmatin.it; Web-site:www.clairmatin.it; Price:A

Hotel la Chance,Viale Duca d'Aosta, 14,11027 Saint-Vincent(AO),Italy; Tel:+39 0166 510110; Email:hotellachance@tiscali.it; Web-site:www.hotellachance.com; Price:A

Hotel Alla Posta,Piazza 28 Aprile, 1,11027 Saint-Vincent(AO),Italy; Tel:+39 0166 512250; Email:info@hotelpostavda.it; Web-site:www.hotelpostavda.it; Price:A

Pensione Serena,Via Ponte Romano, 54,11027 Saint-Vincent(AO),Italy; Tel:+39 0166 512363; Email:pensione.serena@yahoo.it; Price:B

Il Torchio,Frazione Romillod Capard,11027 Saint-Vincent(AO),Italy; Tel:+39 0166 945958; +39 3355 356885; Email:info@iltorchio.info; Web-site:www.iltorchio.info; Price:B

Hotel Zerbion,Via Emile Chanoux, 189,11024 Châtillon(AO),Italy; Tel:+39 0166 540239; Email:info@hotelzerbion.com; Web-site:hotelzerbion.com; Price:A

Hotel Dufour,Via Tollen, 16,11024 Châtillon(AO),Italy; Tel:+39 0166 61467; +39 3408 262390; Email:dufourtaxi@virgilio.it; Web-site:www.htdufour.com; Price:B

B&B il Tiglio,Via Cesare Battisti, 18,11027 Saint-Vincent (AO),Italy; Tel:+39 0166 512194; Email:crosuno@tin.it; Web-site:www.tigliovacanze.it; Price:A

B&B - la Mandorla,Clou de Seran, 10,11020 Quart(AO),Italy; Tel:+39 0165 762163; Price:B

B&B - la Casa Degli Iris,Villaggio Seran, 62,11020 Quart(AO),Italy; +39 3334 329053; Email:info@casadegliris.it; Price:B

Hotel Dujany,Via Risorgimento, 104,11020 Nus(AO),Italy; Tel:+39 0165 767100; Email:info@hoteldujany.com; Web-site:www.hoteldujany.com; Price:B

Hotel Florian,Via Risorgimento, 3,11020 Nus(AO),Italy; Tel:+39 0165 767968; +39 3334 645424; Email:info@hotel-florian.it; Web-site:www.hotel-florian.it; Price:B

Office Regional du Tourisme,Via Roma,11027 Saint-Vincent(AO),Italy; Tel:+39 0166 512239

Unicredit,Piazza Monte Zerbion,11027 Saint-Vincent(AO),Italy; Tel:+39 0166 537646

Banca Sella,Località Soleil, 8,11024 Châtillon(AO),Italy; Tel:+39 0166 563086

Unicredit,Via Emile Chanoux, 15,11024 Châtillon(AO),Italy; Tel:+39 0166 501811

Banca di Credito Cooperativo,Via Aosta, 1,11020 Nus(AO),Italy; Tel:+39 0165 766414; Web-site:www.valdostana.bcc.it

Cavurina - Ambulatorio Medico,Piazza Savini, 5,11027 Saint-Vincent(AO),Italy; Tel:+39 0166 512328

Valente Franco,Via Monsignor Alliod, 43,11027 Saint-Vincent(AO),Italy; Tel:+39 0166 537190

Vert Sport,Via Chanoux, 71,11027 Saint-Vincent(AO),Italy; Tel:+39 0166 510151

Mazzanti Bike di Mazzanti Guido,Via Ponte Romano,11027 Saint-Vincent(AO),Italy; Tel:+39 0166 513558

Taxi Vallz d'Aosta,Via Perret, 8,11027 Saint-Vincent(AO),Italy; +39 3397 113050

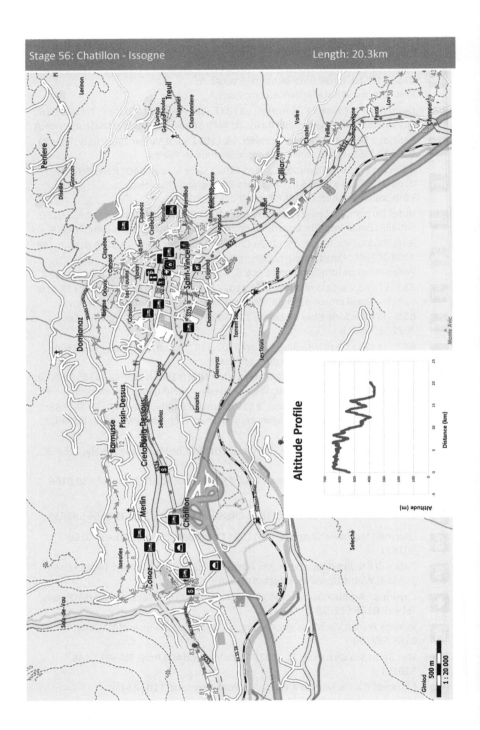

Altitude Profile

Stage Summary: the section returns to the terraced hill-sides on the left of the Aosta valley before descending to the broadening valley floor and following the banks of the Dora Baltea to the small but attractive town of Issogne

Distance from Besançon: 314km

Distance to Vercelli: 120km

Stage Ascent: 981m

Stage Descent: 1124m

Waypoint	Distance between waypoints	Total km	Directions	Verification Point	Compass	Altitude m
56.001	0	0.0	From the front of the church in Chatillon turn left	Up the hill	NW	533
56.002	50	0.0	Pass beside the church and turn left on the road up the hill	Via Gervasone	N	541
56.003	270	0.3	Take the left fork		N	564
56.004	220	0.5	Cross the small bridge and take the tarmac road to the left	Steeply uphill	N	588
56.005	90	0.6	Take the road to the left uphill	Direction Tour de Conoz	NW	602
56.006	200	0.8	After a steep climb on the road take the path to the right	Metal hand rail	E	631
56.007	40	0.9	Turn right on a tarmac road	The road deteriorates into a track	E	637
56.008	400	1.2	At the fork continue straight ahead		E	645
56.009	400	1.6	Continue straight ahead on the track		E	632
56.010	400	2.0	At the T-junction with a tarmac road turn right		E	638
56.011	280	2.3	At the Stop sign, cross straight over the road and take the gravel track		SE	630
56.012	140	2.4	Continue straight ahead on the tarmac	Pass metal gates on your right	NE	628

Waypoint	Distance between waypoints	Total km	Directions	Verification Point	Compass	Altitude m
56.013	300	2.7	Continue straight ahead	Cross a water-course	E	630
56.014	400	3.1	At the crossroads, continue straight ahead		E	624
56.015	800	3.9	Continue straight ahead	Ignore the turning to the right	SE	622
56.016	400	4.2	Enter Saint Vincent and continue straight ahead at the crossroads	Via Monte Bianco	E	618
56.017	200	4.5	Cross the road and bear left uphill		SE	612
56.018	240	4.7	Bear right on the smaller road. Note :- to avoid a flight of steps riders should remain on the road and pass the entrance the Terme, then take the first road to the right – via Battaglione Aosta – and rejoin the "Official Route" as the path emerges from the trees beside house n° 32	Metal railings	SE	610
56.019	180	4.9	Turn right and take the steps to the path below		S	624
56.020	70	4.9	Pass the funicular and the Terme building on your left		SE	620
56.021	400	5.3	At the T-junction with the tarmac road, turn right	Downhill, yellow "F" on left	SW	626
56.022	110	5.4	Turn left towards a yellow house on the small road	Water-course on the left at the junction	S	600
56.023	120	5.5	At the foot of the ramp, bear left onto a steeply ascending tarmac road	Via Trois Mosquettaires	SE	594
56.024	600	6.1	Take the right fork on the small road downhill and then turn left over the bridge	Towards the car park	SE	624

Waypoint	Distance between waypoints	Total km	Directions	Verification Point	Compass	Altitude m
56.025	100	6.2	Continue straight ahead	Near to the chapel	S	615
56.026	40	6.2	Take the track to the left	Beside the water-fountain	SW	613
56.027	120	6.3	Descend through the orchards and take a path to the left		S	605
56.028	140	6.5	After a steep climb, take the track to the left		E	617
56.029	250	6.7	Bear right on the path	Beside the woods	SE	643
56.030	40	6.8	At the T-junction with the road, turn right and then bear right on the small road	Pass sign Feilley	SE	642
56.031	130	6.9	At the first junction bear right onto a path	Beside the stream	S	630
56.032	150	7.1	Cross a track and continue straight ahead on the grass track		S	599
56.033	100	7.2	At the T-junction with the road, turn left on the road and continue downhill	VF sign	SE	579
56.034	180	7.3	In front of the house take the track to the right	Champ de Vigne	SE	574
56.035	240	7.6	Beside the stone house, turn to the left	Through the orchards	SE	541
56.036	180	7.8	Near to the house bear left on the track	Into the trees	SE	556
56.037	120	7.9	After a steep climb in the woods turn left in the clearing		SE	579
56.038	60	7.9	After a short climb bear left on the track	Across the hillside	SE	590
56.039	150	8.1	At the T-junction, bear right on the broad track		SE	616
56.040	180	8.3	Continue straight ahead on the tarmac in Chenal	Ruined castle on the hill to the right	E	631

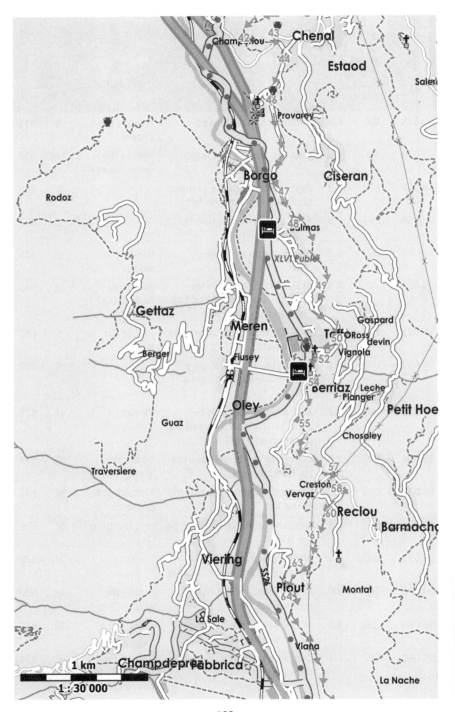

Waypoint	Distance between waypoints	Total km	Directions	Verification Point	Compass	Altitude m
56.041	80	8.4	Take the first turning to the right and immediately right again and continue on the path after passing the small church	Metal railings on the right	SW	640
56.042	500	8.9	Beside the clearing bear left on the cart track	Pass a wooden building on your left	SE	567
56.043	300	9.2	Cross the tarmac road and continue straight ahead on the road	Towards Ruelle	SE	588
56.044	120	9.3	At the junction, bear right, downhill	Pass a shrine on your right	S	578
56.045	220	9.5	Take the right fork	After crossing bridge	SW	564
56.046	140	9.6	Bear left on the road, downhill	Beside Castello di Montjovet	S	550
56.047	1000	10.6	Ignore the track to the right and continue straight ahead on the tarmac	Barmas	SE	448
56.048	120	10.8	Continue straight ahead, on the grass track between terraces	Ignore the small road to the right	S	447
56.049	800	11.6	Continue straight ahead on the tarmac	Toffo	SE	439
56.050	400	11.9	At the top sign, turn right on the stone track before reaching the main road	VF sign	S	427
56.051	170	12.1	Beside a group of houses turn right	Towards church spire	SW	406
56.052	70	12.2	At the T-junction in Montjovet (XLVI), take the road to the left	Uphill	SW	398
56.053	90	12.3	At the first bend to the left take the path to the right	Downhill, towards the church	S	389

Waypoint	Distance between waypoints	Total km	Directions	Verification Point	Compass	Altitude m
56.054	150	12.4	At the junction immediately after passing the church, turn left and then immediately bear right on the track	Cross the hill-side in the trees	S	406
56.055	600	13.0	Join a tarmac road and bear left, uphill	Rock face on the left	SE	484
56.056	500	13.5	Turn left on the path, steeply uphill	Yellow footpath signs	SE	528
56.057	130	13.6	The path emerges at a road junction, continue straight ahead on the road	Towards Quignonaz	SE	556
56.058	40	13.7	At the entry to Reclou, bear right on the track	Yellow footpath sign	SE	555
56.059	130	13.8	At the junction with the tarmac road, turn right	Pass chalet style house on your right	SW	545
56.060	160	14.0	At the crossroads, continue straight ahead on the gravel track	Water trough on the right	S	533
56.061	400	14.3	At the crossroads in the tracks, continue straight ahead	Downhill, through the trees	S	504
56.062	180	14.5	At the junction in the tracks, keep right	Continue downhill	SW	472
56.063	130	14.6	On bend to the right, turn left	Downhill	SW	446
56.064	150	14.8	At the T-junction, turn left		S	419
56.065	230	15.0	Take the left fork and continue across the hill-side parallel to the river and motorway	Pass the hamlet of Viana on your right	SE	423
56.066	1300	16.3	At T-junction, turn right and continue on road through village	Torille	S	484
56.067	500	16.8	Keep right on the road		W	403
56.068	300	17.1	At the T-junction with the SS26 turn left and then right at the traffic lights	Pass under the motorway	SW	370

Waypoint	Distance between waypoints	Total km	Directions	Verification Point	Compass	Altitude m
56.069	300	17.4	Continue straight ahead	Beside the pylon	W	365
56.070	100	17.5	At the T-junction turn left	River immediately to the right	S	366
56.071	800	18.3	Cross a small bridge and bear right	Remain on the bank of the river	S	363
56.072	700	19.0	At the T-junction turn right	Over the river bridge	SW	366
56.073	150	19.2	At the T-junction, after the bridge, turn left	Fleuran	SE	364
56.074	20	19.2	Turn right into a narrow alleyway	Direction Issogne cycle route	SW	364
56.075	130	19.3	Turn left at the junction at the top of the rise		SE	375
56.076	400	19.7	Bear right up the steps	Pass through the church car park	S	378
56.077	100	19.8	At the road junction, continue straight ahead	Pass playground on your left	SE	384
56.078	70	19.9	Continue straight ahead over the bridge	Direction Centro	SE	387
56.079	200	20.1	Turn right	Skirt the grounds of the castle on your left	S	384
56.080	150	20.2	At the T-junction with the road turn left	Towards the church	E	392
56.081	20	20.3	Arrive at Issogne	At the road junction, beside the church		390

Instituto Diocesano,Località le Vieux, 40,11020 Arnad(AO),Italy; Tel:+39 0125 966405; Price:D

Hotel and B&B - il Casello,Via Stazione, 79,11029 Verrès(AO),Italy; Tel:+39 0125 921652; Email:info@ilcaselloverres.com; Web-site:ilcaselloverres.com; Price:B; Note:Price group A in the B&B,

Hotel Napoleon,Località Broccard, 1,11020 Montjovet(AO),Italy; Tel:+39 0166 579111; Web-site:www.napoleonvda.it; Price:B

Hotel il Nigra,Frazione.Berriaz, 13,11020 Montjovet(AO),Italy; Tel:+39 0166 79139; Email:nv1900@nigrahotel.191.it; Web-site:www.ilnigra.it; Price:B

B&B - les Souvenirs,Migot, 1,11020 Issogne(AO),Italy; +39 3389 012043; +39 3391 009572; Email:lessouvenirs@virgilio.it; Web-site:lessouvenirs.altervista.org; Price:B

Maison Lakia - B&B,Frazione.Arnad le Vieux, 40/bis,11020 Arnad(AO),Italy; +39 3486 563509; +39 3468 802155; Email:info@lakia.it; Web-site:www.lakia.it; Price:B

Banca di Credito Cooperativo,Via Franchetè, 95,11029 Verrès(AO),Italy; Tel:+39 0125 920971

San Paolo,Frazinoe Extraz, 2,11020 Arnad(AO),Italy; Tel:+39 0125 966109

Taxi Troilo Marco,Via delle Murasse, 40,11029 Verres(AO),Italy; Tel:+39 3381 473535

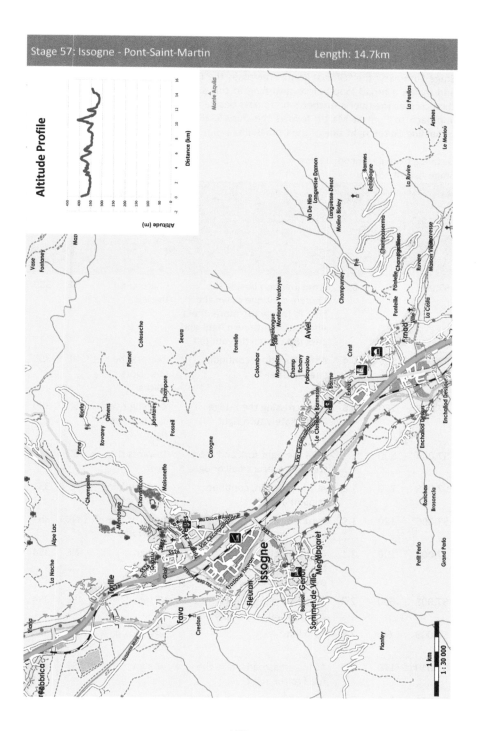

Stage Summary: the "Official Route" recrosses the Dora Baltea, follows the river bank and makes a broad loop before returning to this side of the river near Echallod and then crosses the river a further time to pass beside the dramatic fortress of Bard. The approach to Pont St Martin follows the busy SS26. A more direct Alternate Route remaining on the right side of the Dora Baltea will reduce the journey by 2.3km.

Distance from Besançon: 335km   Distance to Vercelli: 100km
Stage Ascent: 344m   Stage Descent: 388m

Waypoint	Distance between waypoints	Total km	Directions	Verification Point	Compass	Altitude m
57.001	0	0.0	From junction beside the Church, continue down the hill. To follow the more direct Alternate Route turn right and pass the church on your left	Château on the left	NE	389
57.002	500	0.4	At the junction, continue straight ahead	Recross the river Dora Baltea	NE	359
57.003	180	0.6	After crossing the bridge immediately turn right	Keeping river close on the right	SE	359
57.004	500	1.1	Take the right fork and then turn left over a small bridge	Towards the river	SE	356
57.005	700	1.8	At the junction, continue straight ahead	Farm building on the left	E	351
57.006	120	1.9	Turn left	Towards the motorway	NE	351
57.007	190	2.1	At the junction, turn right on the tarmac road and cross over the motorway	VF sign	NE	354
57.008	600	2.7	At the Stop sign turn right and enter Arnad	VF sign	SE	354
57.009	60	2.8	Turn left	Sign Clos de Barme	NE	354
57.010	170	2.9	At the crossroads, take the road to the right	VF sign	SE	370
57.011	280	3.2	At the T-junction turn left	Frazione Torretta	E	357

Waypoint	Distance between waypoints	Total km	Directions	Verification Point	Compass	Altitude m
57.012	400	3.5	Enter Barme and continue straight ahead	Ignore the turning on the right	S	372
57.013	170	3.7	At the Stop sign turn left	Frazione Sisan	SE	365
57.014	500	4.2	Just after the restaurant Buon Convento, take the road to the right	Towards the clock tower	SW	367
57.015	140	4.4	At the T-junction, turn left	Parrocchiale di San Martino	SE	360
57.016	90	4.4	Cross the bridge and then bear right	Pass the school on your left	SE	362
57.017	260	4.7	Shortly after passing house n° 1 and a small shrine on your left, turn left on the road	Towards the corrugated metal barn	SE	368
57.018	110	4.8	At the crossroads, continue straight ahead on the gravel track	Vineyard on your right	E	376
57.019	170	5.0	At the T-junction with the road, turn right and continue on the road	Cross the bridge	SE	389
57.020	130	5.1	Bear right on the small road	Direction La Kiuva	S	393
57.021	230	5.3	Immediately after passing the football field, turn right	Echallod cycle route	SW	391
57.022	190	5.5	Follow the track under the motorway		SW	377
57.023	140	5.7	Take the right fork	Towards main road	W	366
57.024	110	5.8	Cross straight over the main road,SS26 and continue on the track	Gully on the right	SW	359
57.025	80	5.8	Continue straight ahead	Ignore a turning to the left	SW	355
57.026	80	5.9	Continue straight ahead and cross the river bridge	Pass under the railway	W	352

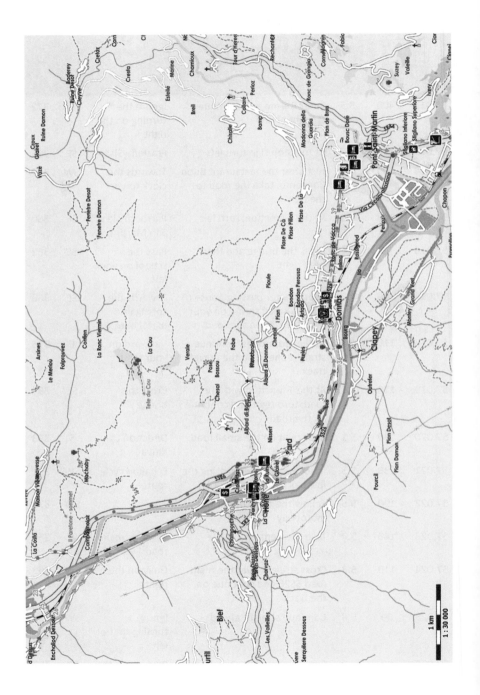

Waypoint	Distance between waypoints	Total km	Directions	Verification Point	Compass	Altitude m
57.027	140	6.1	After crossing the river bridge and turn left. Note:- the Alternate Route joins from the right	Beside the river	SE	354
57.028	1100	7.1	Turn right onto the track just before Autostrada bridge	VF sign	SE	347
57.029	1500	8.6	Proceed straight ahead	Enter Hône	S	344
57.030	400	9.0	Cross the road and continue straight ahead	Via Mario Collard	S	363
57.031	400	9.4	At the crossroads, turn left	Pass under Autostrada bridge	E	353
57.032	180	9.6	Bear right on via E. Chanoux	Between Hotel and car park	E	349
57.033	400	10.0	After crossing the river bridge turn right on SS26 and then immediately bear left on the narrow road into the old town	Fortress on the right	S	356
57.034	500	10.4	Continue straight ahead downhill	Ignore the turning towards the fortress	SE	407
57.035	1000	11.4	At the T-junction with the SS26, turn left and take the pavement on the left	Railway and river to the right of the road	E	331
57.036	500	11.9	Bear away from the main road towards the centre of Donnas	Pass the Arch of Donnas	NE	344
57.037	300	12.3	Pass through the archway and keep right	Lower road	E	325
57.038	190	12.5	At the T-junction with the SS62 turn left on the main road	Via Roma	E	323
57.039	1600	14.1	At the roundabout take the last exit	Direction Pont Saint Martin	E	325
57.040	700	14.7	Arrive at Pont-Saint-Martin	Beside war memorial		345

Length: 3.8km

Stage Summary: this more direct route follows minor roads and tracks on the right side of the Dora Baltea to save 2.3km.

Stage Ascent: 72m   Stage Descent: 102m

Waypoint	Distance between waypoints	Total km	Directions	Verification Point	Compass	Altitude m
57A1.001	0	0.0	Turnright into a narrow street passing the Cafeteria Paninoteca	Château on right before the junction	S	390
57A1.002	50	0.0	Turn left	Frazione Pied-de-Ville	SE	390
57A1.003	500	0.5	Turn left and immediately right onto the Cycle Route, direction Arnad	Parallel to river	SE	363
57A1.004	1300	1.8	Fork left on the track	Closer to river	SE	354
57A1.005	1200	3.0	At the crossroads turn left on the road	Parallel to river	SE	355
57A1.006	290	3.2	Turn right direction Hône	Cross bridge	SE	354
57A1.007	600	3.8	Continue straight ahead. Note:- the "Official Route" joins from the left	River bridge on the left		360

Foresteria Saint Martin,(Signora Angela),Via Schigliatta, 1,11026 Pont-Saint-Martin(AO),Italy; Tel:+39 0125 804433; +39 0125 830611; +39 3472 232039; Web-site:www.comune.pontsaintmartin.ao.it/il-paese/strutture-polivalenti/maison-du-boulodrome; Price:C

Parrocchia San Pietro,Via Roma, 81,11020 Donnas(AO),Italy; Tel:+39 0125 807032; Price:D

Colliard - Agriturismo,Frazione Courtil,11020 Hône(AO),Italy; Tel:+39 0125 809842; Price:B

B&B Mon Reve,Via Aosta, 1,11020 Hone(AO),Italy; Tel:+39 0125 803141; +39 3405 203515; Price:B

Hotel Bordet,Via Emilio Chanoux, 54,11020 Hône(AO),Italy; Tel:+39 0125 803116; Email:info@hotelbordet.191.it; Price:A

Ristorante Albergo del Mulino,Via Emilio Chanoux, 13,11020 Hône(AO),Italy; Tel:+39 0125 803334; Price:A

B&B - le Bon Revei,Via Vittorio Emanuele II,11020 Bard(AO),Italy; Tel:+39 0125 803986; Email:bonreveil@libero.it; Price:B

Crabun Hotel,Via Nazionale Per Donnas, 3,11026 Pont-Saint-Martin(AO),Italy; Tel:+39 0125 806069; Email:info@crabunhotel.it; Web-site:www.crabunhotel.it; Price:A

Ponte Romano,Piazza Iv Novembre, 10,11026 Pont-Saint-Martin(AO),Italy; Tel:+39 0125 804329; Email:info@hotelponteromano.it; Web-site:www.hotelponteromano.it; Price:B

Bed & Breakfast al Castel,(Fabio),Via Castello, 8,11026 Pont-Saint-Martin(AO),Italy; +39 3474 767125; Email:info@alcastel.it; Price:A; PR

Associazione Turistica Pro Loco,Via della Resistenza, 1,11026 Pont-Saint-Martin(AO),Italy; Tel:+39 0165 809912

Istituto Bancario San Paolo di Torino,Via Aosta, 30,11020 Hône(AO),Italy; Tel:+39 0125 803152

Biverbanca,Via Roma, 115,11020 Donnas(AO),Italy; Tel:+39 0125 805269

Banca Monte dei Paschi di Siena,Piazza Primo Maggio, 1,11026 Pont-Saint-Martin(AO),Italy; Tel:+39 0125 809187

Banca di Credito Cooperativo,Via Emile Chanoux, 124,11026 Pont-Saint-Martin(AO),Italy; Tel:+39 0125 805035

Fiorenza - Studio Medico,Piazza 4 Novembre,11026 Pont-Saint-Martin(AO),Italy; Tel:+39 0125 805217

Veterinario,Via Nazionale Per Carema, 17,11026 Pont-Saint-Martin(AO),Italy; Tel:+39 0125 806061

Scavarda,Via Emile Chanoux, 52,11026 Pont-Saint-Martin(AO),Italy; Tel:+39 0125 806168

Ncc Taxivip,Via E.Chanoux, 122,11026 Pont-Saint-Martin(AO),Italy; +39 3459 602287

Altitude Profile

Stage Summary: this section continues on pathways and tracks along the hillsides and through the old vineyards to the east of the Dora Baltea. Extra caution is necessary where the route intersects and briefly follows the busy SS62.

Distance from Besançon:349km
Stage Ascent: 564m

Distance to Vercelli: 85km
Stage Descent: 641m

Waypoint	Distance between waypoints	Total km	Directions	Verification Point	Compass	Altitude m
58.001	0	0.0	From beside the war memorial, continue straight ahead	Via Emile Chanoux	SE	345
58.002	260	0.3	Cross the river bridge	Roman bridge to the left	SE	348
58.003	120	0.4	As the main road bends to the right, bear left on the small road	Via Boschetto, No Through Road	S	353
58.004	170	0.6	Continue straight ahead, between buildings and terraces	Parking area to the right	S	353
58.005	400	0.9	At the junction beside the main road turn left on the smaller road	Rue Sant'Erasmo, pass large fir tree on the right	S	327
58.006	500	1.4	At the T-junction with the main road, bear left	Tabacchi on left	S	317
58.007	50	1.5	Take the first road on the left	Via Schigliatta	E	315
58.008	150	1.6	Bear right on the road	Car park on the right, terraces to the left	S	327
58.009	190	1.8	At the sharp bend in the road to the left, bear right on the steep grass path	Downhill, beside the metal railings	S	316
58.010	90	1.9	After passing the rear of the houses take the pathway to the left	Between vines	E	314

Waypoint	Distance between waypoints	Total km	Directions	Verification Point	Compass	Altitude m
58.011	140	2.1	At the first turning, turn right up the hill	Signed: Sentiero dei Vigneti	SE	340
58.012	150	2.2	Continue straight ahead in the direction of Carema	Beside la Cappella di San Rocco	E	354
58.013	400	2.6	Continue straight ahead into the village of Carema and proceed downhill on via Roma	Stone pillars on your right	SE	349
58.014	300	2.9	At the T-junction, turn left on via Basiglia, uphill	VF sign	NE	342
58.015	70	3.0	In Piazza della Chiesa, turn right on via San Matteo	Pass the church on your left	S	353
58.016	140	3.1	Take the left fork, uphill and then quickly turn right between stone pillared vineyards	VF sign	SW	353
58.017	80	3.2	At the crossroads, turn left, downhill on the tarmac road	VF sign, vines on the left	SW	347
58.018	50	3.3	At the crossroads, bear slightly right on the narrow road	VF sign	SW	341
58.019	140	3.4	Bear left	Between the vines	S	319
58.020	70	3.5	Take the right fork on the paved road		SW	317
58.021	110	3.6	Take the left fork on the track		S	305
58.022	140	3.7	At the junction with the main road turn left and proceed with care beside busy road	SS26, stone pillars on the left	SE	296
58.023	110	3.8	Continue straight ahead behind the crash barrier in the lay-by	Road bears right	S	294
58.024	130	4.0	Return to the main road and continue ahead towards the river	SS26	S	300

Waypoint	Distance between waypoints	Total km	Directions	Verification Point	Compass	Altitude m
58.025	800	4.7	Beside the bus shelter, turn left. Note:- cyclists or walkers wishing to avoid further climbing continue straight ahead on the Alternate Route	Direction Airale, road quickly turns to the right	SE	286
58.026	260	5.0	Continue straight ahead on via Giasso	Beside small church	SE	292
58.027	280	5.3	Continue straight ahead on the track		SE	285
58.028	190	5.5	Continue straight ahead	Cross the small bridge	E	283
58.029	100	5.6	At the T-junction, following the bridge, bear right on a tarmac road	Low stone wall on the left	S	283
58.030	210	5.8	Turn left on the ramp, towards the bell tower	Pass through Torre Daniele	E	276
58.031	100	5.9	Turn right at the edge of the commune	Power lines descend the hill ahead	SE	279
58.032	110	6.0	At the T-junction turn right	VF sign, pass low stone wall on your left	S	276
58.033	90	6.1	Before reaching the main road turn left on the part made road	VF sign, parallel to SS26	SE	276
58.034	700	6.8	Bear left on a track between the vines	Pass two concrete barns on the right	SE	276
58.035	400	7.1	Continue straight ahead	Village of Cesnola	S	309
58.036	80	7.2	At the crossroads, turn right on the narrow road down the hill	Water trough on the left	SW	309
58.037	100	7.3	Take the first turning to the left into the countryside	The way quickly becomes a track, VF sign	S	296

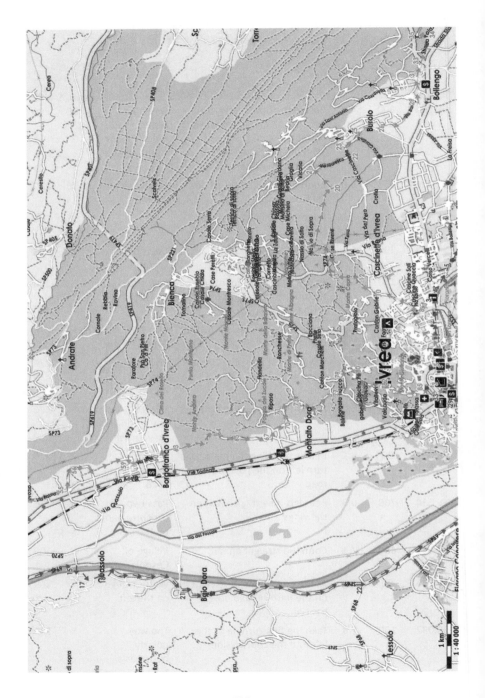

Waypoint	Distance between waypoints	Total km	Directions	Verification Point	Compass	Altitude m
58.038	800	8.1	At the junction turn left, uphill	Beside the ruined church in Settimo Vittonea	E	302
58.039	150	8.2	At the Stop sign, bear left on the road	Uphill	E	319
58.040	280	8.5	Turn left on the cobbled road	VF sign, shrines on the left	E	341
58.041	90	8.6	Turn right	In front of the church	SE	358
58.042	70	8.7	From the car park, turn left, pass through the metal gates and proceed on the unmade road	Pass Castello di Settimo Vittone on the right	E	355
58.043	90	8.8	Bear left on the path		SE	354
58.044	200	9.0	Bear left uphill on the tarmac	Vines above on the right	S	352
58.045	200	9.2	Continue straight ahead on the path	Through the vines	S	352
58.046	400	9.5	Take the pathway to the left	Near a small tarmac road	S	300
58.047	240	9.8	Bear left on the tarmac road	Steeply uphill	SE	306
58.048	160	9.9	Continue straight ahead on the track	Beside the hamlet of Casellino	SE	334
58.049	110	10.0	At the first turning on the track turn right downhill	View of Castello Montestrutto	S	348
58.050	170	10.2	Bear right	Towards Montestrutto	W	321
58.051	300	10.5	Turn left on via Vittorio Emanuele	In the centre of Montestrutto	SE	272
58.052	300	10.8	At the end of the stone pillars, take the track to the left around the house	Beside the electricity pylon	SE	264

Waypoint	Distance between waypoints	Total km	Directions	Verification Point	Compass	Altitude m
58.053	180	11.0	At the crossroads, continue straight ahead on the track		SE	263
58.054	170	11.2	At the crossroads, take the tarmac road to the left	VF sign	SE	263
58.055	1500	12.7	Turn left on via San Germano	Beside the church of San Germano	E	264
58.056	400	13.0	Bear left and then turn right on the stony track	Via del Buonumore	S	273
58.057	500	13.5	Shortly after the road bends to the right, turn left on track	Direction Lago Nero	S	255
58.058	700	14.2	At the Stop sign turn right	Pass the car park on your left	W	256
58.059	130	14.3	At the traffic lights, turn left	VF sign, pass house n° 90 on your left	S	256
58.060	400	14.7	In piazza Ruffini, continue straight ahead on via Marini	Pass Torre Porta on your left	S	259
58.061	230	14.9	At the Stop sign, turn left	Pass house n° 42 on your right	E	257
58.062	70	15.0	Turn right on via Tostre	Gardens on the left and right	S	256
58.063	300	15.3	Continue straight ahead on the track	Towards the trees	SE	251
58.064	700	16.0	At the T-junction in the tracks, turn right		S	269
58.065	600	16.6	Continue straight ahead on the tarmac road	Between industrial buildings	S	254
58.066	300	16.9	At the mini-roundabout, bear left	Via Aldo Balla	S	249
58.067	200	17.1	In the piazza in Montalto Dora, turn left	Via Casana, VF sign	E	253

Waypoint	Distance between waypoints	Total km	Directions	Verification Point	Compass	Altitude m
58.068	120	17.2	Turn right. Note:- at the time of writing a VF sign pointed straight ahead	Via Cappella	S	256
58.069	80	17.3	At the T-junction turn left and then right and then keep left beside the garden wall	Pass house n° 27 on your left	SE	254
58.070	130	17.4	Take the left fork, up the hill	Pass silos on your right	E	259
58.071	300	17.7	At the junction bear right on the larger road	The road quickly makes a double bend	SE	291
58.072	400	18.1	Turn right	Beside the chapel	SW	298
58.073	170	18.3	At the end of the tarmac, continue straight ahead on the track		SW	303
58.074	280	18.6	Turn left on a track	Direction Cappella di San Pietro	SE	307
58.075	290	18.8	At the top of the hill continue straight ahead on the track		SE	334
58.076	260	19.1	Beside Cappella di San Pietro, continue straight ahead on the tarmac road	VF sign	S	311
58.077	150	19.3	At the T-junction, beside the restaurant take the track to the left	Into the woods	E	302
58.078	250	19.5	Continue straight ahead on the tarmac road	Car Park on the left	E	290
58.079	100	19.6	At the Stop sign, bear left on the road	Lake below on the left	SE	283
58.080	170	19.8	Turn right on the small road just before the T-junction	Via Sant'Ulderico	SW	288
58.081	400	20.1	Continue straight ahead on the unmade road	Field on the right, woods on the left	S	279

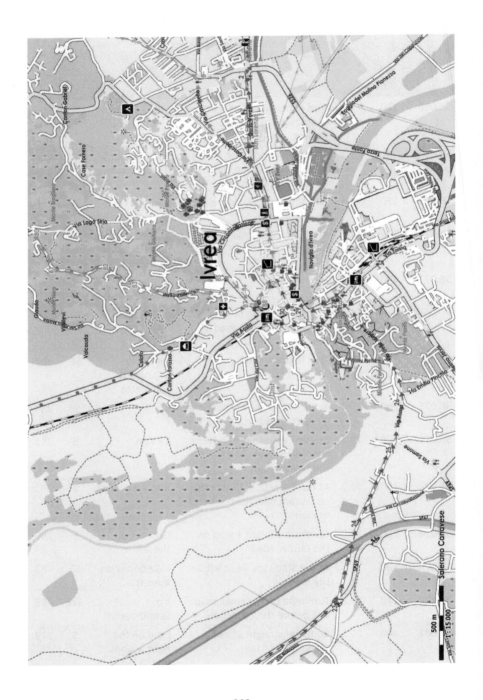

Waypoint	Distance between waypoints	Total km	Directions	Verification Point	Compass	Altitude m
58.082	300	20.4	At the bottom of the hill continue on the tarmac		SW	278
58.083	300	20.7	Continue straight ahead on the pavement on the left of the road		S	265
58.084	600	21.3	Turn left	Car park on your left	E	248
58.085	110	21.4	At the T-junction turn right on the busy road	Beside the old city walls of Ivrea	SW	248
58.086	140	21.5	Cross the road and continue straight ahead	Torre del Castello to the left	SW	255
58.087	120	21.6	At the traffic lights, turn left	Via Amedeo di Castellamonte, No Entry	S	256
58.088	50	21.7	Turn left, under the arch and bear right under the second arch	Castello – Duomo	E	261
58.089	70	21.8	Bear left on the narrow street, uphill towards the castle	Via Torri	SE	266
58.090	40	21.8	Arrive at Ivrea (XLV) centre	Piazza Castello		268

Alternate Route #58.A1				Length:17.8km		
Stage Summary: a less strenuous route but of similar distance to the "Official Route" and better suited to cyclists. The route follows quiet roads and tracks on the western side of the river before taking busier roads on the entry to Ivrea.						
Stage Ascent: 218m				Stage Descent: 237m		
58A1.001	0	0.0	Continue straight ahead on the main road	SS26, pass industrial buildings on your right	S	286
58A1.002	600	0.6	Turn right over the bridge, direction Quincinetto	Cross Dora Baltea	SW	279

Waypoint	Distance between waypoints	Total km	Directions	Verification Point	Compass	Altitude m
58A1.003	400	1.0	Bear right with petrol station on right	Motorway toll station on left	S	285
58A1.004	160	1.2	Bear left, direction Campo Sportivo	Via 4 Novembre	SE	285
58A1.005	400	1.6	At the fork bear left on the ramp	Cross over the Autostrada	NE	282
58A1.006	300	1.9	At the foot of the ramp, after crossing the Autostrada, turn sharp right onto a track	Between the railway and Autostrada	SE	278
58A1.007	700	2.6	Bear right to ford the stream		SE	280
58A1.008	90	2.7	Turn right	Keep Autostrada on your right	S	278
58A1.009	210	2.9	At the T-junction with road turn left and continue beside the Autostrada	Following the overhead power lines	SE	279
58A1.010	900	3.8	At the crossroads turn right under the Autostrada to enter Tavagnasco	Railway to the left at junction	SW	274
58A1.011	100	3.8	At the crossroads turn left	Follow via Roma	S	279
58A1.012	100	3.9	Bear right on via Roma	Mural ahead at the junction	S	277
58A1.013	300	4.3	Turn left beside the large church to recross Autostrada	Piazza del Municipio	E	271
58A1.014	400	4.6	At the T-junction turn right	Pass cemetery on the left	S	267
58A1.015	2400	7.0	At the crossroads, with river bridge to the left, turn right direction Quassolo	Pass under Autostrada	W	257
58A1.016	170	7.2	At the crossroads in Quassolo turn left on via Garibaldi	Pass car park on the left	SW	264

Waypoint	Distance between waypoints	Total km	Directions	Verification Point	Compass	Altitude m
58A1.017	210	7.4	Bear left onto the via San Gregorio	Vines on your right	S	261
58A1.018	400	7.7	Bear left over a small bridge with crash barriers and then turn right at the Stop sign on via San Rocco	Keep Autostrada parallel on your left	S	255
58A1.019	1400	9.1	In Baio Dora, continue straight ahead	Direction Banchette	SW	257
58A1.020	60	9.2	Bear left on via Comm. Pietro Presbitero	Pass fountain on the right	S	258
58A1.021	140	9.3	Follow the road as it bears right and left	Via Presbitero	S	255
58A1.022	3200	12.5	At the T-junction turn left, direction Ivrea	SP69, business park on the left	SE	249
58A1.023	2300	14.8	At the second roundabout take the last exit via Roma	Small road under the Autostrada	E	241
58A1.024	600	15.4	At the roundabout, bear left into the village of Banchette on via Roma	Sports ground to the left	SE	245
58A1.025	600	16.0	At the T-junction, turn left to proceed into Ivrea	Via delle Miniere	E	251
58A1.026	300	16.3	At the Stop sign, continue straight ahead towards Ivrea centre	Via delle Miniere	NE	262
58A1.027	800	17.1	At the roundabout turn left towards Ivrea centre	Piazza Lamarmora, trees in centre of road	N	248
58A1.028	240	17.3	At the T-junction, after crossing Dora Baltea, turn right	Towards metal railway bridge	NE	244
58A1.029	60	17.4	Turn left on the small road, via Riva	Uphill towards bell tower	N	244
58A1.030	100	17.5	At the T-junction, turn right into the narrow street against the traffic flow	Church on the left at the junction	E	263

Waypoint	Distance between waypoints	Total km	Directions	Verification Point	Compass	Altitude m
58A1.031	180	17.7	Take the second turning on the left	Via Quattro Martiri	NW	259
58A1.032	70	17.7	In the small square, turn sharp right and then immediately left up the steps	Via delle Torri	NW	265
58A1.033	80	17.8	Arrive in the centre of Ivrea at the end of the section	Piazza Castello		268

Accommodation & Facilities .... Pont-Saint-Martin - Ivrea

Ostello - Ivrea Canoa Club,(Federico),Via Dora Baltea 1d,10015 Ivrea(TO),Italy; +39 3479 092391; +39 3280 999579; Email:ostelloicc@libero.it ; Web-site:www.parks.it/ost/ivrea; Price:C

Ostello via Francigena,Piazza Santa Marta, 6,10015 Ivrea(TO),Italy; Tel:+39 0125 633040; +39 3402 460722; Email:ostellosangermano@gmail.com; Web-site:cooperativapollicino.it; Price:C

Ostello Salesiano Eporediese,Via San Giovanni Bosco, 58,10015 Ivrea(TO),Italy; Tel:+39 0125 627268; +39 36 6605 2667; Email:ostello.ivrea@ salesianipiemonte.it; Web-site:www.salesiani-icp.net/ivrea/ostello/index.html; Price:C

L'Ospitalità del Castello,Piazza Conte Rinaldo, 7,10010 Settimo-Vittone(TO),Italy; Tel:+39 0125 659083; +39 3484 527017; Email:info@ lospitalitadelcastello.it; Web-site:www.lospitalitadelcastello.it; Price:B

Albergo Luca,Corso Garibaldi, 58,10015 Ivrea(TO),Italy; Tel:+39 0125 48697; Web-site:www.albergolucaivrea.it; Price:A

Hotel Nord,Corso Costantino Nigra, 63,10015 Ivrea(TO),Italy; Tel:+39 0125 40135; Price:B

Camping Mombarone,Frazione Daniele Torre,10010 Settimo-Vittone(TO),Italy; Tel:+39 0125 757907; Email:info@campingmombarone.it; Price:C; Note:Caravan available for pilgrims,

Camping Lago San Michele,Via Lago San Michele, 13,10015 Ivrea(TO),Italy; Tel:+39 0125 616195; Price:C

Ufficio del Turismo,Corso Vercelli, 1,10015 Ivrea(TO),Italy; Tel:+39 0125 618131

$ San Paolo,Via Aosta, 28,10013 Borgofranco-d'Ivrea(TO),Italy;
Tel:+39 0125 751253

$ Unicredit,Via Ganio Vecchiolino Secondo, 2,10016 Montalto-Dora(TO),Italy;
Tel:+39 0125 650017

$ Biverbanca Cassa di Risparmio,Via Statale, 15,10012 Bollengo(TO),Italy;
Tel:+39 0125 676222; Web-site:www.biverbanca.it

$ Istituto Bancario San Paolo di Torino,Corso Massimo d'Azeglio, 1,10015
Ivrea(TO),Italy; Tel:+39 0125 627778

$ Unicredit Banca,Corso Camillo Cavour, 30,10015 Ivrea(TO),Italy;
Tel:+39 0125 418411

H Ospedali Riuniti del Canavese,Piazza Credenza, 2,10015 Ivrea(TO),Italy;
Tel:+39 0125 4141

+ Sartor - Medico,Via Chiappussone, 1,10015 Ivrea(TO),Italy; Tel:+39 0125 40366

🚶 Bazzani Sports,Corso d'Azeglio Massimo, 21,10015 Ivrea(TO),Italy;
Tel:+39 0125 45608

🚲 Bicisport Snc di Aribone Carlo & C,Corso d'Azeglio Massimo, 26,10015
Ivrea(TO),Italy; Tel:+39 0125 40348

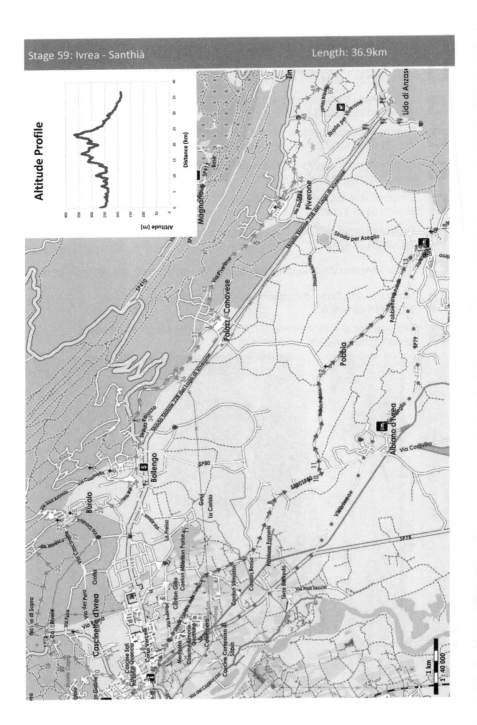

209

Stage Summary: after leaving Ivrea the section continues on minor country roads and tracks. The "Official Route" follows a route chosen by pilgrims in the 12th and 13th century and although it is longer than the more traditional Alternate Route it offers more intermediate accommodation.

Distance from Besançon: 371km   Distance to Vercelli: 64km
Stage Ascent: 498m   Stage Descent: 578m

Waypoint	Distance between waypoints	Total km	Directions	Verification Point	Compass	Altitude m
59.001	0	0.0	From the square below the tower, take via della Torri		SE	268
59.002	50	0.0	At the bottom of the steps turn left	Via Peana	E	265
59.003	100	0.1	Bear right	Via Cattedrale	S	264
59.004	70	0.2	At the T-junction, beside piazza di Città, turn left	Via Palestro	E	258
59.005	400	0.6	In piazza Balla, go straight ahead on via d'Azeglio	Keep trees and large parking area to the right	E	249
59.006	400	0.9	Bear left towards Biella. Note:- The more traditional Alternate Route to the south of lake Piverone bears right	Via Cascinette	NE	245
59.007	290	1.2	At the crossroads, continue straight ahead	Traffic island to the left	E	245
59.008	500	1.7	At the roundabout bear left	Via Cascinette, shrine straight ahead	NE	243
59.009	500	2.1	Shortly after passing the tyre store on the left, bear left onto a smaller road	Via Monte della Guardia	N	241
59.010	400	2.5	At the T-junction turn right	Via Tinasse di Sopra	NE	242
59.011	110	2.6	Take the small road to the left	Into open country	NE	243

Waypoint	Distance between waypoints	Total km	Directions	Verification Point	Compass	Altitude m
59.012	300	2.9	Turn left	Towards lake, woods on the left	N	242
59.013	240	3.1	As the gravel road turns right, continue straight ahead through the barrier	Keep Lago Campagna on the left	NE	245
59.014	400	3.5	At the end of the path keep straight ahead	Across the parking area	SE	246
59.015	100	3.6	Take the tarmac road to the left	Via Lago Campagna	NE	239
59.016	170	3.8	At the T-junction with the main road turn left	Pass house n° 62 on your right	N	239
59.017	40	3.8	On the crown of the bend to the left, turn right	Via Gorrere	E	241
59.018	100	3.9	At the first junction, turn left on the track	Into the woods	N	239
59.019	210	4.1	At the next junction turn right		E	243
59.020	1100	5.2	On leaving the woods take the track to the left	Via Lavatoio, leading back towards the woods	NE	237
59.021	500	5.6	At the Stop sign, turn right on the tarmac	VF sign	SE	238
59.022	700	6.3	At the T-junction with the main road (SP76), cross over, turn left and continue on the right-hand side of the road	Towards the village of Burolo, VF signs	NE	239
59.023	180	6.5	Shortly before the road turns left, turn right	Via Vivier	SE	248
59.024	210	6.7	At the fork keep left	Remain on via Vivier	SE	252
59.025	210	6.9	At the junction with the main road, bear right downhill	Castello Basso to the left at the junction	S	262
59.026	260	7.2	Take the minor road to the left, opposite the bus stop	Via Bollengo	S	248

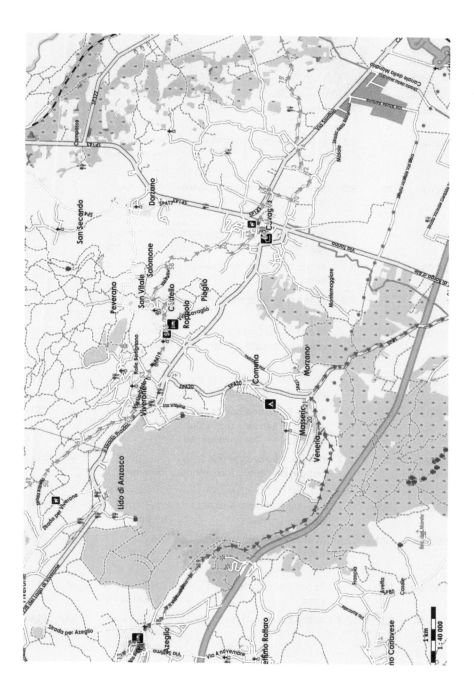

212

Waypoint	Distance between waypoints	Total km	Directions	Verification Point	Compass	Altitude m
59.027	400	7.5	After the bend to the right, turn left	Via Bollengo, VF sign	SE	241
59.028	600	8.1	In Bollengo turn right at the crossroads	Before the chapel of San Rocco	SW	246
59.029	70	8.2	Cross the road and turn sharp left	Via Roma, towards the chapel	E	242
59.030	400	8.5	In the centre of Bollengo, turn right on via P. Cossavella	Direction Biella, VF sign	E	254
59.031	150	8.7	At the fork, keep left towards Biella	Via Scuole	E	249
59.032	140	8.8	At the next fork, keep right	School on your right	E	244
59.033	120	9.0	At the major crossroads, continue straight ahead	Strada Palazzo, direction Piverone	E	242
59.034	500	9.4	On the crown of bend to the right turn left on small path	VF sign, towards trees	N	244
59.035	160	9.6	At the T-junction beside the church of San Pietro e Paolo, turn right on the tarmac road	Strada Piane Inferiore	SE	260
59.036	1600	11.2	At the crossroads at the bottom of the hill, turn left on the main road	Direction Piverone	SE	245
59.037	1000	12.1	Turn right into the village of Palazzo Canavese	Via Garibaldi, VF sign	SE	244
59.038	280	12.4	In piazza Adriano Olivetti turn left on via dei Mulini and immediately right	Via 20 Settembre	SE	246
59.039	150	12.6	At the junction, bear left then right	Pass house n° 15 on the right	SE	246
59.040	120	12.7	At the crossroads, turn left	VF sign, pass car park on your right	NE	241
59.041	80	12.8	At the junction, continue straight ahead	Via Asilo	NE	242

Waypoint	Distance between waypoints	Total km	Directions	Verification Point	Compass	Altitude m
59.042	160	12.9	At the T-junction, turn right	Via Piverone	E	248
59.043	400	13.3	At the Stop sign, turn right	Via Piverone	SE	266
59.044	2000	15.3	Continue straight ahead through the archway in the Piverone tower		SE	308
59.045	80	15.4	Cross the piazza and bear left and right on via Castellazzo	Pass the church close on your left	SE	307
59.046	500	15.9	Bear left on the small road	Downhill, VF sign	E	299
59.047	400	16.2	Beside a farm entrance take the track to the left	Uphill	E	304
59.048	900	17.1	At the junction, beside the small ruined church of Gesiun, turn left and immediately right	Towards the farm, VF sign	SE	327
59.049	700	17.8	At the T-junction turn right	Views of lake Viverone	SW	321
59.050	110	17.9	At the T-junction with the tarmac, road turn left	Towards the towers on the horizon	SE	313
59.051	1100	19.0	Take the right fork	Via Cascine di Ponente	SE	310
59.052	900	19.9	At the Stop sign, bear left on via Umberto I	Towards the centre of Viverone, VF sign	SE	276
59.053	1000	20.8	At the roundabout, continue straight ahead in the direction of Roppolo	VF sign, pass Chiesa di Santa Maria on your left	SE	308
59.054	900	21.7	At the crossroads continue straight ahead into Roppolo	Via G. Massa, direction Poste	SE	309
59.055	90	21.8	In the piazza beside the bell tower, turn left	Towards the castle, via al Castello	E	309

Waypoint	Distance between waypoints	Total km	Directions	Verification Point	Compass	Altitude m
59.056	600	22.4	At the junction, continue straight ahead on the road	Avoid the turning towards Pigglio	N	335
59.057	240	22.6	At the junction beside the well, turn sharp right on the road, towards Salomone	VF sign, large VF pilgrim mural to your right	E	356
59.058	700	23.3	Pass the cemetery and after a brief climb ignore the first track to the right and a little after take the unmade road on the right across the hillside	VF Sign	SE	365
59.059	1100	24.4	After descending on the track through the fields and woods, turn left and then immediately right on the tarmac		S	318
59.060	120	24.5	Take the right fork onto the gravel track, between the fields	VF sign	SW	306
59.061	250	24.7	At the T-junction turn left	Beside house n° 11	SE	296
59.062	250	25.0	At the junction, keep left on the tarmac	Direction Santhià, via Moriando	SE	289
59.063	300	25.3	At the Stop sign turn right	Town of Cavaglià	S	276
59.064	80	25.4	Turn left, towards the town centre	No Entry, VF sign	E	276
59.065	260	25.6	At the end of the road, turn left	VF sign	N	272
59.066	40	25.7	At the mini-roundabout, turn right	Direction Santhià, VF sign	E	272

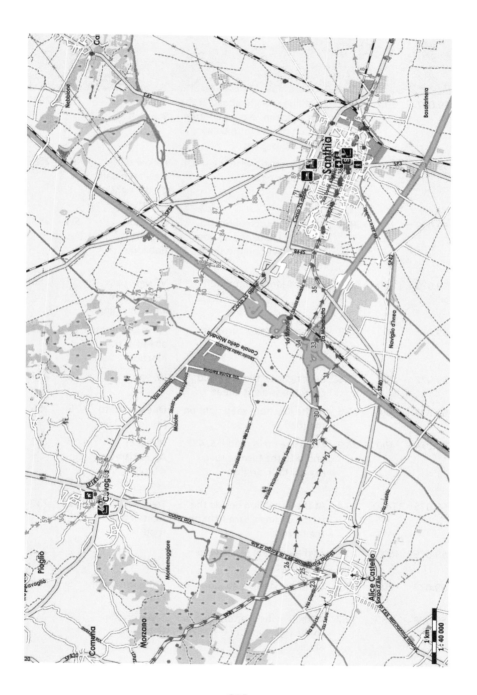

216

Waypoint	Distance between waypoints	Total km	Directions	Verification Point	Compass	Altitude m
59.067	100	25.8	Continue straight ahead at the next junction. Note:- a former version of the route bears right at this point	Vineyard on your left	E	269
59.068	250	26.0	At the junction with the main road, bear right	Follow the tree lined path on the right of the road	SE	259
59.069	280	26.3	With the church of Nostra Signora di Babilone on your left turn right on the small road	Direction Cascine Babilone	SW	257
59.070	400	26.7	At the T-junction turn left	VF sign, pass beside large white building	SE	256
59.071	600	27.3	At the T-junction turn left	Farm buildings ahead at the junction	NE	251
59.072	220	27.6	Bear right on the road and continue straight ahead	VF sign	E	254
59.073	50	27.6	At the junction, keep right on the road	Open fields to the left	E	255
59.074	400	28.0	Cross the main road (SS143) and take the tarmac road slightly to the right	Direction Agriturismo il Molino, VF sign	E	242
59.075	1400	29.4	At the T-junction beside the farm buildings, turn right on the tarmac	Trees on the right of the road	E	239
59.076	500	29.8	At the junction in the woods, keep right		E	232
59.077	700	30.5	Continue straight ahead	Cross the canal bridge	S	217
59.078	180	30.7	At the junction, after the bend to the right, continue straight ahead	Trees on the right	S	217
59.079	500	31.1	At the crossroads, continue straight ahead	Farm to the right	S	213

Waypoint	Distance between waypoints	Total km	Directions	Verification Point	Compass	Altitude m
59.080	800	31.9	At the next crossroads turn left	Towards the motorway bridge	E	208
59.081	240	32.1	Bear left over the Autostrada		SE	204
59.082	500	32.6	Immediately after descending from the bridge turn sharp right. Note:- pedestrians maybe able to eliminate the loop ahead by turning sharp left along the edge of the field and then turning right on the track under the railway	Towards Autostrada	N	202
59.083	190	32.8	At the T-junction turn right	Under bridge, with Autostrada to the left	NE	202
59.084	200	33.0	Turn sharp right on the track		S	201
59.085	190	33.1	Bear left on the track	Pass under railway	E	202
59.086	600	33.8	At the crossroads continue straight ahead	Cross the canal	E	195
59.087	400	34.1	Take the right fork	Towards the electricity pylon	SE	190
59.088	600	34.7	At the junction after passing a farm on your right, keep left on the track	Beside line of trees	SE	188
59.089	1200	35.8	At the T-junction, turn left	Farm buildings on your left, VF sign	SE	184
59.090	280	36.1	At the junction with the main road turn right	Shrine on left at junction, VF sign	S	186
59.091	140	36.3	At the roundabout, continue straight ahead	Pass a sports ground on the left	S	185
59.092	500	36.7	At the traffic lights go straight ahead	Via Svizzera	S	186

Waypoint	Distance between waypoints	Total km	Directions	Verification Point	Compass	Altitude m
59.093	70	36.8	Turn left	Via Edmondo de Amicis, VF sign	E	187
59.094	40	36.8	Turn right	Via Jacapo Durando, VF sign	SE	187
59.095	40	36.9	Arrive at Santhià (XLIV) centre in piazza Roma	Beside chiesa Sant'Agata		187

Alternate Route #59.A1 Length: 30.7km

Stage Summary: this route more closely follows the probable route of Sigeric. The route is shorter (by 5km) than the "Official Route" combining country roads and broad tracks and offering great views of Lake Viverone. Unfortunately the final stages require busier roads to bypass a major motorway intersection.
Stage Ascent: 272m Stage Descent: 329m

Waypoint	Distance between waypoints	Total km	Directions	Verification Point	Compass	Altitude m
59A1.001	0	0.0	Take the right fork on Corso Vercelli	Direction Santhià	E	245
59A1.002	600	0.6	At the roundabout, continue straight ahead	Between the petrol stations	E	237
59A1.003	270	0.9	At the next roundabout, take the first exit	Via Casale	SE	237
59A1.004	210	1.1	Beside the bus stop, turn left	Direction Strada Cascine Forneris	SE	235
59A1.005	500	1.6	Fork right along Strada Vicinale della Fornace	Direction Strada Cascine Forneris	SE	235
59A1.006	1300	2.9	Take the right fork between the trees	Via della Fornace	SE	234
59A1.007	1000	3.9	Beside house n° 1 take the right fork on the small road	Keep hedge on your left	SE	232
59A1.008	1100	5.0	Take the right fork	Pass STT bus stop on your left	SE	233

Waypoint	Distance between waypoints	Total km	Directions	Verification Point	Compass	Altitude m
59A1.009	160	5.1	At the Stop sign, continue straight ahead beside the main road	Pass chapel and large farmhouse on your right	SE	235
59A1.010	800	5.9	Immediately after passing house n° 38 on your left, turn left on the gravel track	Pass white metal fencing on your left	E	235
59A1.011	260	6.2	At the Stop sign, turn left beside the road	Open field on your left, trees to the right	E	236
59A1.012	1800	7.9	At the road junction, continue straight ahead through the village of Pobbia	Towards the church	SE	236
59A1.013	2600	10.6	At the crossroads with the main road, at the top of the hill, continue straight ahead on the small road	Uphill skirting the village of Azeglio	SE	245
59A1.014	400	10.9	At the Stop sign in the centre of the village, turn left. Note:- to the right is the village square with a bar	Via Roma	SE	253
59A1.015	170	11.1	At the crossroads, continue straight ahead	Direction Santuario di S. Antonio Abbate	SE	241
59A1.016	210	11.3	Take the right fork	Direction Santuario S. Antonio	S	234
59A1.017	80	11.4	With the play area directly ahead, take the left fork	Direction Santuario di S. Antonio	SE	235
59A1.018	160	11.6	With the red brick shrine on your right, take the left fork	Direction Santuario di S. Antonio Abbate	SE	239

Waypoint	Distance between waypoints	Total km	Directions	Verification Point	Compass	Altitude m
59A1.019	1300	12.9	Continue straight ahead	Pass S. Antonio on your right	SE	258
59A1.020	4400	17.3	At the T-junction at the top of the hill, turn right on the road	Keep the field on your left and the trees on your right	E	285
59A1.021	300	17.6	Take the right fork	Towards the main road	E	283
59A1.022	70	17.7	At the junction with the main road, turn right and remain beside the road to the town of Alice Castello	Towards fruit trees on trhe brow of the hill	SE	287
59A1.023	3600	21.2	At the crossroads in Alice Castello, turn left	Direction Torino	E	255
59A1.024	160	21.4	At the Stop sign with the chapel on your left, turn left on via Cavaglià	Direction Biella	N	251
59A1.025	260	21.7	At the junction with the main road, continue straight ahead	Towards the petrol station	N	254
59A1.026	290	22.0	Immediately before the exit from Alice Castello, turn right on the gravel road	Direction Agriturismo il Ciliegio	E	254
59A1.027	2200	24.1	At the T-junction with the road, turn left	Silos on your right at the junction	NE	222
59A1.028	300	24.5	At the T-junction, turn right on strada della Benna and keep left after crossing the small bridge	Direction Cascina Ciorlucca	E	220
59A1.029	500	24.9	Take the right fork on the lower road	Avoid the road towards the autostrada bridge	NE	219
59A1.030	170	25.1	Beside Cascina Ciorlucca, continue straight ahead	Autostrada close on your left	E	218

Waypoint	Distance between waypoints	Total km	Directions	Verification Point	Compass	Altitude m
59A1.031	900	26.0	On the crown of the third bend to the right, take the underpass under the autostrada	Shortly after passing a farmhouse on your right	SE	212
59A1.032	270	26.3	At the T-junction with the railway track directly ahead, turn left	Keep embankment on your right	NE	207
59A1.033	600	26.8	With the railway viaduct on your right, turn left	Take the underpass under the autostrada slip road	N	208
59A1.034	300	27.1	After emerging from a further underpass take the next turning to the right through the hamlet of la Mandriotta	Pass between red brick pillars	E	211
59A1.035	1100	28.2	At the junction with the main road, turn left and follow the road to the centre of Santhià	Towards distant commercial buildings	E	198
59A1.036	2300	30.5	At the crossroads, after passing a park on your right, continue straight ahead	Enter the pedestrian zone	E	188
59A1.037	140	30.7	At the crossroads with via Ospedale, continue straight ahead and then take the first road to the left	Towards the piazza	E	189
59A1.038	90	30.7	Arrive in Santhia (XLIV) at the end of the section	Piazza Roma, beside chiesa Sant'Agata		188

Accommodation & Facilities .... Ivrea - Santhià

Ostello Per Pellegrini,Via Generale Pietro Giovanni Salino,13881 Cavaglià(BI),Italy; Tel:+39 0161 96038; +39 0161 967016; +39 3200 736509; Email:biblio.cavaglia@ptb.provincia.biella.it; Price:D; PR

Ostello Degli Amici della via Francigena,Vicolo Madonnetta, 4,13048 Santhià(VC),Italy; +39 3488 403460; +39 3336 162086; Email:info@santhiasullaviafrancigena.it; Web-site:www.santhiasullaviafrancigena.it; Price:D; Note:Collect the keys at Caffé della Piazza(closed Mondays), Immobilcasa - Massimiliano Corradini or call the local police on 0161936220. Minimum donation 5 Euro per person,

Monastero di Bose,Frazione Bose, 6,13887 Magnano(BI),Italy; Tel:+39 0156 79185; Email:ospiti@monasterodibose.it; Web-site:www.monasterodibose.it; Price:D

Villa d'Azeglio Residence Hotel,Via Azeglio, 17,10010 Albiano(TO),Italy; Tel:+39 0125 59760; Email:info@villadazeglio.com; Web-site:villadazeglio.com; Price:A

Il Giardino dei Semplici,Via Roma, 78,10010 Azeglio(TO),Italy; Tel:+39 0125 687549; +39 3398 837233; +39 3407 746520; Email:info@giardinodeisemplici.com; Web-site:www.giardinodeisemplici.com; Price:B

B&B - le Lune,Via Cavaglià, 2,13883 Roppolo(BI),Italy; Tel:+39 0161 980938; +39 3462 109706; Email:bblelune@libero.it; Web-site:www.bblelune.eu/bb; Price:B; PR

Albergo San Massimo,Corso Xxv Aprile, 18,13048 Santhià(VC),Italy; Tel:+39 0161 94253; Price:B

Hotel Piccadilly,Corso Xxv Aprile, 51,13048 Santhià(VC),Italy; Tel:+39 0161 921196; Email:info@ristorantepiccadillysanthia.it; Web-site:www.ristorantepiccadillysanthia.it; Price:B

Camping Internazionale del Sole,Via del Lago, 45,13886 Viverone(BI),Italy; Tel:+39 0161 98169; Email:info@campeggiodelsole.com; Web-site:www.campeggiodelsole.com; Price:C

Agriturismo la Bessa Ippica San Giorgio,Casc.Pianone, 14,13882 Cerrione(BI),Italy; Tel:+39 0156 77156

Comune di Santhià,Piazza Roma, 16,13048 Santhià(VC),Italy; Tel:+39 0161 94267

Banca Sella,Via Giacinto Massa, 21,13883 Roppolo(BI),Italy; Tel:+39 0161 987812

Cassa di Risparmio di Torino,Via Antonia Gramsci, 48,13048 Santhià(VC),Italy; Tel:+39 0161 921120

Banca Mediolanum,Corso Nuova Italia, 174,13048 Santhià(VC),Italy; Tel:+39 0161 939957

Santocono - Studio Medico,Piazza Vittorio Veneto, 4,13048 Santhià(VC),Italy; Tel:+39 0161 921021

Distinto - Medico Veterinario,Strada Per Viverone, 53,10010 Piverone(TO),Italy; Tel:+39 0125 687531

Servizio Veterinario,Via Rollino,13881 Cavaglià(BI),Italy; Tel:+39 0161 96215

Servizio Veterinario,Via Rollino,13881 Cavaglià(BI),Italy; Tel:+39 0161 96215

Basso Laura,Via Gramsci, 64,13048 Santhià(VC),Italy; Tel:+39 0161 921166

Marmony Sport,Via Giacomo Matteotti, 73,13048 Santhià(VC),Italy; Tel:+39 0161 921401

D'Agostino Carmelo,Via Pinerolo, 100,10067 Vigone(TO),Italy; +39 3488 718200

Massimo Bellotti,Corso Nuova Italia, 16,13048 Santhia'(VC),Italy; Tel:+39 0161 94335

Massimo Bellotti,Corso Nuova Italia, 16,13048 Santhia'(VC),Italy; Tel:+39 0161 94335

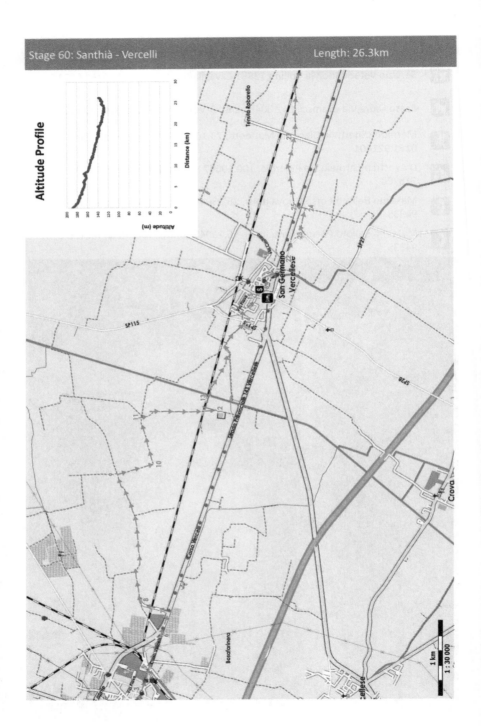

Stage Summary: this section enters the rice fields that will be constant companions until Pavia. The "Official Route" meanders on farm tracks between the rice fields occasionally crossing the busy main road to Vercelli. The VF sign posts are often casualties of the intensive farming in the area and so be sure to keep track of your position in the guide. In hot weather the rice fields are a haven for mosquitoes.

Distance from Besançon: 408km

Distance to Vercelli: 27km

Stage Ascent: 77m

Stage Descent: 126m

Waypoint	Distance between waypoints	Total km	Directions	Verification Point	Compass	Altitude m
60.001	0	0.0	Leave piazza Roma keeping the church to the left	Via Roma, towards the bank	S	188
60.002	50	0.1	At the T-junction, turn left	Pedestrian zone – corso Nuova Italia	E	188
60.003	500	0.6	At the crossroads, continue straight ahead. Note:- to avoid the footbridge ahead, turn left and then right at the traffic island and rejoin the "Official Route" at the turning to cascine Nuova Bella Vittoria	No through road, railway station to the right	E	183
60.004	140	0.7	On reaching the railway track, bear left and then right and cross the railway on the foot-bridge	VF sign	SE	182
60.005	190	0.9	After crossing the bridge, continue straight ahead	Corso Vercelli, large irrigation channel on the right	E	182
60.006	500	1.4	Just before the chapel, cross to the right side of the road and go straight ahead beside the busy SS143	Keep water to the right	E	178
60.007	400	1.7	Turn left, carefully cross the main road and take via Pragilardo over the small bridge	Towards railway line	NE	176

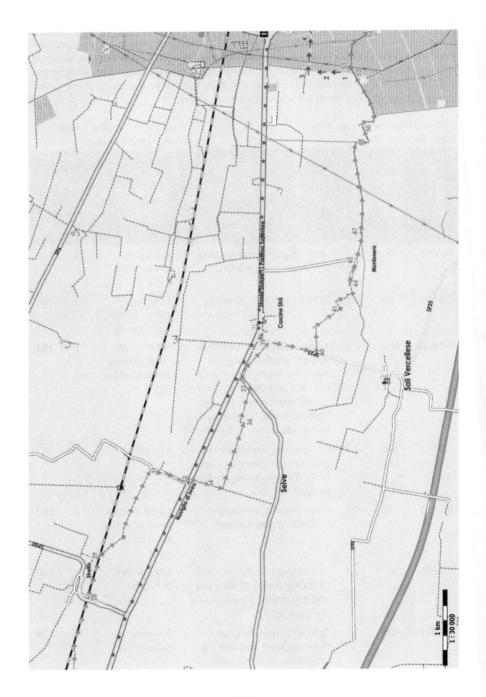

Waypoint	Distance between waypoints	Total km	Directions	Verification Point	Compass	Altitude m
60.008	400	2.1	After crossing the railway bridge bear right on the unmade road	Towards farm	E	175
60.009	1800	3.9	After passing cascina Pragilardo turn right	Beside electricity sub-station	S	170
60.010	500	4.4	At the T-junction turn left		E	168
60.011	700	5.1	At the crossroads turn right		S	167
60.012	1000	6.0	At the junction after crossing the railway track, turn sharp left	The track turns right and continues parallel to the railway	NE	165
60.013	250	6.3	Continues straight ahead	Cross the canal	SE	165
60.014	1300	7.6	At the crossroads, continue straight ahead	Direction Centro	SE	163
60.015	400	8.0	At the crossroads continue straight ahead	Via Antonio Peretti	SE	165
60.016	110	8.1	At the Stop sign turn right and immediately left	Via Cavour, pass arches on your right	SE	165
60.017	170	8.2	Continue straight ahead across piazza Giuseppe Mazzini	Beside the church	E	166
60.018	110	8.3	Beside Palazzo del Commune, in piazza Garibaldi turn right	Towards the main road	S	164
60.019	60	8.4	Cross the main road and turn left	Keep the café on your right	SE	164
60.020	110	8.5	At the end of the small park and turn right	Cross the bridge over the canal	S	163
60.021	40	8.6	After the bridge, immediately turn left on via Franzoi	Returning towards the main road	E	162
60.022	150	8.7	At the junction with the main road turn hard right on the smaller road	Towards Salasco	SE	160

Waypoint	Distance between waypoints	Total km	Directions	Verification Point	Compass	Altitude m
60.023	500	9.2	On the exit from the town and on the crown of the bend to the right, turn sharp left onto a track	Towards main road	E	157
60.024	400	9.6	At the crossroads turn left on the unmade road	Towards the main road	N	156
60.025	80	9.7	Carefully cross the main road and turn left on the pavement	Canal on the right of the pavement	NW	156
60.026	90	9.7	Turn right through the break in the crash barriers, cross over the bridge and bear right on the track	VF sign	E	157
60.027	1100	10.8	At the crossroads continue straight ahead	Obliquely towards the railway on your left	E	154
60.028	1300	12.1	Pass under the road bridge and continue straight ahead at the junction	Railway on your left	E	151
60.029	600	12.7	The track bears right beside the irrigation channel	Channel on your right	SE	149
60.030	1400	14.1	At cascina Castellone turn right	Keep the farm buildings on the left	S	147
60.031	130	14.2	At the entrance to the farm buildings, turn right	Towards the main road	SW	146
60.032	400	14.6	Carefully cross the main road and turn left on the track	Close beside the main road	SE	144
60.033	80	14.7	Follow the track to the right	VF sign, pass pylon on your right	S	145
60.034	200	14.9	Continue straight ahead passing the barrier		S	145
60.035	230	15.2	At the next crossroads turn left	Parallel to main road	E	145

Waypoint	Distance between waypoints	Total km	Directions	Verification Point	Compass	Altitude m
60.036	1000	16.1	At the T-junction turn left and then right	Remain parallel to the main road	E	142
60.037	500	16.6	At the T-junction with the tarmac road, turn left on the road	Towards the main road	NE	140
60.038	170	16.8	Just before reaching the main road turn right on the track	Blue highway sign ahead, VF sign	SE	141
60.039	600	17.4	At the T-junction with the tarmac road, turn right on the road	Cascine Strà to the left at the junction, VF sign	S	138
60.040	700	18.0	Turn left over a small bridge onto a track between fields and skirt the field on your right	VF sign	SE	140
60.041	800	18.8	Bear left on the track	VF sign	NE	137
60.042	110	18.9	Take the right fork over the bridge, towards the farm	Keep the waterway on the right	SE	137
60.043	250	19.1	At the T-junction with the road, turn left. Note:- the via Domitia route, connecting Arles and Santiago de Compostela to the via Francigena, join from the right	Towards Montonero	E	137
60.044	140	19.3	Continue straight ahead on the tarmac road	Pass through Montonero, church on the left	E	137
60.045	300	19.6	Continue straight ahead on the unmade road	VF sign	E	136
60.046	260	19.9	Keep left at the fork in the tracks		E	135
60.047	140	20.0	Take the right fork	Broken VF sign	E	134

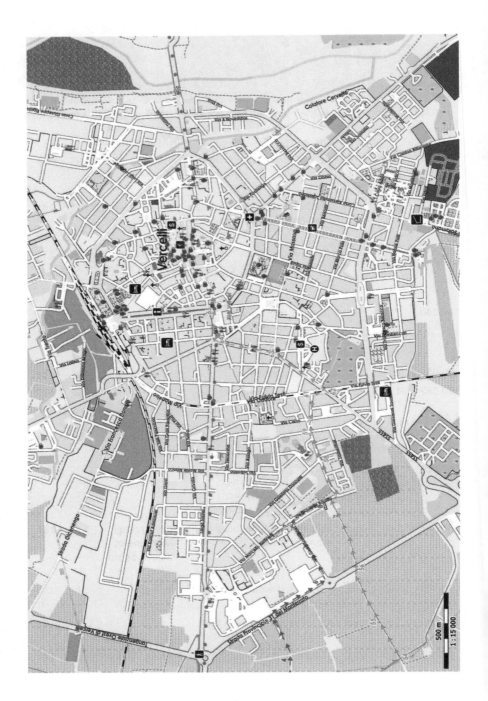

Waypoint	Distance between waypoints	Total km	Directions	Verification Point	Compass	Altitude m
60.048	1200	21.2	Turn right. Note:- riders should cross the broad water course and turn right to the next Waypoint	Cross over the bridge	S	131
60.049	160	21.4	Bear left to cross a sluice gate and a small bridge and then turn right to follow the embankment	Metal safety rails on the bridge	E	131
60.050	220	21.6	Cross a sluice-gate and continue straight ahead	Track will bear right	E	131
60.051	900	22.5	Continue straight ahead	Pass a farm on the right	NE	129
60.052	110	22.6	Continue straight ahead. Note:- at the time of our last survey the "Official Route" was overground and impassable. The Alternate Route to the left bypasses the blockage	Follow embankment	NE	129
60.053	90	22.7	Continue straight ahead beside the waterway	The track widens	SE	129
60.054	500	23.2	At the T-junction turn left on the broad track		NE	129
60.055	270	23.4	Continue straight ahead	Cross the barrier	E	127
60.056	400	23.8	Cross the busy main road and continue straight ahead on the grass track	Brown via Francigena sign on far side of the road	E	127
60.057	500	24.3	At the T-junction with the tarmac road, turn right and immediately left. Note:- the Alternate Route joins from the left	Sports ground ahead	E	129
60.058	400	24.6	At the roundabout continue straight ahead	Via Francigena sign ahead	E	132
60.059	190	24.8	At the next roundabout, again continue straight ahead	Parking area on the right	E	133

Waypoint	Distance between waypoints	Total km	Directions	Verification Point	Compass	Altitude m
60.060	60	24.9	Bear right, cross the road and continue on via Puccini. Note:- there are a number of prior generations of via Francigena signs in the area. For consistency we suggest you follow the instructions in this book	VF sign	E	132
60.061	200	25.1	At the T-junction, turn right	Railway on your left	S	131
60.062	100	25.2	At the T-junction, turn left	Across the railway tracks	NE	132
60.063	400	25.6	At the roundabout, bear left	Direction il Centro, via Guiseppe Paggi	N	134
60.064	400	26.0	At the roundabout, turn right on Largo Brigata Cagliari	Petrol station ahead at the roundabout	E	135
60.065	220	26.3	Arrive at Vercelli (XLIII) centre	Piazza Paietta		138

Alternate Route #60.A1				Length: 2.5km		
Stage Summary: Alternate Route bypassing possible blockage						
Stage Ascent: 15m				Stage Descent: 15m		

Waypoint	Distance between waypoints	Total km	Directions	Verification Point	Compass	Altitude m
60A1.001	0	0.0	Turn left on the broad track	Beside the line of telegraph poles	N	129
60A1.002	220	0.2	At the end of the broad track, continue straight ahead	Cross narrow concrete bridge	N	129
60A1.003	300	0.5	With the farm buildings on your left, turn right onto the grass track. Note:- at the time of writing the track ahead was poorly maintained, but passable, in the event of difficulties continue straight ahead here to join the SS11, then turn right on the ring road to join this track beside the hypermarket	Towards the hypermarket	E	132
60A1.004	500	1.0	Continue straight ahead, across the bridge	Pass houses on your left	NE	130
60A1.005	290	1.3	At the junction with the ring road, cross over the road and turn right in the hypermarket car park	Commercial centre on the left	SE	130
60A1.006	500	1.8	At the road junction, turn left	Via Giulio Sambonet	NE	132
60A1.007	500	2.2	At the crossroads, turn right	Via Giovanni Baratto	SE	130
60A1.008	240	2.5	At the junction, turn left. Note:- rejoin the "Official Route"	Sports ground to the left, via Francigena sign		129

L'Ostello di Billiemme,Corso Alessandro Salamano, 139,13100 Vercelli(VC),Italy; Tel:+39 0161 250167; Email:info@amicidellaviafrancigena. vercelli.it; Web-site:www.amicidellaviafrancigena.vercelli.it/ostello.html; Price:C

Albergo delle Miniere,Corso Giacomo Matteotti, 91,13047 San-Germano-Vercellese(VC),Italy; Tel:+39 0161 933111; Price:B

Hotel Valsesia,Via Galileo Ferraris, 104,13100 Vercelli(VC),Italy; Tel:+39 0161 250842; +39 3493 942427; Email:hotelvalsesia@gmail.com; Web-site:www.hotelvalsesia.wordpress.com; Price:B

Hotel Restorante il Giardinetto,Via Luigi Sereno, 3,13100 Vercelli(VC),Italy; Tel:+39 0161 257230; Email:giardi.dan@libero.it; Web-site:www. ilgiardinettovercelli.com; Price:A

B&B Cascina Erbade,(Carola Gräfin von Hardenberg),Strada Boarone,13100 Vercelli(VC),Italy; Tel:+39 0161 213656; +39 3280 149335; Email:hardenberg@tiscali.it; Web-site:www.bedandbreakfastineurope.com/cascinaerbade; Price:A

Vercelli Palace Hotel,Via Tavallini, 29 ,13100 Vercelli(VC),Italy; Tel:+39 0161 300900; Email:reservation@vercellipalacehotel.it ; Web-site:www.vercellipalacehotel.it; Price:A

Tourist Office,Corso Giuseppe Garibaldi, 90,13100 Vercelli (VC),Italy; Tel:+39 0161 257899; Web-site:www.atlvalsesiavercelli.it

Banca Popolare di Novara,Via Cavour, 9,13047 San-Germano-Vercellese(VC),Italy; Tel:+39 0161 933009

Banca Sella SPA,Via Castelnuovo delle Lanze, 2,13100 Vercelli(VC),Italy; Tel:+39 0161 211397; Web-site:www.sella.it

Biverbanca Cassa di Risparmio,Corso Mario Abbiate, 21,13100 Vercelli(VC),Italy; Tel:+39 0161 210627; Web-site:www.biverbanca.it

Stazione Ferrovie,Piazza Roma, 18,13100 Vercelli(VC),Italy; Tel:+39 06 6847 5475; Web-site:www.renitalia.it

Ospedali Riuniti,Corso Mario Abbiate, 21,13100 Vercelli(VC),Italy; Tel:+39 0161 5931

Salamano - Medico Generico,Piazza Solferino,13100 Vercelli(VC),Italy; Tel:+39 0161 260527

Clinica Veterinaria Sant'Andrea,Viale Rimembranza, 105,13100 Vercelli(VC),Italy; Tel:+39 0161 503331

Decathlon,Corso Torino,13100 Vercelli(VC),Italy; Tel:+39 0161 393687

Bike Shop di Minola Violino Manuel,Via Francesco Crispi, 22,13100 Vercelli(VC),Italy; Tel:+39 0161 503188

Books published by LightFoot Guides

All LightFoot Publications are also available in ebook and kindle and can be ordered directly from www.pilgrimagepublications.com

The complete 2014 LightFoot Guide to the via Francigena consists of 4 books: Canterbury to Besançon, Besançon to Vercelli, Vercelli to Rome, Companion to the Via Francigena

LightFoot Guide to the via Domitia - Arles to Vercelli

Even with the wealth of historical data available to us today, we can only offer an approximate version of yesterday's reality and we claim to do nothing more in this book. The route described runs roughly parallel with a section of the via Domitia between Arles and Montgenévre (a large portion of the original route having been subsumed by the A51), continues along a variety of roads and tracks that together form a modern-day branch of the via Francigena and rejoins the official main route (to Rome) in Vercelli.

The LightFoot Companion to the via Domitia

An optional partner to the guide, providing the additional historical and cultural information that will enhance your experience of the via Domitia and via Francigena

The LightFoot Guide to the Three Saints' Way

The name, Three Saint's Way, has been created by the authors of the LightFoot guide, but is based on the three saints associated with this pilgrimage: St Swithin, St Michael and St James. Far from being a single route, it is in fact a collection of intersecting routes: The Millenium Footpath Trail starting in Winchester and ending in Portsmouth, England. The Chemin Anglais to Mont St Michel and the Plantagenet Way to St Jean d'Angely, where it intersects with the St James Way (starting from Paris).

LightFoot Guide to Foraging
Heiko Vermeulen
"Nowadays if I look at a meadow I think lunch."

A guide to over 130 of the most common edible and medicinal plants in Western Europe, aimed at the long-distance or casual hiker along the main pilgrim routes through Western Europe. The author has had some 40 years of experience in foraging and though a Dutchman by birth, has been at home all over Europe including Germany, Ireland, England and for the last 8 years in Italy along the Via Francigena pilgrim route, where he feeds his family as a subsistence farmer, cultivating a small piece of Ligurian hillside along permaculture principles, and by gathering food from the wild.

Sylvia Nilsen is a South African freelance writer who has been published in numerous local and international publications. She worked as a research agent and editor for a UK-based travel guide publisher and produced several African city and country guides. Sylvia has walked over 5 000 km of Camino trails in France and Spain, as well as from Switzerland to Rome on the Via Francigena pilgrimage. She has served as a volunteer hospitalero in Spain and is a Spanish accredited hospitalero volunteer trainer in South Africa having trained 42 new volunteers. With amaWalkers Camino (Pty) Ltd she leads small groups of pilgrims on slackpacking trails on the Camino Frances.

YOUR CAMINO on foot, bicycle or horseback in France and Spain
A comprehensive Camino planning guide offering advice to pilgrims on choosing a route, how to get to the start, info for people with disabilities, cyclists, walking with children, with a dog, a donkey or doing the Camino on horseback, with 300 pages of advice and information.

CAMINO LINGO
English-Spanish Words and Phrases for Pilgrims on el Camino de Santiago. Compiled by Sylvia Nilsen and her Spanish teacher Reinett e Novóa, this is a cheat's guide to speaking Spanish on the Camino. No complicated verb conjugations or rules on grammar, this book offers over 650 words and phrases just for pilgrims.

SLACKPACKING the Camino Frances
When and where to start walking and how to get there. Three suggested itineraries for hiking daily stages of 10km to 15km: 15km to 20km and 20km to 25km. A 17-day, 5km to 8km per day itinerary for the not-so-able pilgrim wanting to walk the last 100km to Santiago in order to earn a Compostela. A list of Camino Tour Companies and Luggage Transfer services. Contact details for buses, trains and taxis along the route.

Riding the Milky Way

The story of Babette and Paul's journey, but it is not bout hardships and heroes. In fact it was a motley and uninspiring crew that left Le Puy en Velay, France, in July 2005. The humans, broke, burnt-out and vaguely hoping that early retirement would save their health and sanity. The horses, plucked off the equine scrapheap in France and still grappling with their new roles as something between mount and mountain goat. The dog, doing his best to understand why he was there. But 75 days later they reached their destination, overcoming the challenges, and most importantly, finding that they had become an inseparable team. Packed with sketches and photographs, this book will inspire even the most timid traveller, while also giving practical guidelines for someone wanting to do the same or a similar journey. And finally, it is quite simply an excellent, sometimes irreverent, guide to the St James Way. Much more than just a good read.

Riding the Roman Way

"We have good equipment, our horses are fit and we are fully prepared, so why this feeling of dread? Perhaps it has something to do with knowing what to expect." Babette and Paul have come a long way since their first horseback pilgrimage and not just in kilometres. They have learnt a great deal about themselves, their animals and some of the practicalities of long distance riding, but they continue to regard themselves as incompetent amateurs and are still in search of a rationale for their insatiable wanderlust. Common sense and the deteriorating east-west political situation put an end to their original plan, riding on from Santiago de Compostela to Jerusalem in 2006, but Paul has found an equally exciting alternative: the via Francigena pilgrimage to Rome. The good news is that there will be no war zones to contend with, but the bad news is that they will be travelling 2000 kilometres along a relatively unknown route, with a 2,469 metre climb over the Swiss Alps, often under snow, even in August. Riding the Roman Way takes you alongside this intrepid team every step of the way and shares the highs and lows with disarming honesty. It also provides a detailed account of the via Francigena and offers practical guidance for someone wanting to embark on a similar journey. But be warned, this book book will inspire even the most timid traveller and you read it at your own risk.

Lightning Source UK Ltd.
Milton Keynes UK
UKOW06f0828130416

272141UK00003B/5/P